WIN

LEADING PEOPLE IN

WIN

THE NEW WORKPLACE

Management

GEORGE FULLER

PRENTICE HALL PRESS

Library of Congress Cataloging-in-Publication Data

Fuller, George.
    Win/win management : leading people in the new workplace /George Fuller.
       p. cm.
    Includes index.
    ISBN 0-7352-0025-4 (cloth)
    1. Supervision of employees. I. Title.
HF5549.12.F826 1998
658.3'02—dc21   98-13463
                                              CIP

Printed in the United States of America

10 9 8 7 6 5 4 3 2 1

ISBN 0-7352-0025-4

PRENTICE HALL PRESS
Paramus, NJ 07652

A Simon & Schuster Company

Prentice Hall International (UK) Limited, *London*
Prentice Hall of Australia Pty. Limited, *Sydney*
Prentice Hall Canada, Inc., *Toronto*
Prentice Hall Hispanoamericana, S.A., *Mexico*
Prentice Hall of India Private Limited, *New Delhi*
Prentice Hall of Japan, Inc., *Tokyo*
Simon & Schuster Asia Pte. Ltd., *Singapore*
Editora Prentice Hall do Brasil, Ltda., *Rio de Janeiro*

Other Prentice Hall Books by George Fuller

Supervisor's Portable Answer Book

The Supervisor's Big Book of Lists

The First-Time Supervisor's Survival Guide

Manager's Portable Answer Book

The Negotiator's Handbook

The Workplace Survival Guide

Contents

3

HOW TO MOVE AWAY FROM THE OLD WAY OF DOING THINGS   59

4

SUPERVISING EMPLOYEES IN A COOPERATIVE WORK ENVIRONMENT   107

5

SOLVING PERSONNEL ISSUES THE ENLIGHTENED WAY   135

6

MANAGING EMPOWERED EMPLOYEES ON A DAILY BASIS   175

7

ADAPTING TO NEW TECHNOLOGY   209

8

GAINING COOPERATION FROM PEOPLE YOU DON'T SUPERVISE — 239

9

DEALING WITH THE NEW WORKPLACE FROM — 265
A SUPERVISORY PERSPECTIVE

10

REAPING THE BENEFITS OF THE NEW WORKPLACE   **309**

INDEX   **329**

Introduction

Supervising people in the performance of their jobs virtually guarantees that you won't be bored with being a boss. People problems of one sort or another will periodically test both your supervisory skills and your sanity. Nevertheless, after you have supervised employees for a long enough period of time, even dealing with problem employees can seem routine. However, a number of new factors have emerged in recent years to add a more difficult dimension to your role as a supervisor.

Rapid changes in technology and global competition have combined to reshape the corporate landscape. Corporate management has responded to these challenges by initiating sweeping changes, sometimes involving massive layoffs, but at least encompassing substantial reorganization. New ways of changing both the structure of work and the way people are organized to do the job are continually being recommended and adopted. Management techniques are touted, tried, and perhaps even discarded, with continual turmoil in the workplace seeming to be the only constant. Whether the new practices are large or small, practical or ill-thought-out, you as the supervisor are responsible for implementing them within the group you supervise. This, as you may have experienced, isn't easy to do for a number of reasons.

First of all, new tactics are adopted by top management with little or no input from those on the front lines where the work is actually done. As a result, an organizational change may look great on paper, but not work out quite so well in practice. The introduction of new technology may be touted as a productivity booster and turn out instead to be a total bust. Whatever the problem may be, you're the one who has to deal with it on a daily basis.

Even when new ideas are well thought out, there are still problems in putting them into practice within your group. Most people are wary of anything that's new, and some are inclined to offer either active or passive resistance. So even when you try to make a minor revision in how a worker performs his or her job, you may find yourself encountering silent resentment or outright hostility from the affected employee. Apart from that, you have the equally difficult task of finding ways to implement major changes, often with little or no guidance as to how to proceed. The bottom line is that introducing anything new to the workplace can cause a variety of problems which you have to overcome to make it succeed.

Aside from new technology and organizational changes, there are new work force issues you have to deal with. These range from the difficulty of involving employees as participants in determining how the work is done, to the challenge of supervising a multi-cultural work force. Then too, there are issues such as building trust and maintaining loyalty with workers, perhaps even as the group you supervise is being asked to do more work with fewer resources.

The purpose of this book is to provide guidance for you to face the problems of the new workplace with its emphasis on technology and employee empowerment. You will find hundreds of tips on how to deal with these subjects from a supervisory perspective. Among the topics covered are:

- How to successfully supervise telecommuters
- How to adjust the workload after job cuts
- Learning how to let workers control their own work practices
- How to supervise a multi-cultural work force

- What to do when new practices aren't working out
- How to avoid the blame for failed changes
- Seven methods for tackling worker concerns about new technology
- Strategies to prevent worker burnout
- How to avoid the pitfalls of teams
- Ways to preserve employee loyalty through thick and thin
- Nine ways to encourage workers to change the way they work
- How to alter your "old school" management techniques
- Strategies for continuous improvement in daily operations

Perhaps most important of all, the ultimate goal of this book is to assist you in easing the transition when anything new is introduced. There's plenty of practical down-to-earth advice on coping with the supervisory problems of the new workplace environment. Resistance to anything new is natural, but how you deal with it can spell the difference between success or failure. Some actions you take will be downright unpopular with those you supervise, while others will be more easily accepted. However, whatever the level of acceptance may initially be, you may still be held accountable for the success or failure of new practices. For this reason, you will find plenty of advice on how to avoid being the scapegoat for someone else's not so bright idea.

Finally, you will find ample information on the most troublesome aspects of the new workplace, such as having to do more work with fewer people, and coping with new procedures that prove to be unpopular. All of these tips and techniques are recommended based on their real world practicality, not on some textbook notion of how things are in a perfect world. Let's face it. As a supervisor you have to deal with what you have to work with, and the advice in this book is based on that reality. May it help you successfully cope with anything new that comes your way—both now and in the future.

1

The ABC's of the New Workplace— And How to Adjust

The new work environment brought about by a shrinking management structure, a leaner and more flexible work force, and greater emphasis on technology, has a significant impact on your role as a supervisor. You require some adjustment in the way in which you supervise employees. For one thing, you must encourage workers to become active participants in determining how the work is done. This isn't an easy task, since some employees may not want to assume any added responsibilities. Others, although willing to take on more responsibility, may require substantial guidance in learning new roles.

Certain aspects of anything new that affects your job will have more of an impact on your supervisory role than others. Some changes, such as a reorganization, will be a one-time affair, while others, such as encouraging teamwork, will be more subtle and ongoing. Therefore, the adjustments you have to make in your supervisory role will depend largely upon the nature of the change taking place. A company reorganization that affects your department directly is obviously more far reaching and traumatic than redirecting the work procedures of an individual employee. Nevertheless, there are several common threads that are connected with anything

1

new whether it's major or minor. One of these is the fear of change itself.

Many people are instinctively suspicious the moment they hear even the slightest suggestion of anything new taking place. This is a natural enough reaction if you think about it. People get comfortable with the way they do things, and having to alter these patterns is at least inconvenient. Furthermore, if the change is significant enough to threaten some aspect of the employee's livelihood, both fear of and resistance to doing things differently are the end result.

In fact, even something that's beneficial to an employee may be viewed with alarm if the employee perceives it as a threat to his or her continued employment. For example, the introduction of a new machine may serve the dual purpose of making the worker's job both easier and more productive. However, the employee may incorrectly view the new equipment as a means of reducing the work force and eliminating a job. So not only do you have to contend with the natural resistance to doing things differently, but also with the perception in the minds of employees of what the true purpose is. For this reason, you must build trust with your subordinates and this subject is also discussed.

Of course, not every change will be beneficial to you personally, or to those employees you supervise. This is especially true with organizational realignments which result in work force reductions. In these situations, you have to learn how to cope with doing more work with fewer people. This isn't an easy task, since you're likely to be dealing with subordinates whose morale is low. Techniques for dealing with these and other aspects of reorganization are discussed in detail. First, however, let's look at how to overcome the fear of anything new, since the new workplace can cause significant apprehension for everyone.

THE PRACTICAL WAY TO OVERCOME THE FEAR OF ANYTHING NEW

Before you can even attempt to alleviate the anxiety of subordinates over any impending change, you first have to feel comfortable about it yourself. This isn't always easy to do, especially if the change is one you don't agree with. But even if it's a new work procedure you're initiating yourself, there are still hurdles to overcome in convincing workers of the benefits of the change. Some of the factors you have to consider when any change is going to take place are as follows:

Who is initiating the change? The initial acceptance of any change will depend to a large degree on where the idea for the change originated. If the change was suggested by an employee, then the probability is high that there will be little or no resistance, although there may be some disagreement among workers as to whether or not a change should be made. If you are the one who is introducing a change within your own work group, then you have to give some thought to the reaction of the worker or workers who will be affected. In addition, it's important to consider the best approach to take in introducing the change. Of course, it's great if you can reach a consensus agreement within your group about the value of a change before it's implemented. However, this isn't always either practical or possible, so you may have to make the change first and deal with objections afterward. The important point here is to be aware of the possibilities before you take action. That way, you won't be surprised if you encounter resistance in implementing the change.

For the most part, the hardest changes to deal with are those initiated by top management, especially if they involve layoffs, job reassignments, and other personnel actions that have a direct impact on the group you supervise. Even though you may not agree with these changes, it's your job to implement them to the best of your ability. Although it's hard to do, especially if an organizational change will have a negative impact on your group, try to look at such changes from an objective standpoint. For instance, although a work force reduction may make your immediate job harder to do, the long-term advantages of a more competitive company will benefit employees in the future.

What's the purpose of the change? Many changes are obvious, but sometimes changes will be made by upper management that leave you wondering what the purpose is. When this happens, strive to learn as much as you can from your boss and others as to why the change is being made. Unless you know the reason a change is being implemented, it's impossible to defend and promote it with your employees. As a result, when employees ask about the change, you will be forced to shrug and say something such as, "I don't know why the change is being made, but I'm sure there is a good reason." If this happens frequently, workers will soon start to believe that top management is remote, or that you're not in-the-loop and are therefore unable to obtain information on matters that affect employees. If this attitude sets in, then it becomes much harder to successfully implement any sort of change.

What are the benefits of the change? Unless you can clearly identify the benefits, it becomes much harder to justify making the change. The better you're able to convince employees of these benefits, the greater the chances of overcoming any resistance. One problem in this area is when the benefits of a change to the company may be fairly obvious—such as increasing productivity—but not to individual workers. For instance, improving productivity may be great for the company, but it won't sell with employees if they fear it will cost jobs. Therefore, whenever possible, you want to relate the advantages of a change to how and why your workers will benefit from it. Although this isn't always doable, for the most part it can be done if you give it some thought.

Once you have thought through all aspects of a proposed change, you will be better positioned to alleviate the fears and concerns of workers. How to do this will vary in specific situations, but the bottom line in overcoming the fear of anything new is (1) being informed concerning the change, and (2) being able to communicate openly with your workers about the pros and cons of the change and how it will affect them. Doing this effectively in various situations and with different types of changes is discussed at length elsewhere throughout this book. First of all, let's look at some of the problems and pitfalls you have to deal with in the new workplace that has evolved in recent years and will continue to change in the future.

THE PITFALLS AND PROBLEMS OF THE NEW WORKPLACE

Many changes have taken place in the business world in recent years. Some have been sudden and obvious, such as the slimming down of many large and mid-size businesses. Others, such as a more diverse work force, have occurred gradually. Still other changes have come about because of new technology, such as the ability of people to telecommute. A constant search for new management techniques to improve productivity has resulted in other changes such as greater worker participation in decision-making. When you add everything up, what you have is essentially a new workplace different from what formerly existed. Although it didn't happen all at once, and indeed will continue to evolve in the future, you, as a supervisor, have a different working world to deal with.

What are some of the problems of the new workplace you have to confront? Let's look at some of them. Admittedly, they may not all affect you at the present time, and you may be fortunate enough not to ever have to deal with some of them. But for the most part, either now, or in the near future, you will confront the following issues:

- Dealing with a reorganization of your department or group
- Doing more work with fewer people
- Dealing with layoffs
- Retraining workers on new equipment or to do other jobs
- Cutting costs in your department
- Learning how to manage people who work at home
- Using a more flexible work force consisting of many part-time and temporary workers
- Dealing with a wide range of employee personal problems such as parents who want flexible hours to meet child care and other needs
- Training younger workers who lack basic job skills
- Communicating effectively with workers who may not understand English
- Motivating employees who no longer feel their jobs are secure
- Introducing new technology which employees see as a threat to their jobs
- Promoting and encouraging teams and teamwork
- Encouraging workers to operate with less supervisory direction
- Fighting for resources in a cost-conscious operating environment

These are just a few of the problems you will have to resolve to succeed as a supervisor in the new workplace. Unfortunately, you can't count on a great deal of assistance from either a boss or other managers, since they will be struggling with their own problems. Therefore, for the most part, you're on your own in terms of dealing with all of the issues that have to be resolved in order for you to be a successful supervisor in the modern management environment. Making it even more difficult is the need to act as a coach and team leader rather than as someone who gives orders and expects them to be carried out. As you know, that sort of boss is neither tolerated nor wanted in any company where worker participation and involvement are taken seriously. The starting point, therefore, in adapting to the new workplace is to assess how you interact with the people you supervise. So let's first look at what adjustments you may have to consider to be a more team-focused supervisor.

SEVERAL WAYS TO DEAL WITH ADJUSTMENTS IN YOUR ROLE AS A SUPERVISOR

How much of an adjustment is required for you to become a coach and team leader rather than a boss who issues orders depends on your past experience and your current willingness to adjust. Some supervisors always related well with those they supervised, while others followed a more traditional boss/subordinate relationship. No matter what your previous practices may have been, there are a number of measures you can take to become a better team leader.

First and foremost, it's vital to practice what you preach. Your workers will observe how you react in your working relationship with other supervisors and staff personnel. If you are cooperative and work with others in a spirit of teamwork, then this will add credibility to your efforts with those you supervise. If, on the other hand, you frequently criticize your peers behind their backs, then those you supervise have little reason to believe that you won't treat them the same way.

Encourage your subordinates to make suggestions on how their work is done. Be willing to throw problems on the table at group meetings and ask for ideas for solving them. This is one of the best ways to encourage teamwork within your group. When subordinates see the boss ask for help in solving a problem, they know they have a supervisor who doesn't have a big ego. There's a tendency as a supervisor to conceal the fact that you don't have all of the answers. Being able to overcome this trait can go a long way toward gaining the trust of those you supervise.

Let's look at how this plays out in the real world.

Background   Frank and Helen are both first-line supervisors in a large manufacturing facility. Unknown to each other, they both have a similar problem to solve. Helen calls a group meeting, explains the problem she has, and asks if anyone has any ideas on how to solve it. It so happens that Carl, a veteran employee, had encountered a comparable problem several years ago. He mentions what had been done to handle the situation. The group then discusses this, modifies what had been done previously, and comes up with a solution.

Frank, on the other hand, says nothing to his group. Instead, he assigns the problem to Marta and asks that the problem be taken care of. She has no idea of how to handle the matter, and after considerable trial and error finally manages to resolve the problem. About a week later, she casually mentions to Carol, a co-worker, the tough task that was dumped on her. Carol frowns and says, "I handled something like that last year, Marta. I could have told you what to do in fifteen minutes. You know, if Frank treated us more like a team rather than a bunch of robots, it would be a lot easier to work around here."

The result

The different approaches used by the two supervisors yielded different results. Helen's people respect her and willingly offer suggestions on how to be more productive since they know she respects and listens to them. Frank's people resent the lack of the communication necessary for a framework of teamwork to be established. As a result, they aren't likely to volunteer any ideas for workplace improvements.

In one situation we have a team-focused group that takes maximum advantage of the combined experience and skills of its members. The second group, headed by Frank, is a continuation of the traditional boss/subordinate relationship which yields little in the way of cooperative endeavors which can boost productivity and improve morale.

Be Careful with Your Criticism

No one likes to be criticized and everyone recognizes that. Yet some supervisors hand out really harsh criticism when workers make mistakes. Much of this is unintentional and is related to a loss of temper and the resultant emotional outburst. Generally, when things cool down there will be an apology. That's fine, but apology or not, workers will be extremely careful about making mistakes and incurring the wrath of a hot-headed boss. The easiest way for workers to do that is to avoid doing anything that is new or difficult. As a result, employees won't take chances and this can result in reducing the operating efficiency of the department they work in. On the flip side, if you learn to avoid harsh criticism, workers will be willing to take risks without fear of retribution. This approach will eliminate their reluctance to do anything new and different.

In the absence of criticism, how should mistakes be corrected? Rather than berating an employee, concentrate on the problem and proposed solutions. For example, if an employee is making repetitive mistakes when using a certain piece of equipment, consider the possibilities which might include:

- There's something wrong with the machine
- The employee is working too fast
- The employee hasn't been trained properly

Let's look at each of these. If other workers experience no problem in using the machine, then it's not a machine-related difficulty. Direct observation and knowledge of the circumstances will tell you whether the employee is working too fast. Perhaps there has been a recent speed-up in the production line and the employee hasn't yet been able to adjust to the new pace. Talking with the employee about the situation may reveal improper training. There are any number of additional possibilities in a given situation, which can only be explored by looking for the problem and a solution, rather than arbitrarily blaming the worker. Avoiding criticism of employees not only is a sound supervisory technique, but it's also a practical way to encourage risk-taking by employees.

Learn to Let Go

The most fundamental problem you may experience in transitioning from a supervisory order-giver to a coach and team leader is learning how to relinquish some of your duties. It may not be easy for you to let employees make certain decisions relative to their work without first securing your approval. Yet the ability to do this will determine your success in making your group a team-oriented one that works well together to get the job done. Giving workers a greater say in deciding how their jobs are done isn't difficult once you accustom yourself to getting less involved in all of the details.

If you have always found it relatively easy to delegate work to subordinates, then it shouldn't be hard to give employees greater latitude in making decisions involving their work. The fundamental difference is that when you delegate the work, you are basically giving someone else your duties to perform, while in the new environment certain of these duties will become the responsibility of your employees. There is, of course, much more involved in terms of the supervisory techniques for giving your employees more responsibility. This is discussed in greater detail in Chapter Six about ways to let workers control their own work practices. In any event, there are distinct advantages that accrue as you develop confidence in the ability of your workers to operate more independently. One of the biggest benefits is the additional time you will have to deal with more complex problems as you have less and less involvement in the details of day-to-day operations.

HOW TO MAINTAIN TRUST WITH A FLEXIBLE WORK FORCE

As you know, it takes time to build trusting relationships both within and outside of the workplace. Without an adequate level of trust, those who work for you won't be willing to take the risks that are sometimes necessary to get the job done. For example, a worker isn't likely to take a short cut to finish a priority project by a deadline if he or she has to worry about being criticized for doing so. Therefore, the worker will either seek approval from you first, or far more likely, not exercise any initiative and fail to take measures that would allow timely completion of the work. This is especially true if the worker runs the risk of being criticized by managers from outside the department. In this situation, workers need to know they can count on you to back them up if someone outside the department criticizes them.

This is one minor example of what happens when workers know they can count on their boss being there when needed. Many benefits accrue when there's a strong level of trust in a supervisor. Whether it's to fight for new equipment for the department, or to battle for an employee's pay raise, a boss who takes actions that build trust with employees will have a group of workers who are willing to work harder to get the job done.

One of the problems in building trust in the modern workplace is that many supervisors don't have the permanence in their work force that gives them time to gradually build trust. This is especially true in situations where there are a lot of part-time and temporary workers, or a rapid rate of turnover with full-time employees. Sometimes this is the nature of specific companies or industries, which are low-paying or highly seasonal in their workloads. Whatever the cause, a rapidly changing work force makes it more difficult for a supervisor to build trust.

However, even where this occurs, much can be done with a little bit of thought and a great deal of effort. Part-time or full-time temporary workers aren't likely to have great loyalty to their employer. That's to be expected, since for the most part they view their jobs as short-term assignments rather than long-term career opportunities. From their viewpoint you, as their supervisor, are the only link they have to the job. How they react to you is crucial, since they don't feel a need to consider long-term career possibilities.

Since part-timers don't see a long-term future with the company, their relationship with their supervisor is the most important factor as to whether or not they decide to keep working for the company. This is, of course, true to some extent for even full-time career employees, but there's one major difference. Career employees have more at stake with the company and therefore may disregard a poor relationship with a supervisor in the interests of their long-term career goals. Part-timers have no such need, and for this reason may place more reliance on their relationship with a boss in deciding whether or not to look for work elsewhere. For this reason alone, your ability to build trust with part-time and temporary employees is every bit as important as it is with full-time workers.

NOTE: Some companies have a long-standing policy of filling many vacancies from the ranks of part-time or temporary employees. Such employers are likely to have a temporary work force with ambitions to eventually be hired on a full-time basis. As a consequence, these people may work harder than would be the case if they foresaw no opportunity to move to a permanent position. The recommendations in this section apply toward building trust with part-timers where no such incentive is in place.

Be Realistic in Your Expectations

The principal factor in building trust with part-time or full-time temporary workers is to be realistic about what you expect from them. You have to keep in mind that these employees as a group may not have the fervor and dedication of the permanent or core work force. After all, they aren't viewing this job as a career opportunity. There may, of course, be part-timers who work fully as hard as their full-time counterparts, but these are likely to be the exception rather than the rule. This isn't to say that part-timers will slack off, or that they shouldn't be expected to perform up to expectations. It suggests instead that they won't—and shouldn't—be expected to give the extra effort that's sometimes called for from full-time employees. It's sometimes easy to get caught up in this trap without thinking about it.

Along the same lines, it helps a lot to be willing to recognize the special problems that some of your part-timers may have. For instance, students working part-time schedules may sometimes experience trouble in maintaining their regular work schedules because of school requirements that couldn't be anticipated, such as after-school meetings or make-up examinations. Parents working part-time may occasionally run into timing problems coordinating schedules with the other parent. The examples are endless, and although it may be hard to do some of the required juggling of work schedules to get the job done, the more competent you are at meeting the needs of part-timers, the better your opportunity to gain their gratitude and trust.

If you supervise a combination of full-time, part-time, and temporary people, try to treat your contingent workers on the same basis as career employees. Avoid the sometimes prevalent attitude that part-timers don't really matter since they aren't career workers. When this attitude holds sway, sometimes obvious and sometimes subtle, it certainly isn't going to instill trust and encourage workers to do more than is minimally necessary to earn their paychecks. If you notice this second-hand citizen attitude being conveyed by any of your full-time workers, let them know that it's not acceptable. Treat part-timers and temporary workers fairly and show appreciation for their efforts. In the final analysis, you will be able to establish a level of trust that will be the envy of many.

HOW TO BALANCE EMPLOYEE NEEDS AGAINST WORKLOAD DEMANDS

With smaller and more flexible work forces, most companies find themselves in a balancing act, trying to meet increased workload demands with fewer people. At the same time, there are also attempts to accommodate a wide range of employee concerns, ranging from flexibility about taking time off, to better workplace design, and sometimes in managing workers who telecommute.

You, as a supervisor, are on the front line in dealing with these issues. This is further complicated if top management in your company doesn't provide the policies and support that will assist you in meeting these challenges. However, with or without guidance from above, you still have to manage workload demands against employees' abilities to meet those demands.

Use Technology and Workplace Design Wisely

The primary question to answer in attempting to balance employee needs against workload demands is what can be done to help people work more efficiently. One major contributor is obviously technology. Whenever you can use technology to help increase productivity, you've gone a long way to ease your workload burdens. Another aspect is in the facilities management area. How can the work spaces used by employees be better designed to meet modern needs? Greater emphasis on teamwork and cooperation, more flexible work schedules, and off-site assignments such as telecommuting, have all contributed to a need for less and different forms of working space. For this reason, workplace design is a necessary ingredient in the efficiency mix.

In terms of both new technology and workplace design your goals are limited by the willingness of higher level management to make the necessary investments. This places a premium on your ability to prepare proposals and present arguments that are both convincing and cost-effective. Aside from that, let's consider what to look for in these areas. Regarding new technology, you should focus on equipment needs that will provide the means for each employee to increase productivity. That shouldn't be the sole objective, since quality of work and other factors can't be ignored. However, if your number one problem is too much work for too few people, then increasing individual output is paramount.

Incidentally, when considering technology to increase productivity, don't just look for the newest machinery with the most bells and whistles. More often than not, the state-of-the-art stuff being touted hasn't had the kinks ironed out, so if you're on the front lines of using the equipment, you will be the one to experience the initial difficulties. In this case it never hurts to be in the second tier.

Another bad habit is to concentrate on updating to new and expensive technology when your employees are still way behind the curve in terms of having the best of what is currently available. For example, if you have employees working off-site, do they have sufficient equipment in their home offices to operate effectively while telecommuting? One of the keys to telecommuting effectiveness is linking up the off-site location with the office for maximum efficiency.

When it comes to workplace design, companies are always searching for better ways to achieve efficiency. Telecommuting and team building concepts have contributed to this need, but there will always be a continuing search for better ways. On an overall basis, much of the workplace design effort to maximize efficiency will be outside the scope of your duties. However, within your own area of responsibility, there are aspects of workplace design you shouldn't ignore. Always keep an open ear for employee suggestions on how to improve the layout. Most frequently, it's employee discontent with some aspect of the workplace layout that triggers recognition of a problem that if resolved can increase efficiency.

By the way, if you have employees who telecommute or otherwise work out of the office, make sure they have sufficient workspace for those days and times when they will be on-site. Otherwise, they won't be able to work effectively, and it will likely be disruptive for anyone who has to deal with them.

Aside from the technology and workplace aspects of increasing productivity, explore the workload capacity of individual employees. Over the long term, the importance of hiring only the best comes into play when you have an increasing workload and fewer workers to do the job. For more immediate solutions, look for different ways to do the work. Are there steps in the work process that can be eliminated? Are certain employees better at certain tasks than others? If so, assign the work to take advantage of these abilities. What, if anything, can be done about eliminating unnecessary downtime? Is there a better way of scheduling work that is cyclical so it can be more evenly balanced?

Many actions you can take as a supervisor will be based upon the specifics of the work being performed within your unit. It isn't easy by any stretch of the imagination to come up with ways to balance workload demands against the needs of your employees. With some thought, however, and the close cooperation of those who work for you, it's possible to make the situation a lot more tolerable than it may be at present.

TACTICS FOR WORKING WITH LESS SUPPORT
FROM TOP MANAGEMENT

One of the features of slimmed down corporate organizations is, of course, fewer layers of management. Along with that is the likelihood that many former staff functions have been trimmed back or eliminated completely. This may not affect supervisors who work for small companies which have typically sparse management and staff ranks. On the other hand, if you're employed in a mid-size to large corporation, the loss of staff and management support can make your job harder.

Although the theory goes that eliminating layers of management makes top-to-bottom communication quicker, there are also some pitfalls that aren't so readily pointed out. For example, many of the missing middle managers knew how to steer specific requests in the right direction. They were also savvy about what top management was looking for in terms of presentations for such matters as hiring additional people or buying new equipment. Since this form of guidance isn't readily available today, you may find yourself learning how to support your own case when seeking something from upper levels of management.

Also, with fewer middle managers available as gatekeepers for top management, formal requests for action may become backlogged since they will not have been pre-screened prior to presentation. As a result, individual items may actually take longer to go through the approval process. What can happen is that while something can go from the working level to topside more quickly, the time saved this way can be wasted with items waiting around for top managers to complete their reviews.

A related difficulty you may face is having to work without a great deal of staff support in many areas. Corporate trimming may have eliminated staff functions or sharply reduced their scope. Therefore, much of the expertise you used to call upon in specialized areas of personnel services and other staff functions may no longer be available to you. You may find yourself having to spend more time searching for answers that were formerly furnished by a staff member. So, although any slimmed down management structure may have increased your access to higher management, the loss of staff functions and guidance from middle managers may offset this advantage. However, whatever your personal situation may be, there are tactics you can use to counter this drop in support.

Develop Your Own Experts

When cutbacks eliminate staff departments, that doesn't necessarily mean the expertise isn't still available within the company. Frequently, relatively high salaried staff positions are eliminated, and the remaining staff functions are consolidated. In this manner, lower-level people are retained to perform the duties of the old department. Sometimes this is with a lower profile and the remaining employees are reassigned to another group. Therefore, don't arbitrarily assume because a staff department has been abolished that the functions it performs aren't available. This can happen if you work for a large company with many operating locations, or the staff functions are located in another building. Look around and you may be able to find the expert you're looking for operating out of another office.

The obvious question is why information wouldn't be published throughout the company that certain staff functions were still available despite the department's elimination. One possibility may be carelessness, based on the assumption at headquarters that everyone in the hinterlands is aware of the fact. A second likelihood is that top management doesn't want to advertise the retention of functions that were supposedly abolished. After all, sometimes staff functions are reduced in conjunction with large-scale layoffs in the operating groups. On occasion this may be done as a means of demonstrating that the pain of cutbacks is being shared equally throughout the company. When this happens, a particular staff function may be eliminated on the organizational charts, but still remain on a lower profile basis.

Even when staff functions are truly eliminated you may still be able to find expert advice within the company. Frequently, employees are transferred and reassigned to other positions when a reorganization takes place. In this way, you may be able to find people to help you who are now working in other jobs. Naturally they won't be obligated to assist you if their new duties have nothing to do with their former jobs. However, those whom you know from prior business dealings may be willing to give you some informal advice.

Look for Loopholes

When staff and middle management jobs are eliminated, the work that these employees used to do is passed on to someone else, unless it can be combined or eliminated through new technology. Still, in other situations, policies and procedures may be revised to eliminate various approval requirements and reporting procedures. What can often cause trouble is that when middle management or staff jobs are abolished, there is no simultaneous revision of the procedures which these people administered. For example, the employee who was responsible for certain reports is laid off, since top management has determined these reports are no longer necessary. However, the people in charge of such matters don't bother to change the procedure requiring the reports to be prepared. As a result of this oversight, everyone lower down in the organization continues to submit these reports.

When large scale reorganizations or extensive layoffs take place, many of these oversights can occur and they may not be quickly remedied. Simply put, there may be a great deal of confusion as to what requirements have to be met after wholesale changes take place, and until everything gets gradually sorted out, no one is quite sure of what procedures are to be followed. As a result, there is a tendency to try and conduct business as usual, which causes problems when the staff people or middle managers who formerly performed certain jobs are no longer available for assistance.

One of the tactics you can use to operate successfully with less staff and middle management support is to avoid time-consuming procedures on the assumption they don't have to be complied with, since the jobs of the people who administered them have been eliminated. If you're challenged, you can fall back on the fact that you can't send something for approval and/or advice to someone who is no longer with the company. The point is that there may be confusion as to who does what after substantive cutbacks. Rather than spin your wheels trying to do things the old way, take whatever shortcuts you can until you are told to do otherwise.

SUPERVISING YOUR WAY THROUGH AN ORGANIZATIONAL OVERHAUL

Reorganizations, large or small, are one of the unwelcome regularities you have to learn to live with in the business world. If you're fortunate, the reorganizations you have to endure will be few and far between. In any event, whatever their frequency, reorganizations present a particular set of problems for you as a supervisor. How well you learn to deal with these situations will strongly influence your ability to minimize the disruptive impact of a reorganization—both for yourself and those you supervise.

To a large extent, how severe the impact of a reorganization is on your department will depend on whether or not people in your group will be laid off or transferred elsewhere. But even where there is no direct effect on your group, a reorganization in other areas can still cause problems. The obvious example occurs when departments you work with have personnel cutbacks or shifts in work responsibility. This can significantly impact how your group's work is done, and may require substantial adjustments.

Plan Ahead

Long before reorganizations become reality they are generally fodder for the rumor mill. In fact, if you work for an employer where top-to-bottom communications are lacking, the first time you hear about a forthcoming reorganization may be from someone who works for you. Conversely, you may be consulted about a possible reorganization well before it takes place, particularly if it will in some way impact upon the group you supervise. In any event, once you get wind of a forthcoming reorganization, it's time to start planning to minimize its impact upon your own department.

What, if any, action you take will be predicated upon your assessment of how the reorganization will alter your department. For example, if you learn your group will be reporting to a different boss, then it certainly behooves you to maintain good relations with that individual in the interim. From another perspective, perhaps you are told you may lose one or two people from your group. If possible, try to line something up elsewhere within the company for these individuals if the advance information turns out to be correct. The specifics will vary with the circumstances, but the vital point is to do your best to position your department to survive and prosper when the reorganization takes place.

Keep Your Cool

Reorganizations create confusion in the minds of workers. This recedes with time as employees gradually adjust to the new reality in terms of who they work with and who they report to. In the interim, the best way for you to deal with this uncertainty is to remain calm and project a business-as-usual image. This alone will tend to reassure those who work for you that the reorganization isn't something to worry about.

Whenever reorganizations take place, the immediate worry of every employee is job security. "Will I or won't I lose my job?" is the first question every worker wants answered. Therefore, your first priority is to reassure your workers that they won't be losing their jobs, assuming that is true. In some situations, of course, reorganizations do result in job losses, and here you have additional responsibilities.

First of all, handle the termination of anyone who works for your department with both dignity and respect for the individual. The formal procedures will be dictated by company policy. But to the extent that you have any influence on the situation, do your best to see that workers receive the best deal possible. By doing this, you not only earn the gratitude of the departing workers, but also the respect of those who remain. This is important in terms of maintaining morale, since after a layoff workers are edgy about their future. If they have seen terminated co-workers treated fairly, they will be confident in receiving equitable treatment should the same fate befall them at some later date.

Aside from doing what you can for terminated employees, you also have to do your utmost to keep your department running smoothly both during and subsequent to any reorganization. The extent of your efforts in this regard will, of course, be influenced by the impact any layoff has on your unit.

Take Advantage of Opportunities

When reorganizations are in progress, a temporary void takes place where there is uncertainty as to duties and responsibilities. This may present you with the opportunity to adopt new work practices without the need of going through a long and involved approval cycle. After the dust settles, any changes you have made may go unchallenged on the assumption that they were part and parcel of the reorganization and not something you did on your own.

A reorganization may present you as well with an opportunity to unload a segment of your department's workload which has historically caused a great deal of difficulty. To do this successfully, be prepared to show improved efficiency by transferring as part of the reorganization the chore you want to unload. A timely suggestion to your boss that combining X with Z in another department might be met with enthusiasm during a reorganization, whereas in more stable times it would be summarily rejected. The reasoning for this is simple enough. No one wants to deal with change if it's unavoidable, so routine requests for shifts in responsibility tend to be rejected.

On the other hand, during a reorganization it becomes fashionable to recommend changes. Furthermore, from your boss's perspective, your suggestion gives the boss an opportunity to be an active contributor to the reorganization effort. This isn't insignificant, since aside from those who plan the changes, most other managers are reluctant bystanders. Therefore, being a participant marks your boss as someone who is aboard top management's reorganization initiative. If your boss is attuned to organizational politics, he or she will readily recognize any apple polishing possibilities that exist. If you're lucky, you may not only unload an unpleasant task, but also score some points for recommending the change.

PRUDENT WAYS TO COPE IF YOU HAVE TO CUT COSTS

You may well have had your department recently trimmed to the bone, and it seems certain that you have seen the last of cutbacks that will affect your group since it has been reduced as far as it can be. Unfortunately, those in upper management may be back yet again. On the other hand, you may have escaped unscathed in any previous trimming throughout your company. If that's true, there's little guarantee this will hold fast in the future. As a consequence, it pays to know how to make cuts as painless as possible if and when you face them.

Finesse Your Budget

The first step to take in trimming costs involves prevention. Always prepare budget requests with an eye toward the possibility of cutbacks. This isn't always done, particularly when business is good and the future looks bright. This picture can change rapidly for any number of reasons. For example, regardless of how healthy the economy, mergers, consolidations, new competition in the marketplace—all can lead to unforeseen belt tightening in the future. Therefore, always give yourself as much leeway as possible by beefing up your department when times are good. Obviously, you have to offer support for your requests which shouldn't be hard to do if business is brisk. Link your requests to continued expansion and provide plenty of data to support your claims.

All too often there's a tendency to concentrate budgetary efforts on labor costs and capital expenditures for equipment, giving only token or nonexistent recognition to items such as office supplies, training, travel, and so forth. This can create problems later if budget cuts are imposed. The more dollars you have in your budget under different budget categories, the greater your flexibility if you're told to cut your costs. Often budget cuts are stated broadly in across-the-board terms such as "Every department has to reduce costs ten percent." If this happens, then you want as much flexibility as possible in where you reduce your costs. It's a lot better to be in a position to spread reductions throughout categories such as travel and training than to have to reduce labor costs and give someone a termination notice.

Weed Out Waste

When you are faced with having to cut costs, look for ways to eliminate the "nice to have, but not really necessary" items first. These will vary with the nature of your specific work as well as with other factors. For example, if you frequently have employees who travel, perhaps you can combine trips to reduce travel costs. In the same area, maybe rental car expense can be reduced by staying at hotels closer to the visiting site.

Don't just concentrate on the major cost categories, since a lot of money is wasted by "nickel-and-diming" it away without it being noticed. For instance, if you are a heavy user of courier services and express delivery for packages and documents, looking closely may reveal unnecessary expenses for routine correspondence which could be sent by regular mail.

A big expenditure item may be overtime pay which has become a regular habit rather than a one-time emergency necessity. This can happen when employees become conditioned to a minimum number of hours of overtime pay every week. After a period of time, this additional money is viewed as part of the basic paycheck. As a result, workers don't want to lose it and will tend to arbitrarily justify its need. Needless to say, close supervision will prevent this, but occasionally it may have become an ingrained habit almost unknowingly. Therefore, if you do have significant overtime costs, this should be one of the first places to look if you have to make cutbacks.

Look for Ways to Minimize the Pain

No matter how well you cut costs, any significant cutback will require some serious reductions including the necessity to eliminate jobs within your department. Even when that is obvious, you may want to minimize the number of positions eliminated. Beyond that, you still have to consider how to get the same amount of work done with fewer people. This may call for a little creativity in terms of realigning jobs and cross-training employees to handle different tasks.

By carefully juggling and reassigning, you should find yourself able to cope. It may be difficult at first, but as employees become more flexible in handling different assignments the task should be easier. Incidentally, one of the overlooked aspects of cutbacks is the reaction of employees. The brunt of the burden of cutbacks falls upon the shoulders of those doing the work. Frequently, they haven't the foggiest idea of why the cuts are being made in the first place. This is particularly true in situations where they are unrelated to a general economic downturn. When business is bad, everyone knows and expects cuts, but workers don't relate to them just because XYZ Corp. merged with ABC Corp.

Therefore, one burden that comes your way is the need to communicate to your group just why the cutbacks are taking place. If the reasons appear dicey from your own vantage point, then ask your boss for information. Even if you aren't thoroughly convinced by the wisdom of what you hear, steel yourself to talk to your people. Explain in general terms the need for cutbacks to position the company to remain competitive. Emphasize that even though it may be hard to visualize at the present time, the more that is done to better the company's position in the marketplace, the better the chances for job security in the future. At no time, though, should you imply that everyone will have a job long-term because of the present actions. Statements like those may find their way back to haunt you somewhere down the road.

SENSIBLE METHODS FOR ADJUSTING THE WORKLOAD AFTER JOB CUTS

One of the toughest problems to deal with after your department has been reduced by job cuts is reallocating the workload. Typically, you may have lost people, but your group's workload has remained the same. In fact, it's not infrequent to see a reduction in people accompanied by an increase in work beyond what the original group handled. Does it make sense? Perhaps not, but that has never been a prerequisite to job reductions.

The end result is that you probably have more work than your group can absorb. And at the very least there will certainly be inadequacies in the distribution of the work formerly done by the employees who were lost from your group which will have to be addressed. This task alone requires a great deal of sensitivity and diplomacy.

Be Fair About Work Distribution

The easiest—but not the best—route to follow in redistributing work after job cuts is to parcel it out to the best workers in the group. The reasoning is simple enough. First of all, the slackers won't take on more chores, while the average employees are already handling all they can. This leaves only the top performers with the potential for being able to pick up the pace another notch. But adopting this tactic can cause a number of serious problems. First of all, your top performers won't be happy about being assigned additional work. They aren't being rewarded for it, and may feel they are being penalized for working harder than other people. This can lead to even greater problems if your top performers decide to look for work elsewhere because of being overworked and underappreciated. Always spread the work around as best you can when it becomes necessary to redistribute tasks.

Although it's brought about by necessity, job cutbacks can present an opportunity to realign tasks more in keeping with the skills of your employees. If layoffs occur, use this opportunity to create job assignments that best fit the talents of the people you have. By doing this, you can alleviate the problem of having your best workers pick up the slack when job cutbacks take place. Of course, many times there isn't a great deal of realignment that can be done. Yet even reassigning a few tasks here and there can improve the overall output of your unit. Of equal importance, it shows that you are trying to parcel out the additional workload on an equitable basis, which will help to defuse any potential hostility on the part of your more experienced workers.

This is also the opportune time to eliminate any work which borders on being nonessential. Minimize the preparation of reports, cut back on meetings, eliminate any duplication of effort, and take any other measures necessary to free up time so that your remaining employees can handle added duties without being hopelessly overburdened.

Open lines of communication help immeasurably when jobs have been cut and work needs to be reassigned. If you are easily able to discuss matters with your direct reports, then it's useful to have them help plan how the group's workload can be adjusted. Making employees active participants in these decisions encourages teamwork and will prevent the resentment that might arise if you arbitrarily reassigned the workload of departed employees.

Recognize Reality

It's all well and good to try to compensate for job cuts within your department. Nevertheless, there is a limit as to how far you can go and still be able to get the job done. If you don't recognize this, then you will find yourself falling further and further behind in your department's work. You also have to be careful not to push your people too hard, since beyond a certain point it becomes self-defeating. Mistakes will become common, quality will suffer, and careless errors will be made. Furthermore, fatigue will result in increased absences as workers call in sick to get a respite from the hectic pace.

To avoid these problems you have to face reality and recognize when your department has more work than it can possibly handle. Let your boss know this and ask for advice on how to handle the problem. The standard answer you are likely to get is, "Do the best you can," or some variation of that theme. That, of course, doesn't solve your problem. About your only recourse in this situation is to prioritize your work. Concentrate on getting the most important jobs out and let the other work slip. You should also keep your boss posted with memos as to how you are proceeding in the absence of having enough people to do the job. This will protect you should problems arise in the future and your boss suffers a convenient loss of memory about telling you to do the job with the people you have.

2 Dealing with a Changing Work Force

Among the primary issues you have to deal with as a supervisor are the changes taking place in the makeup of the work force, as well as employee needs in terms of their responsibilities beyond the workplace. First and foremost in this regard is the need to recognize and deal with work force diversity issues. This may take on more significance for some supervisors than for others, especially if you're supervising employees with limited English speaking capabilities.

For other supervisors, the main concern may be having to cope with young entrants into the workplace who may lack even the most fundamental working skills. Another imperative is to be able to recognize and make effective use of older workers who offer a wealth of experience, yet may no longer want to work forty or more hours a week. Learning how to best utilize this important source of skills can make a significant contribution toward maintaining a competent and skilled work force.

Beyond these factors are the off-the-job concerns of workers which can play an important part in their productivity. Parents, of course, can require some flexibility in working hours to cope with child-care needs and other parenting concerns. Then there are those employees who may have aging parents to take care of. Whatever someone's personal status may be, everyone encounters problems from time to time. It's easy to establish a rigid policy that everyone must adhere to, but that will send the best and brightest of workers off to work for competitors who offer more enlightened personnel practices. Therefore, it's a fundamental necessity to be both flexible and practical in trying to accommodate employee needs.

Another broad area of change that can't be ignored concerns how the work force is deployed. It used to be that full-time permanent on-site employment was the norm; this is no longer the sole standard. Today there's widespread use of permanent part-time and temporary employees as a regular component of any given business. One of the most important and difficult issues to deal with from a supervisor's perspective is learning how to manage employees who telecommute. As you well know, it's difficult enough to manage people on-site, but when they work at home a new and complex quandary is added to your supervisory role. How to deal with these varied issues from a supervisory viewpoint is the focus of this chapter.

RECOGNIZING AND DEALING WITH WORK FORCE DIVERSITY ISSUES

The make-up of America's work force is, of course, as wide-ranging as the populace in general. Whether it's race, gender, or age differences, there are factors that have to be considered in supervising those who work for you. A lack of sensitivity in this area frequently stems not so much from deliberate intent, but rather from failing to see certain subtleties that may distinguish one worker from another. Everyone isn't cast from the same mold, nor should they be treated as if they were.

For example, something as simple as age differences may require adjustment in dealing with employees. As a group, younger employees may not have the same regard for observing working hours as more mature employees. On the other hand, older employees may not have the ability to maintain the same physical pace as younger workers. Naturally within any group there may be exceptions to certain of these generalizations, which you as the supervisor will readily recognize within individual subordinates. The important point is the need to recognize subtle differences and not to apply the same rigid standards to everyone.

Furthermore, even where there are differences, there may be compensating factors that offset weaknesses in one area with strengths in another. For instance, although older workers may not be able to do physical chores faster than younger employees, they may well offset this disadvantage by their job experience, which in the end allows them to do a better all around job.

Beyond the age variances, there are also needs related to race, gender, and cultural differences. This alone can lead to controversy and confusion over the sorts of problems you have to work through: How flexible can you be? What about the fairness issue concerning other employees? The extent of the guidance in company policy will also influence the approach you take.

Individual diversity issues will vary somewhat according to the composition of your work force. For example, if you supervise a group which has workers who may be foreign-born, who speak little or no English, then language training may be a priority. If the company sponsors English lessons, be sure to encourage the participation of any of your workers who are having language problems. Even if this training isn't available within the company, make the extra effort to help employees find English lessons from private sources within the community. Assisting immigrants in adapting to both the job and the workplace environment isn't all pain with no gain for you as a supervisor. The more you do to help employees assimilate, the more likely it is that you will earn their loyalty. That translates into lower labor turnover and more productive workers.

Challenge Subtle Discrimination

Although blatant discrimination in the workplace has been largely eliminated, subtle discrimination can and still does take place. This can take many forms and some of it stems from historical stereotypes surrounding gender and race. For example, workers ignoring co-workers in casual conversation or in the social gatherings that are part and parcel of the fabric of the workplace, constitutes subtle discrimination. This isn't something that can always be easily identified or dealt with. Often the snubs will be typically denied or shrugged off as an oversight with no intent to discriminate. In fact, that might sometimes be true.

What then can you as a supervisor do to conquer this within your unit? The first and best action you can take is to be a role model in accepting everyone on an equal footing. If you show respect for everyone, you set the tone for people to follow. Beyond that, if you observe instances of subtle discrimination, question them. If someone appears to be habitually excluded from a traditional Friday lunch gathering of your group, bring the person along yourself. In other words, set the tone where everyone is welcomed as a part of your team. Furthermore, let it be known that nothing less will be tolerated.

Above all else, dealing with a diverse work force requires sensitivity. It's important to recognize that cultural backgrounds dictate people's actions in certain situations. This extends to the way people react to those whom they view as being in a position of authority, which includes you as a supervisor. Not recognizing this trait could frustrate you in any attempt to become friendly with a particular worker who happens to be foreign-born. You might assume the person's reticence around you is snobby or standoffish when, in reality, it is a cultural trait involving respect for authority. Therefore, be cautious about jumping to conclusions when dealing with people from other backgrounds. Don't forget, some of your actions are as unusual to them as theirs may be to you. Be patient, extend a helping hand, be respectful of others, and you will succeed in having a united team no matter how diverse the individual backgrounds may be.

ADOPTING NEW SUPERVISION STRATEGIES WHEN EMPLOYEES WORK AT HOME

If you presently have people reporting to you who work from home on either a part-time or full-time basis, you may find it somewhat of a challenge to supervise employees who are not physically on-site. It's admittedly difficult in certain areas such as maintaining adequate communications, but it's certainly not an insurmountable task. In fact, in certain fields such as sales, supervisors have long ago learned how to manage a remote work force.

The biggest problems arise when off-site supervision becomes a reality for supervisors who have always had their subordinates working at the same location. The transition to supervising those who are no longer immediately available for face-to-face discussions on matters large or small can be troubling at first. So whether you have recently had employees start to work from home, or contemplate that possibility in the near future, let's look at some supervisory strategies you can use.

Selecting Workers for At-home Assignments

First of all, you will have to adjust some of your supervisory practices to conform to the needs of off-site workers. Hopefully, the work-at-home option within your company is voluntary, since this will give you the option of selecting those volunteers who have the best chance of success as telecommuters. This alone will make your life a little easier. The best candidates for telecommuting are those who volunteer for a specific reason such as being able to combine telecommuting with parenting duties. These people have a built-in incentive to make telecommuting successful and therefore are more highly motivated to work well independently.

In addition, any employee who tends to work well with minimal direction is better suited to a telecommuting role, as opposed to those workers whom you have to supervise most closely. Therefore, the selection process for at-home assignments shouldn't be too difficult.

It's also preferable to select only experienced workers, since those still learning the job can benefit more from having their problems dealt with on a face-to-face basis. Veteran workers will also have established friendships at work which can be maintained when they start to telecommute. Newer workers who telecommute will find it much harder to have social contacts with peers and in general to gain the advantages of personal interaction within the company.

Manage Performance—Not People

When you have telecommuters to supervise, you must concentrate on work results rather than on impressions from observing the person within the workplace environment. As you know, results count, but sometimes this can be overlooked, especially when someone has personality tendencies that don't appear to jibe with performance. For example, a practical joker may earn a reputation as a goof-off even though he or she easily outperforms any peers. You may well know this, but the same may not hold true for other managers within your company. For this reason, it may be easier to manage some people as telecommuters.

If the nature of the work that telecommuters perform can be easily measured in quantitative terms, then there will be little problem in noticing if any fall-off in output takes place. On the other hand, if the work performed at home can't be easily measured, then you will have to learn to trust your telecommuting subordinates more than you might if they were within the workplace. Nevertheless, this isn't as serious a problem as it might seem. Admittedly it's easier to goof off if you're working from home, but eventually it will catch up with those who aren't performing up to par. In truth, even though it's harder to goof off in the workplace, those intent on doing so can find all kinds of forms of work avoidance.

The fundamentals of a good supervisory strategy for managing at-home workers should also include periodic meetings with telecommuters. These serve several purposes. First and foremost, they provide the opportunity to review work progress, discuss any problems, and facilitate the personal interaction that is missing in a telecommuting environment. In addition, there are certain matters that are best communicated on a person-to-person basis, rather than by phone or e-mail. These include various types of personnel matters, and anything that can be construed as either bad news or good news.

Incidentally, when telecommuting employees are in the office, give them sufficient time for conversation with their peers. This helps tremendously in filling the social void that's created by off-site assignments. It's easy to forget this in the rush to cover everything work-related while the employee is in the office, so make a mental note to allow telecommuters sufficient downtime.

One of the biggest general headaches for many supervisors is giving performance evaluations, which become even more trying with telecommuters. One reason is that many factors on the average performance evaluation form are either totally or partially irrelevant when dealing with telecommuters. "Presents a good appearance" is relatively meaningless in a work-at-home environment. Meanwhile other factors, such as the ability to work well independently, aren't given enough weight. Therefore, unless the form is geared toward telecommuting, make the necessary allowances when you do the evaluation. Aside from that, there really shouldn't be that much of a problem in evaluating at-home workers, especially if they have been telecommuting for any length of time.

One important factor you shouldn't ignore is the training needs of your telecommuters. You can easily forget about at-home workers when seminars and other training sessions are held in-house. It's unintentional, since it's relatively easy to gather your on-site workers for a one-hour training session, but telecommuters have to be notified ahead of time. Furthermore, the timing of the training can ruin the better part of a whole business day. Giving a one-hour training session in the middle of the day means the telecommuter will spend much of the balance of working hours commuting. These minimal problems can be avoided with a little bit of planning. Incidentally, it's also crucial to be certain the equipment needs of your telecommuters are being met. Trying to run a telecommuter program with outdated equipment can seriously reduce worker productivity. Therefore, be sure to stay on top of their equipment needs, even though in most cases they will quickly let you know of any inadequacies.

SENSIBLE WAYS TO MANAGE WORKERS WHO TELECOMMUTE

Along with adopting new operating techniques when workers telecommute, you also need to be practical in how off-site workers are managed. There are advantages for both companies and employees when workers can work part or all of the week from their homes. On the other hand, it's not necessarily as beneficial as it might appear, even for those workers who willingly jumped at the initial opportunity to be home-based. For one thing, work has a social side that is not always evident until employees are thrust into the role of working at home on their own. Not only does this require you as a supervisor to adjust your management practices, but it requires workers to do some adjusting of their own. You as the immediate supervisor can help by carefully monitoring and counseling employees who may be having trouble making the adjustment.

Where do workers' problems most frequently occur? One of the hardest adjustments is being able to discipline themselves to observe a reasonable semblance of working hours. It's very easy for someone to have another cup of coffee, or take a walk in the garden, rather than sit down and tackle a boring project. It may, of course, be equally difficult to get started at the office, but there aren't the enticing alternatives available there that exist at home. Furthermore, the implied threat of a boss dropping by the desk to check on progress is a built-in deterrent to goofing off at work. Even though the phone and computer provide equal access at home or in the office, that's not quite the same level of oversight that a face-to-face encounter can provide.

Even where workers conscientiously work away at home—sometimes even harder than they would at the office—there may be a growing dissatisfaction with being away from the office. Once the newness of telecommuting wears off, workers can start to miss the friendship and office gossip that bring an added social dimension to their lives. There are also seeds of doubt that can form about the career damage to being out of sight on a regular basis. Employees may worry that being out-of-the-loop will harm their chances for promotions and other job opportunities.

Of course, in some situations telecommuting may be the answer to an employee's real personal problem, such as the need to be at home with young children. In such a situation, telecommuting can be a real bonanza. But even beyond working parents, telecommuting can have distinct advantages for any number of employees. For example, someone with a long and difficult commute may find the elimination of this arduous daily trek offsets any potential disadvantages that telecommuting might have.

There may also be cost savings for employees who telecommute, which in some cases can be substantial. In addition to transportation costs, meal expenses and clothing costs can also be cut when employees eat lunch in their own kitchen and dress in what's comfortable and probably a lot less expensive.

All in all, it's easy to see that working from home has both advantages and disadvantages which can vary from worker to worker. For this reason alone, when telecommuting opportunities arise within the operation you supervise, you should carefully counsel employees about the pros and cons. If it is a voluntary option within your department, then you don't want to steer employees in one direction or the other. Naturally, the policy guidelines established within your company will dictate how each situation is handled. In most cases, guidelines will be established as to which groups of employees are eligible for telecommuting, and whatever limitations are instituted as to minimum staffing in the office, periodic reporting for on-site work by telecommuters, and so forth.

Once you have established your new supervision strategies to deal with telecommuters, your on-going management practices won't be all that different from those when you had everyone on-site all of the time. Where you may encounter the most difficulty is in realizing that, just as in the office, telecommuters can't all be managed the same way. Some people need more supervision than others. In addition, not all workers will be as diligent once they are out of the office and beyond the vigilant eye of their boss. You will have to adjust your day-to-day management to attune your supervision to individual quirks.

The thing that work-at-home employees miss most about the office will likely be their interaction with co-workers. From a career standpoint, they may also worry about becoming an unknown quantity in terms of eligibility for promotions and transfers. Both of these problems can be minimized if employees spend one or two days a week in the office on a regular schedule. This, of course, can vary with company policy and the nature of the work. In any event, use these on-site days to go over details that are more easily done in person than by phone or computer. This includes such matters as job performance counseling, work criticism, praise, and so forth. This also provides scheduled time to be used for duties which are more effectively performed in person.

In addition, you should always try to brief employees personally on the general comings and goings of what's been happening within the company. This will help fill the void employees feel about being left out of the loop when they telecommute. Probably the most important facet of managing home-based employees is to be a good communicator with the flexibility to adapt to remote-site supervision.

DEALING WITH THE WORKING HOUR CONSTRAINTS OF PARENTS

As a supervisor, you must make sensitive decisions on various requests from working parents who are trying to juggle the competing demands of employment and child rearing. Naturally, if you work for one of the few companies which still have rigid policies of not allowing any sort of flexibility in time and attendance, then your main function is to listen to criticism and complaints from unhappy workers. However, if like most companies there is built-in flexibility, or it's left to supervisory discretion, then you have the dual role of how best to meet employee needs in this area, while still making certain the workload demands are met.

Your biggest headache is having to reject legitimate requests for time off because of workplace necessities. This is never easy to do, but if you have good rapport with your subordinates, then they are far more likely to be understanding when you have to reject such a request. One of the keys to minimizing problems in this area is for some careful planning on two fronts. First is scheduling workload and being constantly alert to any future changes that can be foreseen. Doing this carefully will give you an idea of any peaks and valleys in workload that may make it either easier or harder to grant requests for time off.

The other aspect of planning is the responsibility of your employees. That is for them to do everything possible to plan for meeting household emergencies without having to request time off in the first place. It's certainly both responsible and practical to be flexible about giving workers time off to meet emergency needs; nevertheless, the primary burden is upon employees to do everything possible to avoid having to ask for unscheduled time off.

For example, parents may need more time off on an unscheduled basis to deal with emergency situations at home. Even something as routine as a sick child can cause a worker to call in absent at the last minute. Therefore, working parents with young children have to be cut a little slack. Nevertheless, it behooves parents to establish networks for emergency needs in addition to regular child-care responsibilities. This means having back-ups available to fill in when a regular child care provider is unavailable, or during school holidays, vacations, and other non-routine occasions. This will help to limit the amount of time a parent has to be away from the job.

How much of a scheduling problem you have with working parents will be greatly influenced by company policy. If your employer offers one or more flexible work schedules, then it becomes much easier for them to cope with their parental responsibilities. Among the types of flexible work schedules are:

- Flextime, which allows workers to have certain core hours during which they work, but otherwise allows flexibility in areas such as starting and finishing times.

- Job sharing, where two people share the same position allowing them both to work less than a full-time work week.

- Traditional part-time employment, which is particularly helpful if workers are able to temporarily shift to part-time status in the same type of job.

- Compressed work weeks such as forty hours in four days, with other variations common.

- Telecommuting, where workers work at home either full-time or some combination of days on-site and at home.

Surprisingly, workers aren't always fully aware of all the possibilities even where flexible scheduling exists. In other instances, they may have an awareness but feel insecure about asking for any assistance. Their reasoning generally centers around the fear that not being in the regular loop will have an adverse impact on their future with the company. It's important for you as their supervisor to take the initiative in assuring workers that they have the full support of both you and the company in meeting their parental duties. Your support and reassurance as a boss can go a long way toward helping your employees cope with parental duties. This sort of assistance is appreciated and workers will respond favorably to a boss who is supportive of their needs.

EIGHT WAYS TO BE FLEXIBLE ABOUT EMPLOYEE FAMILY RESPONSIBILITIES

It's admittedly a lot easier to cope with employee family-related difficulties by basically adhering to a "No exceptions to the rule" policy, whereby everyone goes by a rigid set of standards. That may be easy, but in the long run it won't do much for employee productivity, much less employee retention. And as you well know, supervising unhappy workers doesn't make for pleasant circumstances, either for you or for those you supervise. Therefore, for very practical reasons it's worthwhile to make the effort to be creative in meeting some of the inevitable requests that employees will make. Although how requests are handled will vary with the job requirements and existing workload, a few general ways to be flexible are as follows:

1. *Recognize differences.* There will be differences among the individual problems facing employees in meeting their family responsibilities. Some workers may have time constraints imposed for picking up their children from school or child care which may conflict with working hours on a regular basis. This sort of difficulty requires a permanent solution since it is a repetitive problem. Other people may have an occasional need to take time off to meet a specific obligation such as taking the kids to the dentist or aging parents to medical appointments. These one-time issues frequently require on-the-spot supervisory decisions on how to manage the absentee employee's workload. This is particularly true with requests of an emergency nature. The important point is to recognize differences in worker needs and be willing to deal with each request on an individual basis, while still striving to maintain your group's productivity.

2. *Be willing to compromise with employees in meeting their needs.* When an employee's request can't be met, don't just arbitrarily reject it. Look for ways to work out a compromise that will help resolve the problem. For example, perhaps you can't grant someone's request to work five hours less per week in order to start work an hour

later each morning. However, it may be doable if the employee simply worked an hour later each night to make up the difference. Compromises can be worked out if you make the effort to sit down and sift through the possibilities with employees.

3. *Suggest alternatives.* Apart from working out some form of compromise to deal with employee family problems, make an effort to suggest alternatives. You may come up with an idea that the employee hadn't thought about. But even if you don't, your willingness to discuss various possibilities shows your interest in helping the employee resolve the problem. This thoughtfulness inspires greater worker loyalty than would otherwise be the case.

4. *Expect the unexpected.* One of the most frustrating aspects of dealing with employee family-related problems is that they usually seem to arise at the most inconvenient times. For example, in the same week that a top priority project is due for completion, a key employee suddenly needs time off. This can and does happen, although perhaps not as often as we like to imagine. The important point is to learn to take these things in stride when they do occur. Getting upset isn't good for either you or the employee. It's admittedly a challenge to cope with these crises when they do arise, but anger or outright rejection of an employee's request won't solve the problem.

5. *Exercise patience.* Work-related family problems aren't just a hassle for you as a supervisor. They are, of course, even more troubling to the employee who is trying to cope with the difficulty. For this reason, your ability to be patient with employees who have family responsibilities that conflict with work can go a long way toward easing the situation. The very fact that workers know you are sympathetic and will work with them on a solution to the problem helps ease employee anxieties. It helps create an environment where a satisfactory solution can be worked out. This isn't insignificant since it can mean the difference between retaining a productive employee or having someone quit because of a perceived lack of concern by the boss about a difficult dilemma.

6. *Use care in rejecting requests.* There will be times when employee requests for time off to meet family responsibilities will have to be rejected. Sometimes this will happen because working around the absence of the employee is totally impossible. On rarer occasions,

it may be the result of an employee request which is totally frivolous. As long as you're not violating any constraints imposed by law, and are operating within internal procedures, you have the right to reject employee requests for either time off or an adjustment in working hours. That, however, is of little comfort when you know you have to turn down an employee request because there is no satisfactory solution that would allow you to grant the request. Nevertheless, when this becomes necessary, how you go about rejecting the request will help minimize employee reactions. Let employees know that you sympathize with their predicament, and let them know why it's not possible to grant their request. As long as you're forthright and honest in your dealings with your workers, they may not agree with your decision, but they will likely understand why you made it. Handling rejections isn't important just in terms of the person making the request, because other employees will also watch how you handle these situations. If you are seen as being fair, then rejections will be taken in stride.

7. *Be fair to everyone.* Routinely granting requests for employees to take time off, or at least temporarily adjusting their working hours to cope with family responsibilities can create resentment among other workers. Those who are single may resent the fact that they have to pick up the slack for their married co-workers. Even employees with children who are fortunate enough to have circumstances where they don't require time off can be envious. The thinking may be, "If I can manage without special treatment, why can't so-and-so?" It's nice to think that everyone is charitable enough not to be envious of their peers, but this isn't always the case. Furthermore, if additional work is required of people on a fairly regular basis to compensate for absentee co-workers, then it's reasonable to expect some degree of resentment. To prevent this attitude from developing it's important to be equally considerate of legitimate requests for time off from those who are single and otherwise not in need of working hour exceptions. It's not always possible for people to conveniently conduct all of their personal business on their non-working hours. So if a worker needs some time to run a personal chore be flexible about granting it. This will convey to employees that you are fair across the board, and will minimize any

hostility about unfair treatment for workers with children. Naturally, you have to avoid being taken advantage of by the one or two people who may view your flexibility as an opportunity to take extended lunch hours or leave early on Friday for a round of golf.

8. *Pre-plan.* The better you are able to plan ahead to meet unexpected absences or make adjustments in workers' schedules, the easier it will be to cope with workload priorities when employees ask for time off. Unfortunately, to some extent you're trying to plan the unplannable, since it's impossible to predict the emergency needs of employees. A child care worker not showing up because of illness can't be programmed. Nevertheless, there are many needs that can be anticipated. For example, child care during school holidays can be arranged beforehand by parents, who should not be coming to a supervisor with an emergency request for time off. To this end, get together with employees and encourage them to plan ahead. Furthermore, request that workers notify you well in advance if they know they may need time off. Sometimes employees wait until the last minute simply because they are hesitant about approaching the boss with their request. Letting people know you will be accommodating and asking them to reciprocate by giving you as much advance notice as possible should help to minimize scheduling around absentee workers.

GETTING THE MOST OUT OF PART-TIME WORKERS

You may be in a position to regularly use a large number of part-time workers on either a seasonal or year-round basis. If so, you have long since learned the value of part-timers as well as the special supervisory problems which they create. If you happen to be in a supervisory slot where you haven't had a great deal of past experience in this area, then the benefits and difficulties may be unknown to you.

In any event, whether you do or don't use part-time workers at the present time, they may become a viable option at some time in the future. Therefore, it's to your advantage to know how to maximize their productivity. This isn't something that's always considered, even where part-timers are a regular part of the workforce component. Sometimes in these situations, the part-timers are considered as fill-ins or limited duty contributors with no long-term role. As a result, there is little or no emphasis placed on motivating or training them to render them more profitable to the company. To avoid this it helps to consider how best to make the most of any part-time workers who may be assigned to your supervision, either now or in the future.

Try Before You Buy

There's no better way to evaluate candidates for full-time positions than to have them working for you in a part-time capacity. It gives you a first-hand opportunity to observe their skills and adaptability to the work environment. Therefore, if your position offers you an opportunity to use this strategy as a hiring tool, it's to your advantage to do so.

Part-timers can benefit you in another way when it comes to hiring. For example, let's assume you want to fill a full-time vacancy but your requests are continually turned down on budgetary grounds with standard responses such as, "We can't afford a replacement right now." Once you're convinced you won't be able to fill the position full-time, try for part-time. Say something such as, "Why don't we hire a part-time person on a temporary basis?" Frequently this request will be agreed to as it provides a money-saving solution for your boss, and it eliminates your repetitive requests to fill the vacancy. Later, after you have had the part-timer on the job for a few months you can seek to get the position converted to full-time. This not only provides an opportunity to evaluate the employee before a full-time hire, but it provides an avenue to fill a vacancy through a back-door approach.

Before and beyond any consideration of evaluating part-timers for full-time employment is the basic question of how to find and hire the best possible part-time people. This isn't insignificant, especially if you are using part-time workers on a more or less permanent basis. All too often, carelessness creeps into the hiring process for part-timers based on the assumption that they aren't as important as full-time hires. In reality, they are, with the essential difference that they work fewer hours. Therefore, it pays to exercise equal care in their selection.

Your own employees are an excellent source of part-time help. They may have friends or relatives who are available for part-time work. Assuming they are otherwise qualified, there's an additional advantage in hiring these people. The employee friend or relative will exert subtle pressure on the part-timer not to screw up on the job. Furthermore, full-time employees aren't likely to recommend hiring someone who may be a source of embarrassment for them.

In addition, local schools and colleges are a ready source of part-time help. Close coordination with school guidance counselors can help you pick the cream of the crop for your company.

Incidentally, apart from specific job qualifications, you want to verify the potential for job applicants to stay with the company for a reasonable length of time. This, of course, can't be programmed, but some part-timers, especially students, regularly job hop, especially in good economic times. Therefore, if you are looking to hire someone for an extended period of time, you want to establish the likelihood of the person staying with the company before you hire them. Some can be obviously eliminated since a high school senior going off to college or full-time employment after graduation won't be likely to stay longer than the balance of the academic year. On the other hand, if you are using the part-time opening to evaluate high school seniors for full-time openings, then this is the type of candidate you should be looking for. The point is to interview candidates with the goal of determining how they meet your needs both in terms of skills and potential for retention with the company.

Part-timers Offer Flexibility

Using part-timers in conjunction with your full-time personnel will give you an added degree of flexibility in dealing with scheduling problems. For example, they can be used to fill the gap when a full-time employee asks for time off on short notice—perhaps to deal with a family-related problem or some other crisis. It's usually easy enough to fill the gap by scheduling the part-timer for more hours, or by asking a part-timer who may have the day off to come into work. Obviously, a part-timer may not have the skills to cover for some positions, but if you take the time to familiarize them with various jobs, they should be able to pick up the slack on a temporary basis.

The key to getting the most out of your part-time employees is to deal with them as valued employees rather than relegating them to second-class status. If your company offers benefits to part-timers that are equivalent to those accorded to full-time workers, this makes your job easier. But even if benefits are lacking, the important point is for you to treat both full-timers and part-timers in your group equally. When you do this, part-timers will be more productive and willing to take on new assignments. Incidentally, the more you cross-train part-timers in different jobs, the greater the flexibility you will have to meet scheduling emergencies, and to fill vacant full-time positions with a part-timer who knows how to do the job.

KNOWING HOW TO SUPERVISE AND MOTIVATE CONTINGENT WORKERS

Many companies in the new and ever-changing workplace are emphasizing the use of contingent workers. These are usually temporary workers supplied by agencies or hired directly by the company. They serve a variety of purposes, such as to meet cyclical demands in business volume, or to provide temporary expertise in a particular skill. One prime reason for their use is to buffer the permanent workforce against layoffs. Whatever the purpose of using contingent workers, there can be disadvantages, primarily from the transient nature of these workers which makes them less apt to have the same dedication and loyalty as full-time employees. This makes your job as a supervisor more difficult.

As with permanent part-time workers, every effort should be made to treat temporary employees as valued contributors to the group. Include them in company social activities whenever it's feasible to do so, and don't neglect to have them participate in group meetings. Even though they may be on board for only a relatively short period of time, being asked to participate in meetings will give these people a sense of belonging to your unit and will help to motivate them to greater productivity.

Of course, you have to be practical in terms of how much effort you put into making temporaries an inclusive part of your group. This largely depends upon the length of time they will spend on the job. If it's only a fill-in assignment for a few days, it probably isn't worthwhile to include contingent workers in meetings covering issues which won't affect them. On the other hand, if temporary workers will be on board for a month or longer, then it makes sense for them to fully participate in the activities of the department. In fact, certain temporary employees may perform specific duties on a recurring basis for your company. This is particularly true when individuals are hired by a company as independent contractors to provide specific skills which the company requires on a periodic basis but doesn't need or want to hire permanent help to perform. This concept has led to employment of temporary workers in a wide variety of professional and technical areas. Naturally, someone like this who is working closely with you within your group should be treated as a full-fledged contributor to the group's efforts.

Always make certain to give temporary workers a brief orientation including basics, such as where employees eat lunch, location of rest rooms, introductions to people they will interact with and so forth. This not only makes the temporary worker feel more at ease, but it also spares you from frequent interruptions to answer basic questions.

As difficult as it may be to motivate temporary workers, it becomes even harder if they are openly ignored or resented by permanent employees. This may occur in situations where permanent workers perceive the temporary people as filling permanent job slots. This may, in fact, be the case in many instances, since one of the reasons for using temporary workers is to avoid the periodic hiring and firing of permanent employees as a business experiences its ups and downs. For this reason, it's necessary to point out to your permanent employees that the use of temporary workers contributes to their job security by minimizing the need for layoffs when business is slow. Taking the time to explain this will spare you unnecessary supervisory problems.

COPING WITH YOUNG WORKERS WHO LACK FUNDAMENTAL WORKING SKILLS

Business leaders are prone to periodic griping about the quality of public education which turns out high school graduates who often lack even the basic skills necessary for employment. That, of course, isn't news to any supervisor who has had to cope with young workers, some of whom don't even have the motivation to report for work on time. Sometimes supervisory wrath over the inadequacies of new workers is directed at the human resources department with comments such as, "If personnel would give us some decent job candidates, we wouldn't have these headaches." Personnel people will often retort, "You made the hiring decision, so don't blame us."

Unfortunately, this back-and-forth stream of indignation and accusations is generally misguided, since the pool of job candidates is where the problem lies. And if the quality of the job applicant pool is low, the end result is that you as a supervisor have to live with what's available. This places the burden on you as the immediate supervisor to take whatever action is necessary to bring young workers up to an acceptable level of performance. It means you have to spend a great deal more time and effort than you might like to in this area. But with no available alternatives, there is little else you can do.

If you, along with other supervisors, have a continuing stream of young workers lacking basic work skills, then you should lobby for support systems to be set up within the company to provide adequate training systems. For example, perhaps formal classes can be held in basic language and math skills. In fact, even general tutorials on what is expected from employees, such as adhering to time and attendance policies and other basic fundamentals, are of value. Also, liberal question and answer sessions where young workers can get their most basic questions answered help to educate new employees as to the expectations of the company. Classes held regularly by staff people are cost-effective where large numbers of young workers are entering company employment on a regular basis. However, if only an occasional younger worker is hired, then you as the supervisor may have to do most of the "heavy lifting" in terms of basic skills training. In fact, even where formal structured assistance is provided by staff members, you will still have job-related responsibilities in terms of training young workers in their specific duties. Along with that, you will also have to supervise younger workers more closely to help them become valued employees.

To address some specifics for dealing with younger employees, the following are a few of the most prevalent problems you will encounter:

1. Younger workers may display an indifferent attitude about working hours and may have little hesitancy about coming in late, leaving early, or taking an occasional day off—most often Fridays and Mondays. Deal with this problem right away before the employee gets into a permanent bad habit. Emphasize the importance of respecting working hours in your initial orientation with young employees. At the first violation, sit down with the employee and reemphasize the rules. If the abuse continues, gradually increase the pressure with sanctions such as docking pay and formal reprimands. The point is to emphasize that you have no intention of letting the employees set their own working hours. You may find some younger workers quit in a huff over such matters. This isn't uncommon with those new to the workforce, as they tend to job hop initially. Don't panic over younger workers quitting rather than observing basic policies on time and attendance. Eventually you will find someone who has greater employability skills.

2. Being a good listener is a skill that many mature adults haven't mastered, so there should be little reason to expect that those in their teens or early twenties will listen attentively to what you or anyone else has to say. In fact, many of those in these age brackets assume they already know everything there is to know. The point here is that you have to exercise a great deal of patience along with a lot of repetition to make your point with this group. Hang in there though, as, believe it or not, these people are capable of understanding what you're saying.

3. Don't assume too much in terms of what younger workers know. It's easy to overlook the fact that young workers new to the job market have no knowledge of even the most fundamental basics of the workplace. Everything from manner of dress to office politics is in the realm of the unknown for them. Therefore, be prepared to spend a good deal of time in on-the-job training in basic workplace fundamentals as well as in the standard job-specific training any new employee would receive. Because of the time involved, if it's at all possible, try to pair newly hired young workers with an experienced mentor. Be careful here, though, since you want them teamed up with someone who has both knowledge, communications skills, and most of all, a positive attitude toward the job and company.

4. Those new to the workplace will tend to act casually. What this means is that they are just as likely to challenge the knowledge of a senior manager as that of a co-worker; they may easily insult someone, and in general may relate to people at work much as they would outside of work. This is to be expected and is solely due to inexperience with the formalities and nuances of the workplace. All you can do here is to provide sufficient oversight, along with a little guidance, to avoid any big blunders. As a preventive measure, it helps to specifically identify to whom the employee should go with problems, which for the most part will be either you or someone you have appointed as a mentor.

There's a Positive Side to the Effort Involved

Although there is a lot more work involved in training younger workers there is a bright side that can make the effort worthwhile. Hiring an experienced worker generally means a smooth transition into the organization; however, that person comes aboard with workplace skills learned elsewhere. These may not necessarily jibe with your notions of how certain things should be done. Remember the common refrain of newly hired experienced workers, which is, "That's not the way I used to do it at the XYZ Corp." Having someone who doesn't want to abandon an old way of doing things can truly be a real headache.

By contrast, a young employee, new to the workplace, will be trained to do things the way you want them done. You will eventually have someone who has been trained in your mold. Over the long-term this should give you a valued team member who best meets the standards you have set for your department.

RECOGNIZING AND ADJUSTING TO THE NEEDS OF OLDER WORKERS

Just as there are special problems associated with supervising younger workers, there are also certain considerations related to managing the more mature members of your group. As it happens, though, the uncommon needs of older employees are often ignored.

For one thing, these are veteran employees with a wealth of experience so there's little realization of any difficulty. Alternatively, when it gets to the point that an older worker may appear to be slowing down on the job, the assumption is that it's just another case of someone nearing retirement. With that thought in mind, no action of any sort appears to be warranted.

What can happen is that a supervisor may consciously or unconsciously give difficult assignments to younger workers. This is often done with the best interests of the mature worker in mind, even though the worker, if queried, might respond otherwise. In fact, this form of pandering might be seen by an older worker as a gentle attempt to nudge him or her out the door to retirement. The end result may be the loss of a valuable worker who wasn't yet ready to retire.

Don't Neglect Training for Older Workers

There may also be an unconscious tendency to favor younger employees for training in new technology. Where this happens, older workers are left at an obvious disadvantage since over time their technical skills will become outdated. Make sure to keep older workers abreast of changes in technology. The unspoken reason for overlooking mature workers in technology training is that they may be retiring shortly, so investing the money in training them would be uneconomic.

First of all, that's a decision that should be left to the worker. Those with plans for retirement in the near future are unlikely to invest time and energy in attending training courses to update technical skills. Rather, they're more than likely going to defer when additional training is offered, and may explicitly inform their supervisor they don't want to take further courses because they are planning to retire in the near-term. Furthermore, the argument that training is being wasted on an older employee who may retire makes no more sense than saying that training shouldn't be wasted on younger workers since they are liable to use their newly acquired skills to job-hop. From that standpoint, the company would be educating an employee for another employer's benefit.

Older Workers Offer Advantages

There's a lot to be gained by any supervisor who strives to recognize and deal with problems of more mature workers. The greatest motivation for you as a supervisor is to consider the advantages to be gained by adopting some flexibility in dealing with older employees. For one thing, you don't want to lose highly skilled experienced workers since, as you know, they aren't easy to come by. If you think otherwise, you may want to reflect upon some of the headaches you have in bringing new workers up to standard.

Older employees tend to have a stronger "work ethic" in terms of factors such as company loyalty, adhering to time and attendance standards, general adherence to policies and procedures, and a higher regard for quality of work. Furthermore, chronological age has never had a direct correlation with the ability to do a particular job. Someone aged sixty-five can have equivalent or better stamina than a peer who is twenty or more years junior in age. The relating of chronological age to competence continues—or at least it should—to diminish as advances in medicine continue to extend both longevity and quality of life. The average sixty-five-year-old man or woman is in a lot better physical condition today than peers of earlier generations. Working longer has become a very viable option.

Make Adjustments to Accommodate Older Workers

What you as a supervisor can do in this area is to make any necessary adjustments, such as accommodating an older worker who may want a shorter work week. The individuals themselves will be reluctant to approach you in this regard, so it really requires your initiative to open any dialogue. It may be a subject that's easy to neglect, but it can be a costly one for any supervisor who wants to retain the best possible workers.

The key to adjusting to the needs of mature workers is for you as the supervisor to keep the lines of personal communication open. Try to pick up on hints from an older worker. For instance, if one of your veteran employees mentions the possibility of retiring in six months or so, seize the opportunity to open a dialogue about the individual's plans. Perhaps say something such as, "Have you given this a lot of thought, Barbara? What are your future plans?"

In the course of this and subsequent discussions you may learn that employees have well-defined and long thought-out plans for retirement. You may then choose to do little other than tell the workers that if partial retirement in terms of working fewer hours is something they would be interested in, then the possibility is open for discussion. Incidentally, there are people who retire and after six months or so decide they didn't make the right move. Therefore, always encourage retirees to contact you if they might be interested in returning to work at a later date, perhaps with a reduced work schedule. Of course, never hold out false hope if there's little likelihood of any vacancy being available.

If during discussions an employee seizes on the suggestion of working shorter hours, then work together to come up with a satisfactory schedule. In some situations, it may not be hours of work as much as some aspect of the job that is making it difficult for a mature worker. This is something that would be more evident in highly physical jobs. In this type of situation, try to look for ways to adjust the worker's duties to make them easier to perform. There are all sorts of creative ways to redeploy the skills and experience of mature workers if given the necessary thought.

There are a couple of general considerations that shouldn't be ignored in dealing with mature workers. One is to diligently avoid age discrimination and to take strong exception to any age-related statements made by those working within your group. This goes beyond the letter of the law; you must insist that those who work for you avoid any form of age-related comments that are disrespectful of people—old or young. For example, saying "He's too young to know what he's doing" may be just as offensive to a young employee as saying "She's getting old for that job" to a more mature employee. Tolerating such remarks sets the tone for an environment which encourages disparaging age-related comments.

The second major consideration when discussing the future plans of mature workers is to be extremely sensitive to their desires. On the one hand, you may want to encourage them to continue working even in a part-time capacity. Conversely, you don't want to urge them to continue working if they would really prefer to retire. Naturally, all your urgings won't deter those who have long since planned for the day they could look forward to a leisurely drive to the golf course rather than to a lengthy commute to work. But there may be some people who have worked closely with you for years and who feel an extreme sense of loyalty, and if you're particularly convincing, they may decide to stay on for a while longer. If that's their true wish, fine, but you don't want to unduly influence someone. It's a sensitive area, since, as retirement time draws near, some folks find it more difficult than others to make the right decision. Of course, in some situations the decision hinges largely upon financial considerations and company-wide policy on retirement also comes into play.

HOW TO HANDLE THE NEEDS OF EMPLOYEES WITH AGING PARENT DUTIES

The child care and parental duties of working parents are common, and most supervisors recognizing these problems try to make adjustments to accommodate employees. But a less frequent responsibility which people are learning to cope with is the care of aging parents. This should become more prevalent as life expectancies increase and growing numbers of employees have a parent or parents who need various forms of assistance. Supervisors can therefore expect to see more of their employees facing these responsibilities.

To some extent employees' needs in terms of caring for aging parents will be similar to those of workers with child-care responsibilities, and will center around requests for time off. But there will be differences. The illness and frailty of aging parents will be the major problems employees have to react to, which may result in unexpected absences and workload adjustments on short notice to compensate for an absent employee.

One often overlooked way in which a supervisor can contribute greatly to the needs of employees with aging parents is by being sympathetic and understanding. It can be very trying for an employee who is working hard to juggle the competitive demands of the job and the needs of an elderly parent. The emotional trauma can take its toll. For this reason alone, the empathy displayed by someone's immediate boss can help a great deal in coping with the situation. Therefore, try to be available as a source of reassurance and, if nothing else, at least be a willing listener.

The initial arrangements of eldercare for a parent, although a one-time problem, can be time-consuming and energy-consuming for employees. So even though a worker may be on the job, productivity may lessen during this period. Knowing and understanding the reason will prevent an unnecessary boss\subordinate clash. In fact, do what you can to put the employee in contact with local resources that can provide assistance. This may be no further away than your own personnel office where staffers may be able to supply agencies and others that the employee can contact.

Many employees may be contributing financial assistance to care for aging parents. Even though they could have unpaid time off, that might not be of much help if they are struggling financially. Therefore, if employees eligible for unpaid leave prefer to work, do what you can to help them work out a flexible schedule until they are able to get the situation under control. There's no question that being helpful will take away from time you might spend on more productive tasks. In the long run, however, the loyalty you build with this approach will pay dividends in terms of lower employee turnover and higher morale. It also can make you feel pretty good knowing you're helping someone out in a moment of need. That alone can make the extra effort worthwhile.

KNOWING WHEN AND HOW TO DRAW THE LINE ON EMPLOYEE PROBLEMS

Accommodating the needs of employees with personal problems of one sort or another is beneficial for a number of reasons beyond the notion that it's the right thing to do. Workers who know their boss will be flexible in a pinch will be far more loyal. They will be willing to pitch in and go that extra yard when you most need them. They are also less likely to take days off here and there for frivolous purposes. And, aside from being generally more productive than unhappy, employees who are accorded understanding in dealing with personal problems are more likely to remain with their present employer. This means you will spend less time hiring and training replacements which, as you know, is both burdensome and time consuming.

Nevertheless, you are managing a business unit and on occasion there will have to be limits as to how accommodating you can be in meeting employees' personal needs when they conflict with business operations. This can be tough to do, but if it's handled properly, then workers will generally understand your inability to agree with their every request.

Establish Limits

One of the first steps you should take in this area is to let those who work for you know that you will be as flexible as possible in accommodating their needs, but it can only be done within the constraints of making certain the workload is accomplished. Incidentally, be sure that you aren't violating any federal or state laws or company regulations whenever you turn down an employee's request. If there's any doubt in your mind, be sure to consult with the appropriate expert in your employer's personnel or legal office.

How easy or difficult it is to cover for the absent person is a major factor in determining whether or not to grant a request for time off. If you communicate openly with your subordinates, you should be able to establish the sort of teamwork where other employees readily pitch in to pick up the slack when someone will be absent on short notice. However, this doesn't always suffice due to the nature of the job. In some situations, either because of the job itself or the skills of the employee, substitution isn't possible. Under these circumstances, the work will have to wait until the person returns.

Although you want to cooperate with employees in meeting their personal needs for time off, it's their responsibility to be on the job during working hours. When there are emergencies of one sort or another it's reasonable to be lenient. However, some employees may take advantage of your flexibility about taking time off rather than accept their own responsibility for finding a solution to their problem. If it seems as if a worker isn't doing anything to resolve a recurring problem, confront the individual, discuss alternatives, and insist that the employee take action to find a solution other than taking time off from work on a repetitive basis. Let's look at how such an encounter may play out.

Background   Carolyn is the supervisor of a fifteen-person group in a mid-size manufacturing company. She prides herself on being reasonable in accommodating employee needs within the bounds of getting the job done. Both her boss and the company are generally supportive of these efforts. Lately though, Carolyn has become frustrated with Betsy, one of her workers, who, two or three times a week for the past four weeks, has been leaving at 2:00 P.M. to pick up her daughter at school. This is three hours prior to quitting time so someone else has to double up and do Betsy's work. Although this wasn't a problem the first few times, lately the other workers have started to complain. As a result, Carolyn has decided to do something about this situation since it is causing dissension within the group.

The discussion

Betsy has been called into Carolyn's office, and after the exchange of pleasantries and some small talk, the following conversation takes place:

Carolyn: "Betsy, I've been wanting to talk to you about your leaving early to pick up your daughter at school. It wouldn't be a problem if it was on an occasional basis, as I can understand how emergencies can come about. However, I see from the records where you have left at 2:00 P.M. ten times in the past four weeks. That's thirty hours of personal time you have taken in a month. Naturally, that's your time and you can take it for any purpose. The problem I have is that you're leaving on short notice and I can't plan adequate coverage for your job. Furthermore, the frequency of your early departures indicates this is more than an occasional emergency. What seems to be the problem, and is there some other alternative we can work on to help you out?"

Betsy: "I don't know what else I could do. The mother who usually drives my daughter home from school has taken a part-time job, which means there are two or three days a week she can't drive my daughter. Therefore, I have to pick her up. The woman doesn't know until the day before which days she will be working. I didn't think there would be a problem since I'm using my leave time."

Carolyn: "My problem is not having advance notice so I can cover for you. Besides that, it seems you have a permanent problem rather than a temporary one. You are only entitled to 120 hours of personal time a year to cover illness, vacations, and instances such as this. At the current rate you will use your personal time up very quickly. Do you know how much time you have left this year?"

Betsy: "I've used 110 hours so far this year."

Carolyn: "In that case, you only have 10 hours left. Then you will have to take time off without pay. Rather than do that, aren't there other alternatives to deal with your daughter's transportation problem? What about the school bus?"

Betsy: "She's a junior in high school now and at the age where taking a school bus doesn't fit in with her age bracket. You know how teenagers are."

Carolyn: "Perhaps so, but there are other considerations here so other possibilities can't be ruled out. Can't she get a ride with someone else, or can't someone else pick her up?"

Betsy: "I guess I'll have to discuss this with her."

Carolyn: "I'd appreciate it if you would and let me know what you come up with. I certainly want to be helpful and if you can't work it out then perhaps I could get you reassigned to another shift where there wouldn't be any conflict. In any event, let me know tomorrow, Betsy, and if necessary we'll talk over what our alternatives are."

The outcome

The following day Betsy tells Carolyn the problem is resolved and Betsy's daughter will get a ride with someone else. Unfortunately, not all of the problems of this nature that you face will work out this easily. However, sometimes as in this instance, employees make little effort to search for alternatives until they are forced to do so. Therefore, always explore alternatives whenever something other than a one-time emergency requires employees to take time off.

A few other points to consider from this example. Notice how Carolyn avoided making any mention of the fact that Betsy's co-workers were unhappy about having to cover for her. There was no point in unnecessarily causing employee conflict by bringing this up. It was a problem for Carolyn as the supervisor and she treated it as such and didn't try to pin the blame on Betsy's co-workers. It's also worth noting that sometimes unpleasant alternatives can motivate workers to find solutions they might not otherwise consider. For instance, in the example Carolyn mentioned the possibility of Betsy having to work a different shift. Betsy may well have viewed this as a bad choice and therefore made more of an effort to solve the problem. This wasn't brought up by Carolyn to be a deliberately unpleasant alternative, and of course this tactic shouldn't be routinely used. However, in situations where an employee is taking advantage of your flexibility in granting time off, you may want to think about options for changing the worker's bad habits.

Finally, many situations in which an employee has a personal problem which requires time off involve close calls as to whether to routinely grant the request or reject it. For instance, in the example, if Betsy only had an occasional requirement to pick her daughter up then it would have been easier for Carolyn to live with. This is why requests shouldn't be arbitrarily denied. If it's feasible to help out, by all means do so, but when it's beyond the bounds of practicality, then be firm but understanding about rejecting employee requests.

Dealing with Deadbeats

Although most employees will be sincere about personal problems that require time off from work, you may run into a deadbeat or two who is taking advantage of your flexibility to miss work for reasons unrelated to any valid personal problem. Of course, you can't lower the boom on someone without being positive that you are being taken advantage of. For the most part, that isn't hard to do.

Loyalty will be high in a working environment where a supervisor consistently tries to accommodate the legitimate needs of subordinates. For this reason, a deadbeat's co-workers will either blow the whistle or exert peer pressure on the culprit to knock off the nonsense. After all, employees readily recognize that if privileges are abused they will be withdrawn. Therefore, co-workers are going to be unwilling to tolerate the nonsense of people trying to con their way into time off on the justification that it's for emergency purposes. So your biggest allies in your efforts to avoid the abuse of your flexibility are those who work for you. As a result, if you do take an employee to task for attempting to take advantage of your flexibility you will likely receive the wholehearted backing of other employees.

3 How to Move Away from the Old Way of Doing Things

One of the most difficult aspects of change in the workplace is weaning employees away from the old way of doing things. Change of any sort isn't something that's readily accepted. When workers are accustomed to doing their jobs a certain way, it's not an easy task to convince them that there is a better way to do their work. Whether it's a change in policy or a change in work procedures, employee resistance can be expected. How effective you are as a supervisor will be largely dictated by your success in selling change to those you supervise.

One of the many issues that have to be addressed is how to cope with worker criticism of change. In some cases, this may mean learning how to handle worker anger. There may even be situations where it will be necessary to directly confront any die-hards who stubbornly refuse to adjust to new practices. Generally, however, most of your efforts will be focused on tactics to overcome the natural resistance to change that can and should be expected. The following topics discuss numerous ways to do this effectively.

HOW TO BREAK BAD HABITS THAT INTERFERE WITH NEW PRACTICES

Your efforts to encourage workers to adopt new technology and accept changes in the way their work is accomplished will encounter roadblocks in one form or another. These bottlenecks can indicate the need for additional training, or simply be the natural resistance to change that is part of human nature. In fact, the major hurdle may be nothing more complex than changing habits that have become second nature over a long period of time.

Unfortunately, whether it's at work or elsewhere, habits aren't that easy to change. It takes time and patience, and these are the most important tools you have to work with when it comes to weaning workers away from the old way of doing things. However, before you even get to changing the work habits of subordinates, you should first look for any ingrained work routines you personally have adopted which interfere with maximizing your own efficiency as a supervisor. Then, and only then, will you be in a position to attack bad practices that may exist in employees' work patterns. After all, unless your own house is in order, it's neither practical nor prudent to attempt to straighten out someone else's habits.

Take a Hard Look at How You Do Things

Naturally, it's easy enough to immediately decide that you don't have any ingrained work habits that aren't useful or efficient. This is, of course, what most people would conclude if they don't take the time to think about the tasks they perform on a routine basis. However, once you start to give some thought to your daily routine it won't be long before you discover some things you do that can be done differently.

Although your goal is to basically eliminate or revise poor work habits, this can't be done arbitrarily. Careful thought should be given to what you do that could perhaps be done more effectively. Think about the work habits and procedures that consume every minute of your working day. Are there things you do that could be eliminated? Do you do work that probably should be delegated to subordinates? Is your group doing work that is better done by other departments? These are the types of questions you have to ask yourself before you can come to grips with some of the ingrained practices that hamper your ability to function effectively. Otherwise you will be handicapped in adapting to a work environment that emphasizes teamwork, the implementation of change, and the ever expanding use of technology.

Let's look at some of the work habits that can be overhauled if you find yourself engaging in any of these practices.

1. *Are you using technology rationally?* The introduction of new and improved equipment will be a continuing process both in the office and on the factory floor. The key to using it effectively is to carefully think through the advantages and disadvantages of every new item which is being touted as the next best way to do your work. You have to look at the latest technology with a moderate viewpoint and not operate at one of the two extremes which entrap some managers.

   At one extreme are those who embrace every new and improved version of equipment as the key to maximum performance. These people tend to give little thought as to whether the equipment will do what is promised, or whether it will do so as effectively as that which it will be replacing. Simply put, their philosophy is to "buy before they try" on the misguided assumption that because the equipment is new it will be an improvement over the existing technology.

   At the other extreme are those who refuse to accept any new technology and stubbornly stick to antiquated operating practices. These managers often justify the refusal to try new equipment on the basis of the expense involved or the training required. They may even try to justify their reluctance by claiming the inability of their workers to adapt to the new equipment. This attitude exists even where it has been proven beyond a doubt that the technology in question will improve operations and is essential to remain competitive.

   The best approach in dealing with new equipment and technology is somewhere between these two extremes. You should always attempt to objectively determine the advantages and disadvantages as they apply to your particular department. Don't be pressured into adopting something you know won't work; on the other hand, don't hesitate to try something that offers potential improvements. Be willing to accept the fact that when new equipment is introduced there may be kinks that need to be ironed out and things may go more slowly initially if there is an extensive learning process involved.

2. *Do you neglect to delegate work?* With teamwork being an essential element of the new workplace, it's worth thinking about what sort of attitude toward teamwork you demonstrate in the eyes of those who work for you. If you habitually do things yourself, rather than delegate them to subordinates, then you have a bad habit that needs to be changed in order to promote teamwork and cooperation. This is true even in situations where a supervisor may be openly promoting the concept of teamwork. It's of little value to talk up teamwork if you do everything yourself. Subordinates will tend to do what they see you doing; not what they hear you saying.

3. *Do you listen effectively?* Historically, many supervisors pretty much issued orders and paid little or no attention to anything subordinates might have suggested in terms of improving operations. This was generally accepted as the way things were done and for this reason workers seldom volunteered alternative ways to do their work more effectively. These conditions made it unlikely that a supervisor would become a very effective listener. Today, however, with the focus on encouraging employees to contribute their ideas on how jobs should be done, it's essential to be an effective listener. If for whatever reason you don't consider yourself to be a good listener, it's time to break this habit.

4. *Modify ineffective work routines.* Many of the bad habits that hamper new ways of doing things are nothing more than a collection of work routines that you have developed over a long period of time. Unless you carefully review your actions you may not even realize some of the time-wasting habits you practice on a daily basis. These can range from wasting time on low priority paperwork, to not controlling needless interruptions, which can be one of the biggest time eaters of the business day. Learning to change any of these bad habits will free up time you can put to use in implementing changes that improve the operations of your group.

Exercise Time and Patience with Employees

Along with weaning yourself of bad habits that interfere with your effectiveness, you must also encourage the same with your subordinates. However, they are the ones who have to change their habits, and it may take some time in certain situations. In fact, time and patience are the main tools you need. Whatever you do, avoid getting angry when an employee has trouble learning a new technique and opts to lapse back into the old way of doing things. It may take a number of attempts over a period of time before the old method is finally put to rest for good.

Offering encouragement is one of the simplest and best approaches you can take in helping employees to overcome old habits. Where this is most noticeable is when you succeed in getting workers to do one or more steps differently. Often, without even meaning to, workers will go back to their old way of performing the function that has been changed. At other times workers will revert to the old way of doing something out of sheer frustration at learning the new approach. You have to keep in mind that employees may have been doing something a certain way for months or years. Therefore, it's not that easy to start doing the task differently. For this reason it helps to let employees know that you recognize the difficulty in changing over to the new practice. If they know you are sympathetic, they will be more willing to be upfront about any problems they may be experiencing.

FIVE WAYS TO ELIMINATE PRACTICES THAT DON'T ENHANCE PERFORMANCE

In your search for ways to increase the efficiency of the group you supervise, you will be revising or eliminating practices that are specific to the work done by your unit. On a more general basis, there are a number of approaches you can take to help you work through the process of deciding what can be changed for the better. Among the questions you should raise are the following:

1. *Will eliminating the procedure save time?* The ability to make better use of time is increasingly important as supervisors are asked to do

more work with fewer people. Technology will fill the gap to some extent, but in large measure eliminating and combining unnecessary actions is of paramount importance. Beware of a trap: eliminating a procedure will not automatically save time. We all think that not doing something should free up that segment of time to do something else, but this rationale isn't necessarily so. For example, saving time by eliminating a quality control procedure may result in a large increase in product defects and rework which more than offset the time initially saved. Therefore, when you consider approaches to saving time, look at the complete picture and not at just one aspect of the process.

2. *What happens if you eliminate something?* Surprisingly, much of the time eliminating a work procedure creates no adverse consequences. In searching for what can be reduced or eliminated you may be surprised to learn that when you start asking questions as to why certain practices take place no one will have an answer. Even when you do discover the origin of a specific practice it may turn out to be a requirement that no longer exists. Many of these outmoded practices can be eliminated in the interests of improving efficiency.

3. *Is there duplication of efforts?* Two or more groups may be engaged in collecting the same information, preparing similar reports, or in some fashion needlessly duplicating the work of others. Combining efforts can yield benefits in improved efficiency.

4. *Can a more efficient method be substituted for a less efficient one?* Sometimes what's being done is proper, but the method of doing it is inefficient. A simple example might be sending time-consuming written messages rather than using the more efficient e-mail. On a one-time basis this is insignificant, but repeated many times these bad habits can be costly in terms of the time involved.

5. *Are workers assigned to duties that play to their strengths?* Sometimes workers aren't performing up to their peak because they are assigned to jobs which they don't do well. Everyone has their strengths and weaknesses, and by trying to align people with jobs that best suit their abilities you will improve the overall performance of your unit. For example, someone who has poor hand/eye coordination shouldn't be doing a job requiring that skill. This does-

n't mean, however, that people shouldn't be cross-trained to handle other work. The point simply is that workers shouldn't be arbitrarily assigned to jobs for which they are ill-suited.

COPING WITH WORKER CRITICISM OF NEW PROCEDURES

Whenever you're introducing new technology, realigning your unit's workload after a reorganization, or updating operating procedures, the task isn't easy. To complicate matters, you have to cope with varying forms of worker criticism, some open and overt, some silent and subtle. While the former may appear to be more troublesome, it's the latter that can cause you the most grief over the long haul. After all, if worker complaints are openly expressed, you can usually resolve the problems in some way.

It's when workers say little or nothing about their dissatisfaction that effective implementation of changes becomes difficult. While you are assuming there isn't any problem and that the change will go smoothly, workers silently resent what is being done and make little effort to adopt the new practices. When this happens, new procedures never live up to their promise, or do so only after a long period of learning and adaptation by workers.

As with so much else in the area of successful supervision, good communication is the key to encouraging open criticism of changes by employees. If you have laid the groundwork over a period of time by establishing a work environment where your subordinates are encouraged to express their opinions, then there's far less chance of meeting hidden resistance to any changes that take place. It's only when employees feel threatened by making their thoughts known that silent resistance will prosper.

Assuming you have established a work climate where people who report to you feel comfortable about making their thoughts known, the next question is how do you deal with the criticism that will come your way. That, of course, will be largely determined by its nature and the specifics of the situation. There are, however, common general criticisms whenever anything new is introduced. Here are a few ways to deal with these complaints.

Generic criticism related to changes in general

Example

> *Employee:* "This new procedure stinks."
>
> *Your response:* "What's wrong with it, Tim?"
>
> *Employee:* "Aw, nothing really. I just get tired of all of the changes they make around here."

Comment: Often employees will gripe when a change is made only because of the fact they are required to do something differently. It's only a way of blowing off steam and doesn't require a detailed response. All you have to watch for here is to be certain it's just general griping and not a specific complaint.

Criticism that the change is confusing

Example

> *Employee:* "I can't do this job using the new procedure."
>
> *Your response:* "What seems to be the problem, Pamela?"

Comment: When the employee responds with the specifics of what is causing the problem, explore with the worker what can be done to resolve the difficulty. It may be that the employee is just blowing off steam. On the other hand, there may be some difficulty in learning the new technique. If the learning process is complicated, formal training may be required. However, for the most part it's a question of learning by repetition. If that's the case, then reassure the employee by saying something such as, "Stick with it, Pamela. It will get easier with time."

Criticism that the change makes things worse

Example

> *Employee:* "This new machine isn't working right. We were better off with the other equipment."
>
> *Your response:* "What isn't working right, Miguel?"
>
> *Employee:* "It takes a minute per unit longer with the new machine. The new equipment was supposed to speed up the process, not slow it down."

Comment: Frequently when new equipment is introduced workers will be critical in their comments. Usually this criticism will fade as they become adept at using the new machinery. However, once in a while complaints that the machinery won't do the job right turn out to be something other than learning curve griping. Equipment is sometimes introduced into the workplace without ascertaining its ability to perform the required function. This most frequently happens when new equipment decisions are made without consulting those who actually do the work. At other times, the equipment has glitches which weren't foreseen when it was procured. Whatever the reason, in these situations always determine the validity of the criticism. If it turns out to be nothing more than griping about learning to operate the equipment, reassure the worker by saying something such as, "Don't worry about slowing down the line, Frank. You will gradually pick up the pace as you become familiar with the equipment." This form of reassurance will help keep workers from trying to move too fast on new equipment and making careless mistakes.

Criticism about being singled out to test new equipment

Example

Employee: "Why am I always the one to get stuck testing new equipment?"

Your response: "You're the best when it comes to working with something new, Carolyn."

Comment: It's logical to select the most competent workers when you want to try out new equipment, but try to choose employees who like to try something new. You can lessen criticism of this sort by reassuring workers of the valued contribution they're making by being the first to use the machinery.

Criticism about being the only department to get new working procedures

Example

Employee: "Why does our department always get new procedures before anyone else?"

Your response: "Because we're the best group in the company. Besides, by being first, we're able to recommend any adjustments that are needed rather than having to live with procedures developed by some other department."

Comment: When you're a top-notch supervisor running an outstanding department, you may find yourself and your group being used to try out various new procedures before they are adopted company-wide. This can lead to griping by one or more members of your group. Remind them of the advantages of being the trial group and thus being able to recommend adjustments that make the procedures more workable. Emphasize that this is preferable to not having a voice in making changes in new procedures. You can also, of course, use this argument along with the "superior performance" argument which plays to workers' egos.

Criticism about being overburdened by additional work assignments after a reorganization

Example

Employee: "I'm being asked to take on more than my share of the additional work due to the layoffs."

Your response: "Do the best you can, Cristy. If it doesn't work out then we'll have to see what we can do."

Comment: Whenever you have to parcel out work after a reorganization that increases the workload of your group, the criticism is apt to be long and loud. About all you can do in these trying situations is ask for people's patience along with their best efforts. You should also look for work that can be simplified or eliminated. When your employees see you are making a concerted effort to minimize the impact of additional work, they will be more inclined to limit their complaints.

These are just a few general areas in which worker criticism can be expected when anything new is introduced. The important point is not to brush off the criticism lightly. Be willing to listen to employee complaints and do whatever is possible to alleviate their concerns. Obviously, you won't always be able to satisfy their gripes, but as long as you show you are trying they will be satisfied.

IDENTIFYING WHAT'S NEEDED TO OVERCOME RESISTANCE TO NEW IDEAS

One of the time-honored burdens of introducing anything different within the workplace, whether it be a new piece of equipment or a new idea on how to do an old job, is the need to overcome worker resistance. No matter how much easier new techniques might make it for workers to do their jobs, there's going to be reluctance to accept these suggestions. The best way to tackle this hurdle is to identify the best approach to convince workers that the changes being made will benefit them.

Remember that the overall benefits to the company from new operating procedures, reorganizations, and other changes may be of little or no interest to employees on an individual basis. For example, reorganizing a department to make it more productive may mean little to a worker, especially if the changes have a direct personal impact. Basically, from an individual employee's viewpoint, you have to sell new ideas in terms of their benefit to the worker. It's the simple self-interest argument of "What's in it for me?" If you want to overcome worker resistance to anything new, then you need to come up with arguments that show the change is to the worker's advantage. This isn't always easy to do, but with some thought you can usually make a good case for accepting the change.

One trap some supervisors fall into is mimicking senior management's rationale for the change in an effort to convince workers of the virtues of doing things differently. For instance, they use arguments such as how new equipment will improve the company's competitive position and so forth. This may be quite true, but the average worker could care less. *"How will this impact my job?"* is what the average worker is thinking. The closer you can come to making an argument that answers this question in a positive way, the better your chances of overcoming resistance to whatever the change may be.

Your ability to overcome resistance to changes will depend to a large extent on how workers view the company as an employer. Resistance to change will be high when employees perceive they are being treated as disposable assets to be terminated whenever doing so will improve the company's bottom line. Conversely, if the company is a respected employer which treats its workers well, then a greater spirit of cooperation is bound to exist. Of course, as a supervisor you are charged with implementing changes whether the employer/employee climate is fair or foul. Therefore, learn to use your own credibility to gain the confidence of your subordinates.

Be Honest About Changes

Above all else, learn to level with employees about the reasons changes are taking place. First of all, they may know as much or more than you do from the office grapevine. Second, if you tell employees something and it turns out to be wrong, you will lose your future believability. You don't always have to give a blow-by-blow account of why a change is taking place, but don't distort what's happening in the interests of trying to smooth things over with your workers. For example, if the introduction of new equipment will eventually mean fewer jobs in the future, don't steadfastly deny this. Instead, try to counteract that possibility by pointing out that those who become proficient in using the equipment are most likely to have a secure future.

Major reorganizations are relatively rare, so the sort of resistance to change you most frequently have to deal with as a supervisor will be of the one-on-one kind—a change in an individual worker's job in terms of doing something differently or learning how to use a new piece of equipment. Most often the worker's reluctance to do things differently is due to the natural resistance to change. Simply put, the argument goes, "Why should I do it differently when I already know a perfectly good way to do it?" How do you counter this? Your answers can vary and could be based upon:

- Showing how the employee will save time.
- Pointing out how much easier the new procedure will be for the worker.
- Emphasizing that less maintenance will be required.
- Speeding things up and helping eliminate required overtime which many employees don't like.

Of course, the last isn't a good argument at all for workers who like using overtime to supplement their earnings.

It's foolish to believe that a valid reason can always be found to convince each and every worker of the benefits of some change. The fact is that some potential benefits are remote such as saving future jobs, while at other times benefits are nonexistent in terms of the employee. When this is the case, don't try too hard to do a selling job since it will only ruin your credibility. When something is being introduced to increase productivity or otherwise benefit the company, the employees affected know it as well as everyone in management. They may not like these changes, but they will usually conform even though they aren't in wholehearted agreement with what's being done. Of course, there will be instances where resistance is deep-seated and this is discussed in the next topic.

WORKING WITH—NOT AGAINST—RESISTANCE TO NEW PRACTICES

It's all too easy to take the attitude that even though some or all of your employees aren't happy about certain changes, they will gradually come around to accept them with the passage of time. In many cases this will be true, while at other times it won't work out that way. Some new practices may be so objectionable to certain workers that their resistance will only harden with time.

Of course, your initial approach will be to try and sell new ideas as discussed in the preceding section. However, it's foolish to assume that this will always be successful. For instance, if a reorganization is about to take place that will result in people losing their jobs, it's a bit naive to expect employees to readily accept this as a beneficial change. And the age-old argument to layoff survivors that their jobs are now more secure can ring pretty hollow. This is especially true in companies where one layoff has been followed by another.

The fact of the matter is that certain changes may not even be acceptable to you as the supervisor. This alone makes it difficult for you to convince your subordinates of the benefits of the change. Even where this isn't the situation, there will be new practices introduced into the workplace which will engender a great deal of resistance from workers. In some cases where it's impractical to convince workers of the value of the change, your best approach to gaining eventual acceptance is to not get involved in trying to defend the new practices whatever they may be. Don't express your own dissatisfaction with the changes if you yourself are unhappy with them, since this will only encourage further resistance from those who work for you. Instead, in a low key way encourage workers to find the best way to live with the new practices. Doing this will gradually break down the resistance and the new practices will gradually be accepted as the status quo.

Let's look at an example of how you can accomplish this:

Background   The shipping and receiving department of a small manufacturer starts and finishes work one hour ahead of the regular working hours observed by the rest of the company. This is a carryover of a policy which has been in existence for years. It was supposedly initiated to allow the group to schedule early morning deliveries. However, now deliveries are made throughout the day on an as-needed basis, eliminating any valid reason for the department to work hours that differ from those of other groups. Mark, the shipping department's supervisor, calls his six workers together to tell them of a new company directive which requires the department to start work one hour later beginning in two weeks. This will bring the department into conformance with the working hours observed by the rest of the company.

The discussion

Mark:	(*the supervisor*) "It's been rumored about for months but it's now official. In two weeks we will be on the same work schedule as the rest of the company. That means we start and finish one hour later than we now do."
Herb:	"I car pool with three people who work at other companies. Can I continue coming in early so I don't lose my car pool?"
Alice:	"Me too. I have to drop my kids off at school."
Mark:	"Let's hold it right there. I'm sure everyone has commitments based upon current working hours. I do myself. Unfortunately, Harris [the division manager who is Mark's

boss] made it quite clear there would be no exceptions. Naturally, Herb, you can still come in an hour early but you won't go on the clock until the regular working day starts. We're all just going to have to make some adjustments. That's why the starting date is two weeks down the road."

Alice: "I just can't do it. There's no other way for me to get my kids to school. I'll have to look for a job somewhere else."

Mark: "Don't do anything rash, Alice. Why don't you see what you can do about some alternative way to get your children to school. Look, everybody. I know it's a big adjustment for all of us, but we don't have any choice. So I suggest everyone make whatever arrangements are necessary during the next two weeks."

Herb: "This stinks. Other companies are starting up flextime programs to give people flexibility while this company is getting more rigid. It doesn't even make any sense."

Mark: "You know, Herb, that flextime wouldn't work here because of the multi-shift scheduling. Aside from flexible hours, the company has a very liberal benefits policy compared with other employers in the area. In any event, that's it for now unless anyone else has questions."

The result

Over the next two weeks Mark heard some griping, particularly from Alice and Herb. Eventually, everyone worked the situation out. Alice found another parent willing to take her kids to school, and Herb came in an hour early and had breakfast in the company cafeteria so he could keep his car pool. The other four workers made whatever adjustments they had to.

Comments

There are several things to note here that apply equally to other new procedures which meet with resistance. First of all, notice that Mark, the supervisor, made no comment as to his opinion on the new working hours. By so doing he avoided adding fuel to the fire in terms of the workers' dissatisfaction. If he agreed the new hours were better, then workers might blame him for suggesting the change. On the other hand, if he openly expressed dissatisfaction, it would have encouraged employees to agitate further against the change. By remaining more or less noncommittal, he conveyed the impression that compliance was mandatory with no exceptions to the rule.

In most situations, as here, not everyone will openly object. That, of course, doesn't mean there aren't other workers who disagree, but not everyone will express resistance freely. The important point is to give everyone an opportunity to voice their concerns. Depending upon the type of change, it may be beneficial to follow up at a later date to see how each employee is adapting to the change.

Another important point demonstrated in this example is that you can't be willy-nilly about compliance when a change is made. Mark made no offer of flexibility in terms of people gradually adopting the new working hours. Later on, after the new policy was in effect, he might have made a temporary adjustment on a one-to-one basis with a worker, but this would depend upon individual circumstances. Making an open offer to deviate from a change is an invitation for everyone to come up with an excuse as to why they can't comply. Therefore, for the most part it pays to insist that the change be adopted without exception.

NINE WAYS TO ENCOURAGE WORKERS TO CHANGE THE WAY THEY WORK

Every worker has an individual work routine and any outside attempt to change this pattern automatically has people putting their guard up. So even the simplest of changes can become an irritant. There are, however, a number of ways to encourage employees to change the way they do their jobs that generally can overcome the natural resistance to change. These practices would include:

1. Create a working environment where trying out new ways of doing things is encouraged. Talk it up and praise people for trying different approaches. Somewhere in your career you may have had a boss who wanted everything done in a certain way. These sticklers for detail refuse to accept any deviation from the established rules for

performing tasks. To cope with this sort of attitude, subordinates often spend an excessive amount of time making certain they have done everything according to the set procedures established by the boss. In this environment people will not be willing to accept—much less initiate—any form of change. This attitude is the opposite of that, which you want to encourage to foster change within your unit. So let everyone know that you are willing to consider changes in the way people do their jobs. In fact, demonstrate by your own actions that this is the type of working environment you encourage.

2. Whenever possible encourage worker participation in making decisions about potential changes. This helps make workers active participants when it comes time to implement the change. It also identifies which workers will offer the greatest resistance to a particular change.

3. Don't be critical when workers make mistakes. Whenever anything new is adopted, errors are inevitable as people proceed through the learning process. By letting workers know mistakes are acceptable, you'll lessen their reluctance to take chances.

4. Explain the purpose of the change and the goals to be accomplished by its implementation.

5. Be flexible about modifying changes to accommodate the suggestions of workers. This is particularly true when it involves changes in how an individual does his or her job.

6. Listen to the feedback you get from workers when changes are implemented so that necessary adjustments can be made to correct problems.

7. Identify the benefits of a change, but don't oversell the notion. The more an employee can see its direct result, the greater the odds of accepting it as something positive. For example, a change in how an employee does his or her job that makes it physically easier to do is an obvious benefit. Another change without any obvious gain for the worker isn't as likely to be accepted on some vague assertion that it will increase productivity.

8. Identify the problems associated with changes. Workers will have to deal with these hurdles anyway, so to ignore them until they come up is a sure-fire way to stiffen resistance to a change.

9. Follow up frequently to help employees resolve any problems they may be having. Many workers will be reluctant to come to you if they are having difficulty working with a new technique. They may fear that you will think they don't have the ability to handle the change. Frequent follow up will allow you to see for yourself if there are problems which aren't being brought to your attention.

GETTING WORKERS TO ADMIT THEY DISLIKE DOING THINGS DIFFERENTLY

You might well be wondering why you would want to get employees to admit dislike of some change in how they do their job. After all, supervisors have enough gripes coming their way without going out and encouraging employees to express their displeasure. There are situations, however, where new procedures don't seem to appeal to employees even though you have received no feedback that would indicate workers' unhappiness. Unfortunately, it's impossible to do anything to correct this sort of problem unless you know the basis for employee discontent. Only by learning what's bothering them in terms of the new working procedures will you be able to devise a plan for dealing with it. Therefore, it becomes necessary for you to seek out bad news—unpleasant as this task may be.

Naturally, if workers were going to freely discuss their dislike for new practices, they would have come to you with their gripes. When they don't, there can be any number of reasons. Obviously if the lines of communication are poor, then that alone would be the cause. No one but a fool will approach a boss who doesn't like to hear bad news with a complaint. Then again, the reason for a lack of communication could be just the opposite. Perhaps you have good relations with your subordinates and they like and respect you. In such situations, workers sometimes hold back from griping to a boss on the basis that they believe there's nothing that can be done anyway, so why make the boss miserable over a lost cause.

Whatever the reason, encouraging workers to be forthright in their concerns over new work practices requires a bit of diplomacy. Most of all, it requires you to take the initiative to inquire about your suspicions. Let's look at a couple of different approaches you can take.

Ask the Office Gossip

As you know, office gossips are a constant source of information who are always ready to divulge what they know—even on occasions when you don't want to hear it. The problem here is that the credibility of office gossips generally isn't too high. For this reason, be careful how you phrase your questions, since they are likely to give you the answer they assume you want to hear, irrespective of whether or not it is true.

Try to be relatively vague about what you're interested in and see if anything is volunteered without your asking a direct question on the subject. For example, don't say, "Charlie, I think there are problems with the new procedures that I haven't heard about. Is this true?" Whether or not it is, many an office gossip will confirm it is and shower you with examples. Instead, say something such as, "Charlie, everything seems to be going smoothly with the new working procedures." Here, unless Charlie has actually heard otherwise, it's unlikely he will fabricate anything since you have planted the idea that you think everything is all right. For this reason, Charlie is unlikely to want to challenge your beliefs unless he has concrete information to the contrary. If he does, he will divulge it to prove how knowledgeable he is about the comings and goings of the workplace. However, he will most likely not make any self-claims about dissatisfaction with the new procedures, but instead tell you anecdotes of discussions with other workers. If this happens, it can get you started on the right track toward finding out what is happening behind the scenes.

Ask for Help

Another tactic you can try is to raise the issue directly in a group meeting with your subordinates. Say something such as, "These new working procedures don't seem to be going too well, although I can't put my finger on the reason. If some changes need to be made, I'd like some information to use when I approach Jones (your boss) about it. Can anyone help me out with some examples of the problems we're dealing with?"

This may open up the group to discussing the issue since it now knows you sense there is a problem. Incidentally, notice that the focus was on "we're," not "you," in mentioning problems. After all, a worker may be reluctant to admit he or she is having problems because they might reflect on the individual's ability. Making it a team problem removes this sort of obstacle to any admission and to subsequent open discussion about what can be done.

Ask a Trusted Employee in Confidence

If you have been supervising a group for any length of time, you probably have developed particularly good rapport with at least one or two of your direct reports. If so, you might want to approach one of them and ask in confidence if there are any problems with adopting the new procedures. The only pitfall here is that it's usually the best workers with whom a supervisor has such close rapport, and it's entirely possible these people are experiencing no problems. Unless they have heard about difficulties from others, the answer you get could be misleading.

All in all, it may be highly unusual for workers not to voice their complaints about changes in any form. Nevertheless, it's quite common for such information to be kept from a boss, so from time to time you may have to seek out answers when feedback isn't readily available. In any event, whether it's in the short-term or over the long haul, whenever workers are dissatisfied about changes, sooner or later that fact will surface. The advantage of hearing it sooner is that it makes it that much easier to resolve.

LEARNING TO LIVE WITH EMPLOYEE SKEPTICISM ABOUT ANYTHING NEW

You may be the most enthusiastic supervisor in the universe in terms of accepting change. As a consequence, this fervent devotion to anything new may leave you bewildered about why your workers don't feel the same way. In fact, your very enthusiasm may lead you to go to great lengths to encourage your subordinates to happily embrace change within the workplace. To some degree, of course, this makes sense. But you have to realize that no matter how beneficial something new may be, there may be some degree of employee skepticism about the benefits of changes in a constantly evolving workplace.

Reasons for Skepticism

Although your first and foremost task is to convince employees of the benefits of doing things differently, you have to accept a certain level of skepticism that may prevail for some time after changes are introduced into the workplace. To do this effectively, sit back and reflect upon the reasons why workers may not be quite as enthusiastic as you are about any given change that takes place.

The most obvious reason will come from the history of the company in terms of worker treatment. Where layoffs have been common, benefits scanty, and pay practices below the industry average, it stands to reason that employees aren't likely to see the introduction of new machinery as benefiting them. Rather, and realistically so, they are likely to view such equipment as one more threat to their job security.

In some circumstances such as organizational change, particularly where wholesale reorganizations are in the works, employee skepticism is sometimes fueled by the rumor mill. Then you have to take the initiative to combat these rumors or they will spread like wildfires. Learn to keep the lines of communication open so employees can come to you for confirmation or denial of any rumor.

Another reason workers often display skepticism for anything new is when it's designed solely to get more work out of them on an individual basis. This won't inspire enthusiasm, especially in situations where workers are already overloaded. Worker suspicions about changes in their work methods are also influenced by the degree to which they have or haven't been consulted about the changes beforehand. Thrusting changes, whether in the form of operating practices or new equipment, upon workers who had no prior knowledge of the change won't be met with glee. Employees know—and they are right about it—that no one knows their job better than they do. Therefore, any change that comes about without their prior knowledge is almost automatically guaranteed to earn a hefty dose of skepticism—along with a few choice words about the wisdom of senior management within the company.

Therefore, you have to be alert to recognize when the limits have been reached in trying to convince workers of the wisdom of any given change. At that point, learn to accept worker skepticism and, if it suits your personality, be willing to joke about it. In fact, making light of worker hesitation to accept the benefits of anything new can go a long way toward reluctant acceptance of changes by skeptical workers.

Keep Your Sense of Humor

Actually a good dose of humor is a wonderful remedy for the pressures brought about by change. Being able to joke about it helps defuse worker anger, and it can relieve the frustrations of dealing with a thousand excuses as to why a change can't be implemented. In fact, the bigger the change the more excuses there will be as to why it won't work. What you have to do is concentrate on countering every excuse one by one. This can be a trying experience, and after you've heard what seems like a million excuses, you will recognize why it's so difficult to implement any form of radical change.

It requires a lot of patience, but one of the keys to ultimate success is to counter excuses from workers who will give you all sorts of reasons why a change isn't working as it should. Carefully explaining why each and every excuse isn't valid is time-consuming, but it shows workers that you have faith in the change. With workers inclined to be naturally skeptical about changes, displaying your confidence will lead employees to question their doubts. And as you painstakingly explain why excuses have no validity, you will gradually convince all but the most stubborn of the naysayers in your department.

DEALING WITH "WHAT'S IN IT FOR ME" ATTITUDES TOWARD CHANGE

As mentioned previously, the bottom line in dealing with changes in the workplace is responding to the natural self-interest of workers. After all, if employees don't see any personal benefit in changes taking place, there's no valid reason to embrace them. Often when it's difficult, if not impossible, to show how changes will benefit the individual worker, there's a tendency to generalize with statements such as, "Increased productivity makes the company more competitive, and gives everyone greater job security." No matter how valid, it's a stretch to readily expect employees to accept these arguments.

Accept the difficulty of relating some changes to the personal welfare of individual workers. Time and patience are necessary to deal with "What's in it for me" attitudes. Actually, for the most part, workers will accept change even if it's with some degree of reluctance. Frequently, those who do the most complaining about changes are those who are least productive. Therefore, although you certainly want to communicate the benefits of a change that is being made, it shouldn't become an all-consuming passion to convince every worker of its virtues.

Frankly, beyond a certain point, it becomes "Put up or shut up time" for disgruntled workers. Anyone who unreasonably refuses to adopt changes in working practices should be told either to work within the new guidelines or to seek employment elsewhere. The bottom line is that it's certainly advantageous for employees to embrace change, but even if they don't, they should be expected to adopt the new practices whether they agree with them or not.

Whenever possible, try to introduce changes gradually so employees can adapt at a slower pace rather than having an abrupt change thrust upon them. This is especially true if the change involves new machinery or technology where substantial training is necessary. The less that has to be learned at one time, the easier it is to overcome employee resistance. It also helps to sell a change if you can enlist the support of one or two senior employees, since their acceptance will influence the attitudes of other workers.

Let's look at a couple of examples showing how a supervisor can explain the potential benefits of a change to workers who don't see any obvious gain for themselves.

Background   Chuck is a supervisor for a large wholesaler that is relocating its facilities ten miles from the present location. This will allow for substantial expansion of operations. This relocation is acceptable to most employees, but Marty, who works for Chuck, is complaining loudly about the move.

One-on-one encounter

> *Marty:*   "Chuck, how am I supposed to get to work on time when we move? It will take me thirty minutes longer to get there from my house."

> *Chuck:*   "I thought you took the Interstate to work now, Marty. The new location is only two exits further up the road. That's another ten minutes. Why would it take you thirty minutes?"

Marty: "Because I pick Finley up on the way to work, I come in the back way now instead of using the Interstate."

Chuck: "Even so, Marty, we're right off the Interstate here and so is the new facility. It's still ten minutes from here."

Marty: "Well, I don't plan on going by the Interstate. So it will take me thirty minutes."

Chuck: "That's your choice, Marty, but you will still have to be to work on time. If it's going to take you another thirty minutes, I guess you'll have to get up thirty minutes earlier in the morning."

Marty: "The company moves to save money, but it's going to cost me additional money for gasoline. That stinks."

Chuck: "The company had to find larger quarters to meet our needs. Don't forget that the company will be growing significantly now that it has the facilities. That will provide a lot more job security for us all. It will also open up more promotional possibilities and improve all the other opportunities that go along with an expanding business. Didn't you mention a while back that you want to switch from driving to an inside position in a year or two? Well, with the company growing at its new location, that will give you more of a chance to do so. Also, don't forget that your profit-sharing bonus is tied to profits, so the better the company does the more money you get for a bonus. All in all, Marty, there are several reasons why the move is good for every employee."

Marty: *(mumbling somewhat grudgingly)* "I suppose so, but I sure wish it didn't mean a longer drive for me."

Comments

Notice how Chuck relates the growth of the company at the new location to factors that will personally benefit Marty. When employees such as Marty see a change that is not in their present interests, they may fail to see the longer-term benefits. Pointing these out may lessen the resistance to the change.

Incidentally, prior to the announcement of the company relocation, it would have been beneficial to survey employees about its potential impact. Even though it might not have changed a decision, consulting employees beforehand would have made them more willing to understand the reasons for the decision.

Background Mary supervises ten people in the accounting department of a major retailer. They have just been told they have to learn a new software program. Here Camilla approaches Mary to complain.

One-on-one encounter

Camilla: "Mary, why do we have to learn another system? Every time I become familiar with a computer program, someone makes a decision to chuck it and substitute something else. I don't think I can change again. It seems to me as if computer programs keep changing for the sake of change. It's all bells and whistles just so software producers can make more money."

Mary: "This program will be easier to use and give us better capabilities. I appreciate how difficult it is to keep learning new programs. However, as technology changes we have to adapt to it or we won't be competitive. Incidentally, this program has good tutorials built-in and a company representative will be here next week to walk us through everything step-by-step."

Camilla: "Come on, Mary, you know how many times in the past glitches have developed with programs. We'll have the same old hassles all over again. Then when we finally get everything ironed out, the program will be dumped and replaced by something else. All of this aggravation isn't doing me any good. Change, change, change, that's all we get around here. Someone upstairs decides to change something to justify their job and us poor slobs get stuck having to do things differently for the umpteenth time."

Mary: "Come on in my office, Camilla. I want to show you something." [They move to Mary's office where Mary pulls out a lengthy magazine article that she hands to Camilla.]

Camilla: "What's this?"

Mary: "Take it back to your desk and read it. It points out the career advantages of knowing a wide variety of accounting programs. The important point is that it specifically mentions the new program as one which everyone in accounting should know how to use. To make a long story short, Camilla, it's personally good for your career to learn how to use this program."

Camilla: "That may be true, Mary, but I'm happy working here, so what benefit is it to learn skills that can help me land a job somewhere else?"

Mary: "You never know when you will need all the skills you can get. Besides that, learning new skills is one of the considerations on your semi-annual performance evaluation. The more you know, the better the chances of getting a decent raise, or getting promoted. So there are distinct benefits to learn these new programs even though it's a hassle to disrupt your routine."

Camilla: *(smiling)* "I guess you're right, Mary. It's sometimes hard to see the personal benefits in all of these changes. It's frustrating when you learn one system to have to start all over again, but as you say it's probably worth it over the long haul."

Comments

Change after change is frustrating, and it can dull the perspective of employees so much that they fail to see any personal benefit from a change. Taking the time to point out these benefits can overcome opposition. In other instances, workers are so wrapped up with the problems associated with a change that they don't even consider whether or not there are any advantages. As Mary did here, it's necessary to point out these benefits.

It's also advantageous, when it's possible to do so, to use the "show and tell" tactic as Mary did when she gave Camilla the magazine article. Anytime you can prove the benefits of a change by producing third party documentation supporting your claim, it will go a long way toward convincing employees that what you're saying is correct. Of course, as hard as you try, on occasion you may have to deal with a change that can't be shown to personally benefit workers. In fact, changes such as reorganizations which result in layoffs are a distinct detriment to some workers. In these situations you may have to deal with worker anger, so let's look next at how that can be handled.

OVERCOMING WORKER ANGER AND CONFUSION RELATED TO CHANGE

On occasion you may have the misfortune to have to deal with a change in the workpace which generates a great deal of hostility and resentment. Sometimes these problems are individual in nature, such as changes in how an individual worker does his or her job. In other instances, the change may impact your entire unit, such as a reduction in fringe benefits or a change in working hours. At other times, a change may be such that even you as the supervisor aren't happy, as in a reorganization of your department.

Your displeasure will, to a great extent, determine how you deal with it. In most instances, simply letting employees blow off steam over their frustration with a change will release most of the tension. For this reason, it's useful to always have a meeting to discuss any change. Even when it is obviously distasteful, provide the opportunity for employees to discuss their grievances. By having an open forum workers will be able to express their dissatisfaction. On rare occasions, the feedback may prove valuable in providing information that can get a change overturned. Aside from that, however, the real value is in openly recognizing the anger over the change and going on from there.

Incidentally, if the change is one that you find unsatisfactory, don't join in a chorus of displeasure along with those you supervise. For the most part remain noncommittal. Naturally, if the change is of such a nature that you wouldn't be expected to accept it, don't fake it. For example, a reduction in company paid health benefits affects you as well as your subordinates. Therefore, don't pretend the change is personally beneficial, since it's not believable and only serves to destroy your credibility. On the other hand, don't openly express opposition. For instance, your comment on a health benefit reduction might be something such as, "I don't like it personally, but I can understand why the company has to reduce costs." This sort of response is one of grudging acceptance, and you hope to generate the same from your subordinates.

Advance Information Prevents Later Problems

Many times worker hostility toward change is grounded in unfamiliarity with its purpose and scope. Employees will relate better to changes that have been discussed with them before being implemented. More often than not, managers announce changes and then are surprised by the negative reaction when the changes take place. Yet much of this anger and confusion could be prevented by prior discussion with workers to point out in the most basic way (1) what the change is, (2) why it is needed or what it will accomplish, and (3) the impact on anyone affected by the change.

When employees aren't aware of a change beforehand, the rumor mill springs into action. In this fashion, even distasteful changes such as layoffs become blown out of proportion. For instance, the rumor mill will greatly exaggerate the number of employees being released. Even worse, when scuttlebutt indicates a reorganization is in the works, even if it doesn't involve layoffs, the rumor of large scale job losses may start to circulate. The problem is that once these rumors get going they often take on a life of their own. It then becomes that much more difficult to counteract their impact. For this reason, it's important to get the details of any change out early.

Let Employees Know the Impact of Changes

Every change is disruptive to some extent, but when a change has a negative impact on employees, it becomes much more difficult for them to accept. If the goal isn't spelled out, then workers have no reason for accepting it on its face value. For example, a reorganization may be well thought out and hold much promise for increasing the efficiency of a company. Nevertheless, if the reasons for this aren't clearly pointed out to employees, then chances are the reorganization will be pegged as one more change for the sake of change. Unfortunately, it's this sort of attitude that can destroy the chances of success long before a change even takes place. For changes to succeed it's necessary to let employees know what will be accomplished by their implementation.

Finally, every employee should be advised of the personal impact of any change. Many employees oppose changes, believing erroneously that the change will have a negative impact on their jobs. This may not be true, but unless the worker knows this beforehand, he or she will be a crusader against making the change a success. This is totally unnecessary and results from the failure to openly and honestly communicate with employees. Even in situations where the change will have an impact on a worker it's important to sit down and discuss what will happen. If a worker is being transferred, then it's important that the worker not learn this at the last minute. Otherwise, the anger that results can mean a lot of lost productivity just because no one took the time to communicate what was going to take place.

WHAT TO DO WHEN CHANGES AREN'T BEING ACCEPTED

There may be certain changes in the workplace that employees refuse to accept. They may not openly rebel, which might constitute insubordination and, depending upon the circumstances, could be grounds for dismissal. They also wish to avoid confrontation with a boss. Instead, the lack of acceptance of changes is far more subtle and also more prevalent than is generally realized. For example, a worker may receive job instructions revising certain work procedures. Nonetheless, when not being directly observed, the employee may revert to the old method of doing the job. Sometimes this is intentional, while on other occasions it's the natural inclination to fall back into old habits.

There are times when employees do this because they firmly believe the old way of doing things was better. In reality, they are not always wrong. This is especially true when changes are made without any prior consultation with the people who do the work. This is regrettable, since the person working at a job has the best knowledge of its intricacies.

Other times, employees do recognize that the new procedure may be better. But they will do things the old way simply because they weren't consulted about the changes.

Whatever the cause may be, when changes aren't being accepted by employees, your first task is to find out why. Be patient, and keep your cool. It's easy to get hot under the collar when workers knowingly ignore changes that have been made. Despite that, getting emotional and initiating heated discussions about how things should be done won't solve anything. In fact, it's as likely as not to stiffen worker resistance of workers to acceptance of the change.

First of all, what you want to do is gain a firm understanding of why employees aren't accepting the change. The reason may actually be relatively simple. Perhaps there wasn't sufficient training when a new technique was introduced and, as a result, some employees are uncomfortable about using the new procedure. In other instances, workers may need a little reassurance that you won't criticize them for making mistakes as they learn to do things differently.

Sometimes you may have to dig more deeply for the reason why a particular change is meeting resistance. Perhaps a new procedure isn't as effective as the old way, but no one wants to be the person who tells you the change should be eliminated. Sometimes the magnitude of the change is such that it will take some time for employees to fully adapt. This is particularly true with substantial reorganizations, a complete realignment of how a job is performed, or the introduction of new technology.

Use Patience and Persuasion

Whatever the problem may be in getting changes accepted, sometimes lowered expectations and patience are all that is required of you. On occasion, changes are initiated, and when the expected results aren't immediately forthcoming, there's a tendency to blame it on the employees. However, major changes require getting used to; the learning curve may be longer than was anticipated. Be willing to recognize this and resist unreasonable demands from upper management to push things along. The more pressure exerted to speed things up, the greater the likelihood that a difficult change will be even harder to implement.

Frequently, when changes are meeting more than the normal amount of resistance, a little bit of gentle persuasion will work. Whatever the nature of the change, your own actions toward the employees who are having difficulty adjusting will be the main ingredient for overcoming resistance. Be ready to listen to criticism whenever anything new is introduced. After all, the refusal or inability to cope with change isn't necessarily bad. It can turn up problems that weren't anticipated when the change was first considered. Issues may be raised which require a revision in the change itself. Your willingness to seek out potential problems and search for creative solutions is essential to overcoming the reluctance of employees to accept changes in the way their work is being done.

WHEN TO CLAMP DOWN ON DIEHARDS WHO RESIST ANYTHING NEW

As was just discussed, there are a variety of reasons why workers may not accept changes within the workplace. In addition, every supervisor may have the misfortune from time to time to supervise one or more employees who resist anything new and cannot be dissuaded to do otherwise. At some point, no matter how patient you may be, there will come a time when these people have to be told to get on board or ship out. In other words, just do it.

Some people show reluctance, since many find it difficult to adjust to anything new. But there's a distinct difference between these individuals and those who will unceasingly resist—at least until you lay down the law. On occasion, you won't realize you're dealing with this type of individual until you have done everything possible to establish that the problem is nothing more than the employee's outright refusal to adapt. In other instances, the employee may let you know right from the beginning that he or she isn't about to cooperate with the change being made. Apart from the outright insubordination, this situation presents an additional problem. Unless you quickly quell the objections of the individual, you may discover greater resistance from other employees who aren't particularly enthusiastic either about a new work procedure.

Use the following techniques when you have to deal with an individual who adamantly resists doing something differently:

- Confront the individual in a calm and reasoned manner to determine his or her objections to the change that's being made.

- Challenge the reasons given for not accepting the change. Don't let excuses as to why the individual won't comply go unanswered. Otherwise, the employee will take this as agreement with his or her position.

- Give the employee explicit directions that the change must be complied with.

- After allowing time to comply with your instructions, confront the worker if there is noncompliance. State calmly but firmly that further refusal to perform the work in accordance with the new procedures will be grounds for possible disciplinary action.

- Keep your boss posted about the problem if it appears that disciplinary action may become necessary. It also makes sense to coordinate with your Human Resources personnel to be certain the correct procedures are followed in terms of disciplinary actions in general and particularly in termination of the employee.

Let's look at an example of how to deal with this type of situation.

Background Miriam is the supervisor of a group in the billing department of a large wholesaler. Certain changes in work procedures were implemented two weeks ago, and they have gone smoothly with one exception. That concerns Becky who twice a day is supposed to pick up copies of billings and take them to the auditing group. This is a task that was formerly performed by each of the five billing clerks within the group. It was decided that it was more efficient for one person to do this and the change was discussed with the clerks before being implemented. At the time there were a few questions and no specific objections, although Becky made a couple of snide remarks and intimated that she thought the change was stupid.

In the two weeks since the change was put in place, Becky hasn't done the job. Initially, the other clerks just ignored this and took their own billings to auditing rather than confront Becky about it. This wasn't unusual since Becky was known to get angry whenever she was challenged about her work. Finally the matter was brought to Miriam's attention. She decided to talk to Becky.

One-on-one encounter

Miriam: "How's everything going, Becky? Are the new work procedures going all right?"

Becky: "Yeah. Everything's OK."

Miriam: "Joe [the audit group supervisor] tells me he's getting billings a half dozen times a day rather than twice a day. He also says everyone is bringing their own invoices to auditing. That's supposed to be your job under the new procedures."

Becky: "Everyone decided it was easier to do it the old way. Those people in auditing complain about everything. Why don't they pick the billings up themselves in the first place?"

Miriam: "Well, I'll talk to everyone else, but the fact is that the new procedure was discussed and thrashed out before we implemented it. Therefore, I want you to start doing it twice a day beginning tomorrow. I'll talk to everyone else to let them know the same thing."

(Miriam then goes to each of the other workers and tells them not to take their billings to auditing if Becky doesn't pick them up. At three the following afternoon, Miriam gets a call from Joe who says he doesn't have the day's billings. She checks with the other clerks and discovers that Becky hasn't picked up their billings. She then goes to Becky.)

Miriam: "Why haven't you picked up the billings, Becky? We discussed this yesterday."

Becky: "I just forgot. I'll get them tomorrow."

Miriam: "You will have to get them now as they're needed in auditing. Furthermore, you're going to have to do this regularly as you're supposed to. If you don't start doing the job right, then I'll have to take some form of action."

Becky: "Gee, can't a person be forgetful?" (She then stalks off to collect everyone's billings. From then on she performed this task as she was supposed to.)

Comments

Note that Miriam took the time to check what was happening even though she already knew that Becky was responsible. It's important to be certain when you are going to challenge an employee for noncompliance with a new procedure. It's also worth noting that Miriam made no mention that employees had complained to her, since that would only heighten dissension within the group. Finally, when Miriam confronted Becky the second time she was deliberately vague about what would happen if Becky didn't do what she was told. This left the options open while still letting Becky know that something would happen.

It's highly unlikely that most situations will progress much beyond your initial admonition to comply with a change. After all, most employees aren't going to refuse to follow a new work procedure if it means bucking the boss. Therefore, the only time this situation is likely to arise is with an individual who is already a troublemaker and is just using the introduction of new work procedures as an excuse to create more trouble. In reality, the employee's resistance to change becomes the catalyst for you to take action which would have been forthcoming at some other time in the near future. For this reason alone, don't waste any time worrying about why you couldn't convince someone of something that seemed relatively simple.

LOOKING FOR ALTERNATIVES TO MAKE NEW PROCEDURES SUCCESSFUL

Sometimes changes aren't working out, but for one reason or another you can't just scuttle them. One good example is new equipment which was purchased at great expense. For reasons unseen beforehand, it may not quite do the job it was expected to do. However, it may not be prudent to just chuck the equipment and go back to the old way of doing things. There can be any number of reasons why this is so, but none so telling as you being the one who urged the procurement of the equipment in the first place. Telling top management that it won't do the job in such a situation might not be such a good idea, particularly if you have a number of payments left on your mortgage.

For this and other practical reasons, often when a change isn't working it becomes necessary to look for adjustments that can be made to make it successful, whether it involves new equipment or revised working procedures. This isn't unusual and in fact is to be expected when new ways of doing things are introduced. No matter how carefully everything has been planned prior to the introduction of something new, it's inevitable that minor glitches will develop. When this happens, you must look for ways to make any necessary adjustments.

Avoid Blame

The first thing you want to do is avoid placing blame on anyone. Reassure workers not to worry and let them know they aren't to blame for the lack of success with the new equipment or procedures. Even when it appears that at least part of the problem may be employee-related, don't point fingers. Keep your composure and address the issue as a team problem. Some good and bad ways of commenting on the situation are:

Bad: "Hector, you really screwed this up."

Good: "We need to correct what we did wrong here."

Comment: This identifies it as a joint problem and depersonalizes it. Pinning blame on the worker is just going to put him on the defensive and make him less cooperative in resolving the matter.

Bad: "Martha, you knew that wasn't the right way to do it."

Good: "Don't worry about it, Martha. We need to provide more training on how to use this equipment."

Comment: All too often workers are blamed for problems when the failure is actually the result of insufficient training. One point to keep in mind is that everyone doesn't learn at the same pace. So even where training has proved successful with some people, others need more intensive training.

Bad: "This should be simple for you to do. John didn't have any trouble with it."

Good: "It takes time to learn new techniques so just keep trying and don't worry about getting it wrong."

Comment: Don't make comparisons with one of your better workers. Be able to recognize that it may take longer for some people to get it right. Employees who are having trouble learning something new need reassurance. They know that some of their peers aren't having any difficulty, and harsh criticism will further weaken their confidence in being able to do the task right.

Seek Solutions with a Team Approach

The best approach in searching for alternatives to make new machinery or procedures effective is to enlist the support of your employees. Call them together as a group and brainstorm ideas for solving the problem. Be careful to steer the discussion toward positive changes since it's easy for such a meeting to evolve into a bull session as to why the new item won't work. Obviously, there will be a few blunt remarks made at the beginning of the session, such as, "That machine's a piece of junk. It'll never do the job," or "That procedure's wrong. The job can't be done that way." This is all right to release tension but try to quickly shift everyone's focus to a positive approach by saying something such as, "Fine, we all know it's not working, but let's see if we can work together to come up with some ideas on how to make it work."

Incidentally, always get all of your employees involved in recommending solutions. Some people tend to dominate meetings while others remain quietly in the background. Encourage everyone to contribute, since it may be the person who seldom says anything who has the perfect solution. Even if that doesn't happen, it's always good practice to encourage contributions from everyone. This helps to cement the team concept.

USING FLEXIBILITY TO GAIN ACCEPTANCE OF CHANGE

One of the keys to gaining rapid acceptance when anything new is introduced into the workplace is to be flexible about dealing with the problems and issues that are sure to arise. It's easy to accept the notion that some new change just won't work, particularly when the idea originated elsewhere. The "not invented here" syndrome can frequently be a subconscious contributor to rejecting change. This is another of the many reasons why changes should be discussed with those people who will be directly affected. This gives them the opportunity to be contributors to the change or, at the very least, the opportunity to voice their objections beforehand.

Listen to Employee Suggestions

The flexibility needed to get changes accepted will, of course, vary with the specific circumstances. There are, however, some common elements to gaining acceptance of workers. First of all, listen to what employees are saying about the change. If there are strong objections in one particular area, look for ways to make adjustments. Even when an employee suggestion isn't particularly significant, adopting it can have value beyond the suggestion itself. When employee ideas are incorporated into the change taking place, the employees are buying into the idea. Since the idea partly belongs to them, there is every incentive for them to make it work. Their attitude becomes, "Of course it will work. It's my idea." For this reason, it's often useful to incorporate suggestions just to enlist this sort of cooperative attitude toward making the change work.

Less Can Be More with New Technology

Another area where flexibility comes into play is in the introduction of new equipment. Frequently, the expectations are much greater than the reality with new technology. Reasons for this are commonplace. First and foremost are the sales and marketing tactics which sometimes promote technology as the cure-all for all sorts of problems, with little or no actual recognition of the potential for solving the problem. This, of course, can result in a great deal of fingerpointing at manufacturers and technology developers. No one seems to stop and think that these people are supposed to promote their equipment. They aren't the only culprits if things don't work out as planned. Often-times, the blame should be jointly shared by those who buy into the cure-all notions that are promoted.

The end result is that new equipment and technology may be procured that doesn't meet the preplanned expectations of those who bought it. This causes problems and it's here that flexibility is needed to try to adapt the equipment and technology to meet your needs. At the supervisory level, you're sometimes caught in the middle. This is particularly true where new technology is foisted upon you when you weren't even consulted before it was bought.

The people responsible for buying the equipment probably did a big selling job with top management to justify the expenditure. The pitch probably included detailed projections of the great things that would happen if the new technology was bought. This sales pitch would have included estimates of cost savings, increased production, or whatever else was related to the purpose of the purchase. Unfortunately, you as an operating level supervisor may be responsible for meeting unrealistic goals that other people projected.

It's at this juncture that problems develop and, when it looks like the new wizardry isn't working as planned, the pie-in-the-sky procurers of the new equipment start putting pressure on you. Their interest, of course, is in making the equipment do what it said it would do so as to avoid the wrath of top management. When these people start pressuring you it's easy to get angry and bluntly blame them for making a dumb purchase. Doing that, however, doesn't solve any problems. It's far better for both you at the operating level and those who sponsored the new technology to work together and come up with alternatives for making it work as best you can. This requires flexibility both on your part and by those who bought the equipment. You have to be willing to work with the sponsors of the technology to see if you can make it fit the intended application. They have to be willing to recognize that there are unforeseen glitches to be ironed out. In summary, there's a great deal of political flexibility that has to be used when changes are introduced.

PINPOINTING NEW TECHNIQUES THAT AREN'T PANNING OUT

With the inevitable glitches that will occur when new techniques are introduced into the workplace, it becomes essential to spot problems as early in the process as possible. Otherwise, they may become more severe, and employees may be even more reluctant to accept the changes when they see that the changes are not working out as planned. Therefore, you have to monitor new techniques closely when they are first placed into practice. Furthermore, you can't always count on employees alerting you to problem areas, since the changes may be such that workers wouldn't be at all disappointed if things didn't go as planned.

The key to catching problems early on is to closely monitor any new changes when they take place. Ask lots of questions to satisfy yourself that everything is going smoothly. Employees should also be encouraged to let you know if they see any problems developing. This is a simple enough pattern to follow, but there are a couple of factors which make it easier said than done. For one thing, you have your normal workload to accomplish, which may not leave you much time to closely monitoring something such as new work procedures. Again, too much oversight of workers will produce a negative reaction. If they perceive you're essentially standing there and watching them every minute of the day, they are likely to assume you have little or no faith in their abilities.

Both of these potential pitfalls can be dealt with. As far as your workload is concerned, you may have to let it back-up a bit whenever new changes are introduced within your unit. This may be burdensome initially, but it can compensate for the time you may save later by not having to correct problems which develop when a change doesn't work out. In terms of your workers resenting your presence, try to be as unobtrusive as possible. Your attitude is also important. Don't be constantly questioning one thing after the other. Instead, solicit opinions and intersperse discussions of the change with conversation on other matters. You can also be selective in terms of monitoring individual workers.

You will know from the start which people in your unit can be counted upon to adapt to the change. These people won't require the same level of supervision. They shouldn't be entirely ignored, however, for one very important reason. Your best performers may be the ones who most quickly adapt to changes, but they may be the last people to let you know when problems develop with something new. The reason is that they may tend to be more confident in their own abilities to work the problems out and will be reluctant to ask you for assistance. This is a factor that is often overlooked on the assumption that the best workers don't really need to be monitored when something new is introduced.

Sometimes it will be long after the introduction of something new that the problems start to surface. For example, a new piece of equipment may work entirely as planned—at least initially. Later, you may discover that it tends to fall apart after extended use. This is just one example of new techniques and changes that may not work out well but that can't be foreseen. If you encounter changes of this nature, don't worry too much about it. Not everything will work perfectly. The greater danger lies in not taking a chance on something new for fear it will fail.

HOW TO AVOID SOMETHING NEW WHEN YOU KNOW IT WON'T WORK

There are times when changes are made in the workplace that just don't pan out. In some instances you may know ahead of time that a new procedure won't work, or that a new piece of equipment won't do the job. Obviously, if you're able to avoid the introduction of the procedure or equipment before the fact, it will make life much easier both for you and for those you supervise. That, unfortunately, isn't always easy to do, since sometimes decisions are made at senior management levels with little or no prior input from the supervisors who will be responsible for integrating new procedures and equipment into the workplace. There are, however, a number of measures you can take in terms of problem avoidance.

Don't Volunteer

One of the best ways to avoid problems in this area is to dodge being a volunteer for testing new equipment. Supervisors are always battling to get the latest equipment for their departments. There's an almost irresistible urge to secure the newest version with all of its attendant bells and whistles. This is only fine, however, if you know for a fact that it will actually improve the operational efficiency of your group.

Frequently, state-of-the-art equipment arrives on the scene without the inevitable glitches worked out. This causes everything from minor difficulties to major havoc for those using the equipment. The irony is that many a supervisor may have fought long and hard, including any number of budgetary battles, to secure approval to procure it. The point here is to be not too hasty about trying to get the latest equipment. Stick with battling to get only the equipment which you know is effective for your particular operating environment. Let others be the guinea pigs for equipment which is new and essentially untested in the workplace. You're far better off fighting for limited resources that you know will be beneficial to your group's productivity.

Unfortunately for you, the very efficiency of your group may make it the prime choice for trying out new equipment or work procedures. After all, to demonstrate that something is going to work effectively, top management wants to select the most productive and best-managed department for any trial runs before implementing anything new on a company-wide basis. You may thus find yourself as the first choice for testing out new equipment and ideas. This can cause you some serious problems.

The Problem of Being First

Among the headaches associated with being selected as a departmental guinea pig is that your group is in the spotlight. Upper-level managers will be hovering around constantly checking out the progress of the latest "gee-whiz" technology or management fad. You will be besieged with questions and find the entire experience to be generally disruptive. The downside to this is that both your personal and the group's productivity may be seriously affected.

If being under close scrutiny by top management isn't bad enough, there are other difficulties that can't be ignored. The learning curve involved, whether you're talking about new equipment or procedures, can temporarily reduce the productivity of your unit. And depending upon the success or failure of the new item, future productivity may be affected over the long-term. For example, if new equipment works out well, it may improve the output of your group. Even that can turn out to be a mixed blessing. How so?

Management may decide that the new equipment is a labor-saver and cut the number of people assigned to your department. That may be both prudent and practical from the distant viewpoint of higher-level managers massaging numbers, but a total disaster in your eyes. After all, you may value the person more than the machine. Furthermore, you're the one on the front line dealing with the morale and employee productivity problems when machines replace people. Naturally, this may be inevitable but you may not want your group to be the test case by always being the group to try out new equipment.

Another potential pitfall with trying out new equipment is that if it doesn't work—or is only marginally effective—you may find yourself stuck with it. This is especially true if significant sums have been spent, and is compounded if the idea was the brainchild of upper management. Unless you're dealing with stand-up top managers who are willing to admit mistakes, management failure won't be recognized at that level. Therefore, the equipment will stay and you will be forced to make the best of it. What's more, to add insult to injury, you may be blamed for the failure of the equipment to work as planned. Incidentally, this same scenario is even more likely in terms of a reorganization planned by upper management. You will find your department reorganized, and if it doesn't work out, then you may be blamed.

Look at Both Negatives and Positives

Does all of this mean that you should be a disciple of the status quo and rebel against any attempts to bring progress to the unit you supervise? Of course not, but it's important to recognize there are two sides to the coin, and not everyone tends to look at the negative aspects associated with introducing either new machinery or new operating procedures. You should look at both the negatives and the positives and, whenever possible, avoid situations where you're convinced that being the first to try something new might not be in the best interests of your group. How to avoid getting stuck? A few general guidelines include:

1. Beg off by telling your boss that your group's productivity would suffer. Suggest that a group with a lighter workload might be a better bet. If your group is handling critical jobs that must be completed within a short time frame, this argument can carry the day.

2. Tell your boss why you think the new equipment won't work. Sometimes this alone will get you off the hook. After all, the boss will recognize that the equipment might not get a fair trial if you don't like it from the start. He or she may prefer to put it in a group where the supervisor is more favorably inclined. Needless to say, be careful how you handle this situation since you don't want to ignore the politics involved in criticizing something new.

3. Make your argument on a factual basis. For instance, point out to the boss that some aspect of your plant location such as lighting makes it impractical for the test case.

4. Perhaps you can show in some way where the workers in your group aren't representative of most other groups. For example, maybe you have mostly inexperienced workers while the average group has significantly more seniority. Emphasize that a more representative group would provide more valid results in terms of testing the new equipment or trying out a new procedure.

There are, of course, any number of specifics you may be able to come up with in your own situation. Let's go on to look at the best ways to tell your boss that something won't work, either before or after it has been introduced into your unit.

THE PRUDENT WAY TO TELL YOUR BOSS "IT ISN'T GOING TO WORK"

We have just discussed dodging problems with equipment and procedures you know won't work by avoiding their introduction into your unit beforehand. But once in a while it might just be necessary to tell your boss directly that something won't work. At times you may be able to do this before changes are implemented, but more likely you will have this task after the change has been introduced into the workplace. Not an easy thing to do, particularly if your boss was influential in planning for the new equipment or procedure. Even if it isn't your boss's pet idea, if it originated at higher levels of management, your boss will be less than enthusiastic about having to convey the word that some top manager's bright idea is a dud. The bottom line here is to be as diplomatic as possible and to have plenty of available evidence to back up your assertion.

Object Early and Often

The best way to avoid changes you know won't work is to short circuit them with the boss at the earliest opportunity. For example, perhaps you know a certain type of equipment has a tendency to break down frequently, resulting in excessive downtime for repair and maintenance. In a staff meeting, your boss asks if you would be interested in updating to this equipment. Make your viewpoint known then and emphasize that, despite the promise of increased volume that the machine offers, this advantage is more than offset by reliability problems.

Another benefit of making your objections known before changes are implemented is that even if it's decided to go ahead despite your disapproval, you avoid later blame if the new equipment doesn't pan out. This isn't insignificant since when something goes wrong and expensive equipment proves to be useless for the intended purpose, everyone is looking for someone to blame. At times like these it's nice to be in a position to say, "Don't look at me. I told you so beforehand." Needless to say, barring the need to defend yourself from being a scapegoat, don't openly exult about predicting failure. Upper-level managers who made the wrong decision won't appreciate being ridiculed and they will hold it in for you in the future.

Don't Point Fingers

When new equipment or procedures have been introduced and show no promise of succeeding, you have to let your boss know that something has to be done. There are a couple of tricky aspects about doing this. One is that it may be your boss's idea. The other is that even if it isn't, the boss still has the problem of passing the bad news along to upper-level management. First, let's look at how to deal with this problem if the new procedure or equipment was your boss's idea. A main consideration in how you handle this is the personality of your boss. If he or she is someone you can readily confide in, then there should be little difficulty in laying it on the line. On the other hand, if your boss doesn't cotton well to criticism, then a more subtle approach is called for.

One way to get the point across is to let the boss be the one to discover the problem with the equipment. When you're asked why productivity has slowed, quality has deteriorated, or whatever other troubling problem has been caused by the introduction of the new equipment or procedure, subtly point the boss in the direction of realizing what is causing the difficulty. It also helps if you can provide some rationale as to why the new equipment didn't work. This will make the boss more receptive to accepting that fact. Otherwise, the boss may keep insisting that kinks need to be ironed out, training is needed, or any other justification short of admitting the equipment just doesn't hack it.

When the equipment or procedure that's not working out originated at management levels above your boss, the problem is a little easier for you. Since it wasn't your boss's idea, there isn't any personal issue involved in pointing out the new item isn't doing the job.

Nevertheless, as you know, corporate cultures are political and it's not pleasant to be the bearer of bad news. This will be foremost on the mind of your boss, and it's this issue you want to work on. One way to be effective here is to give your boss some options for explaining why the new equipment or procedure won't work. The more remote these reasons are from laying any blame on senior management for a bad decision, then the better off you are.

Whenever possible, provide as much documentation as possible to support your argument that a change isn't working out. It also helps to offer alternatives for curing the problem. For example, in lieu of removing new equipment, suggest possibilities that exist in terms of equipment modification or training that might solve the situation. Of course, don't do this if the evidence conclusively shows that this won't resolve the matter. Whatever else you do, don't be hesitant about challenging the viability of new equipment and/or procedures if they're not working. It's admittedly difficult to do so, but if you let things drag it will work to your detriment. When it's finally decided to pull the plug, you may be criticized for not letting people know about the problem sooner.

HOW TO AVOID THE BLAME WHEN SOMETHING DOESN'T WORK OUT

Whether it's an extensive reorganization, new policies and procedures, or the use of new technology, not all of the changes in the workplace will succeed. This should be expected, since despite all of the planning and preparation, the introduction of anything new can cause unforeseen difficulties. Although this seems obvious, within the workplace there's a tendency to point fingers and assess blame. Rather than determine what went wrong and why, there's a scrambling to avoid blame for the failure. This, of course, isn't the right approach, but if you work in such an environment, you have to look out for your own interests. This means you don't want to be the scapegoat when something doesn't work out quite the way it was planned.

All too often the shunting of blame bounces all the way down to the supervisory level where the equipment or procedure is being used. This can happen even though the operating level supervisor was never consulted beforehand and was merely the recipient of direction from higher levels of management. This is most likely to happen in a working environment where mistakes result in blame, and praise is seldom heard.

Use Facts to Prove Your Innocence

The best way to avoid being the victim of blame is to be able to objectively prove you weren't responsible. This is why it's important to let your objections be known beforehand when anything new is being implemented. It's especially useful to document your objections at the beginning. Be sure to save e-mail messages or written memos which can prove your earlier assertions. When the time comes to defend yourself against erroneous accusations, this is your evidence to show you knew the idea or equipment wouldn't work. Be tactful, however, when you point this out, since no one likes to hear "I told you so," especially someone who is at a higher management level. So use any ammunition you have to protect your interests without inferring any superiority of judgment.

There may be a sound reason why something didn't work out as planned which was beyond your control. For instance, maybe a new piece of equipment needed frequent maintenance but the supplier of the machine failed to provide it in a timely manner. That may have caused extensive downtime which lowered productivity for which you are being berated by your boss. Point out—and be ready to prove—that you did what you could but the supplier didn't fulfill a contractual responsibility for timely maintenance. Whatever the specific situation may be, always be prepared with facts to support assertions that the fault lies beyond the confines of your department.

Be Careful When Responding to Accusations

Above all else, always remain calm when you're accused of being responsible for the failure of a new idea or procedure. When you know you're unfairly accused, it's not easy to keep your cool, but it's an essential ingredient for keeping your job. Decide which one you want to keep. Stick with the facts and learn how to ward off accusatory statements. Here are three essentials for avoiding trouble when someone blames you by an accusatory remark:

1. Take your time and think before you reply. If you feel you need some time before answering, then respond with a general remark such as, "We certainly made every effort to make that equipment work properly." This gives you time to think about the specific reasons you want to cite.

2. Don't point a finger at someone else. Even though the fault may lie elsewhere, you don't want to specifically say so if you are accused as being responsible. If the accuser doesn't know the facts, he or she will assume you are just trying to pass the buck. Instead, you can respond in a general way that sends the message you want to convey. For instance, say something such as, "We just followed the procedures as they were written," rather than bluntly stating, "Tom B's group gave us faulty procedures." This prevents your accuser from going back and stating you said the procedures were wrong. It avoids creating internal problems with people you have to work with on a continuing basis.

3. Don't try to wing your response. If you need to work up details to support your claim of innocence, issue a general denial and let the person know you need more time to furnish the facts supporting your position. For example, say something such as, "We made every effort to make the reorganization work, but were faced with a sharp increase in workload at the same time that we lost two slots. I'll have to look up the figures which show the increase in our work compared with the same period a year ago." Incidentally, if the person asks for a date by which to receive the information, give a realistic date which can be met.

One thing you always want to avoid in these situations is pinning the blame for failure on the people who work for you. Whatever you do, accept the responsibility as the boss. Frequently, people making accusations try to finesse it by saying something such as, "Jones and Brown really messed this thing up." The thinking is that the supervisor will be less likely to react strongly if a subordinate is blamed rather than accusing the department or the supervisor. As the supervisor you're responsible for what happens within your group and part of that responsibility rests in defending them against unfair allegations.

4 Supervising Employees in a Cooperative Work Environment

One of the main attributes that distinguishes the new workplace from the rigid by-the-book management practices of the past is the degree to which cooperation is practiced in getting the job done. Savvy supervisors have learned that productivity, quality, morale, and other factors all improve when employees feel they are part of a team working together to meet job objectives. To some extent, however, the degree of cooperation is determined by broad corporate policy and the emphasis placed on teamwork by top management. Therefore, the cooperative spirit of those who report to you as a supervisor is partly determined by corporate practices beyond your control.

Nevertheless, even where company-wide emphasis on teamwork and cooperation could be better, you as an individual can still secure a high degree of harmony within your own group. It's admittedly harder to do without top management backing, but it can be accomplished as long as you demonstrate a willingness to listen and respond to employee suggestions and complaints.

You may supervise employees who are organized into structured work teams. In this situation you will have to learn how to hold teams accountable for their assigned projects. And on a larger scale, you will have to be able to recognize and deal with some of the pitfalls that teams can create with both their positive and negative aspects. As is the case with many other useful practices, teams can be seen as a potential cure for a variety of unrelated problems. It behooves you to know where and when they can be most effective.

Beyond the structured practice of work teams, cooperation and teamwork can be encouraged in a number of ways. Within this chapter you will find useful techniques to empower employees and promote group problem solving. You will also find tips and tactics for dealing with the need to say "no" in sensitive situations, as well as the best way to deal with the inevitable mistakes that will happen along the way.

SEVERAL SOUND WAYS TO EMPOWER EMPLOYEES

Giving greater authority and responsibility to those who work for you has a two-fold advantage. First, workers who feel they are vital contributors to the operations of your group will be inclined to work both harder and smarter because they will feel greater responsibility for the work they do. The second benefit accrues to you. Being able to assign duties to direct reports which you formerly did yourself will relieve you of some of the burdens of the job. This will allow you to spend more time guiding the group and resolving issues that in the past may have been ignored.

Delegate Based on Skills and Temperament

Although giving workers greater responsibility sounds simple enough, there are a number of pitfalls that have to be avoided. For one thing, not every worker will have an equal desire to assume responsibility. A few people will take on as much additional responsibility as you're willing to give them—some perhaps assuming more duties than they can handle. What you have to watch for here is that people don't dig themselves into a hole by overdoing it.

At the other extreme will be a few people who really don't want any responsibility. They may be perfectly happy to have a supervisor who tells them what to do and when to do it. They don't want to make decisions and they want someone to go to when they need answers. When you have workers who exhibit these traits refrain from forcing them to become more independent. This may only serve to unsettle them and make matters worse.

It is obvious, then, that the first thing to watch for in giving greater freedom to your workers to self-direct their work is their willingness to accept greater responsibility. Beyond that you will have to assess degrees of ability to handle additional duties. This isn't insignificant, since a worker who is empowered to do more than he or she is capable of may fall flat at the outset and may become discouraged from attempting to assume any further responsibility. Try at the beginning to delegate these duties to subordinates that best fit their skills and temperament. Some folks lack people skills, others can't handle details, and still others buckle under pressure situations. The point is simply to empower your subordinates at first to assume the duties they are best qualified to handle. Doing it this way will build their confidence, and over a period of time you will be able to gradually add to the scope of their assignments.

Assess Your Own Attitude

Aside from the difficulties employees may experience in adjusting to the acceptance of greater responsibility, your own attitude has to be considered. Many supervisors find it extremely difficult to adjust to a role where they are no longer directly involved in making every decision. Even though they may have a larger number of direct reports than was the case prior to the days of empowerment, they still try to micro-manage. This leads to longer hours at work and a heavier workload for the supervisor, as well as frustration by subordinates who aren't allowed to operate with any degree of independence. Once supervisors learn to relinquish control they quickly realize how much more efficient everyone becomes. Therefore, the first step in empowering your employees is to be willing to relinquish duties and the decision-making that goes along with it.

In addition to adopting an attitude conducive to empowerment, you must watch your sensibility toward mistakes. One of the hardest parts of relinquishing control is the ability to let subordinates learn by doing, which sometimes means making mistakes. It's easy to get drawn into the trap of closely monitoring subordinates so they either don't make mistakes or they can be quickly corrected. The problem here is that this discourages the very independent action you want to encourage. Sometimes workers have to be allowed to make mistakes as that is how they will learn not to repeat the same error. For this reason you may on occasion have to swallow hard and accept employee errors as part of the learning process. Naturally, you don't want a calamity to happen, and in situations where it becomes obvious an employee is in over his or her head you may have to step in to do some coaching. Nevertheless, for run-of-the-mill situations try to train yourself to stay on the sidelines and let the employee flounder around until the problem is solved.

Although the idea of empowering employees sounds simple enough, it's not all that easy to implement. It certainly isn't something that can be changed overnight by issuing a management directive, but is a process that is best implemented gradually for long-term success. This is particularly true in companies where tight controls and close supervision have been practiced for years. Trying to overturn such a culture overnight simply leads to confusion, misunderstanding, and ultimate failure to change anything. For this reason, both on a company and personal basis it's far better to empower employees gradually. This approach allows both supervisors and subordinates to change their ways in a positive and productive fashion.

USEFUL TACTICS TO PROMOTE GROUP PROBLEM SOLVING

As you work to establish the most cohesive working group you can, one worthwhile goal should be to encourage group problem solving. This can best be done by demonstrating your confidence in the ability of employees to come up with solutions to varied problems that periodically arise. It takes time to establish this sort of rapport and sometimes may require patience on your part in letting employees work the problem out.

This is particularly true when you may have strong opinions of your own about what should be done. By voicing these opinions too loudly, you can discourage workers from trying to solve problems, since they may feel their contributions aren't being taken seriously. For this reason, it pays to be low key about volunteering your own contributions; when necessary, try to subtly steer the discussions in the right direction without giving the appearance of trying to dominate the discussion. Let's look at an example of how to do this:

Background Several of the people who work for Frank (the supervisor) are gathered together in an impromptu meeting. They are trying to figure out the best way to eliminate a particular step in the work process that habitually obstructs its smooth flow. Frank has an idea about combining the function done by one worker while giving part of that same worker's job requirements to someone else. However, the conversation within the group is lively and Frank doesn't want to arbitrarily stick in his two-cents-worth. Only after the discussion starts to slow down and there's little evidence that the group feels it has a solution does Frank voice his opinion. Even here, though, he does so cautiously as a suggestion and lets the group pick up on his idea.

The discussion

Harry: "Well, gang, it doesn't look like there's anything we can do to cure this bottleneck."

Frank: "I wasn't here at the beginning, so you people probably already considered it, but I was wondering whether combining steps three and four under John and giving Mary step five would help. It seems like the flow of work might be smoother, but you people would know more about it than me."

Mary: "Hey, we didn't talk about that. It just might work. What do you think, John?"

John: "It certainly wouldn't hurt to try. Has anyone got a better idea? If not, let's give this a trial run and see what happens."

The result

The suggestion works and the problem is solved. By being diplomatic about making the suggestion, Frank avoids giving the impression he is asserting his authority as the boss to dictate a solution. By being low-key about his contribution to the solution, Frank keeps his group interested in continuing to contribute. By contrast, if a boss is assertive in injecting an opinion, the group will feel that lip service is being given to their suggestions and that in the end the boss will do what he or she wants.

The advantage from a practical standpoint of getting employees involved in group problem solving is that it leads everyone toward working together as a group. By reaching joint decisions, there's less likelihood of dissension among group members. In terms of general techniques for these sessions, the following tactics are useful:

- Don't cut people short even if their suggestions are off-the-mark. Unlike other gatherings where you're trying to keep the meeting moving along on course, group problem solving discussions require some flexibility. If you rein people in too quickly, they may become reluctant to make further contributions. And the more reticent among them may decide you aren't really interested in hearing what they have to say.

- Don't let the discussions become heated when there's a disagreement between one or more members as to the proper course of action. After all, you don't want to end up with a situation where group members become enemies since that defeats the purpose of promoting teamwork. Try to placate both parties with some form of acknowledgment that both positions have some validity.

- Try to be low-key about stating your position. If you start a meeting off by announcing what you think should be done, it will be interpreted as what you want to have done. There won't be any discussion of alternatives and the group will just second what you proposed. You will have to keep control of the meeting to keep it going in the right direction, but do so in as casual a manner as possible.

- When you have to veto an idea because it's impractical, be sure you explain the reasons why the solution won't work. Workers will understand if they know why something can't be done, but they will think you are being arbitrary if you just say "no." It also helps to convey the impression that the idea had validity. For example, say something such as, "That's not a bad idea, but there's no budget available for additional equipment." This leaves people feeling good about having made a valid recommendation even though it couldn't be implemented because of circumstances beyond their control.

- Express your appreciation for the contributions made by the group. Don't be phony about this, but when the opportunity arises, say things such as, "That's a good idea, Frank," or "You really know how to figure these things out, Ann." People like to have their contributions acknowledged, and by doing so you're encouraging them to make further contributions.

Of course, not every problem is amenable to being resolved in a group problem-solving meeting with the people who report to you. However, whenever it's possible and practical to work things out in this fashion, seize the opportunity to promote teamwork.

EIGHT WAYS TO BE FLEXIBLE IN DEALING WITH EMPLOYEE WORK PROBLEMS

One of the constants of supervision is that you will habitually be confronted with one workplace problem after another for resolution. Despite whatever success you may have in encouraging employees to work as a team in solving work problems, there will be situations where you alone will have to make the decision: when the workers themselves are unable to come up with a solution, or perhaps because the nature of the problem is such that it requires your input. Whatever the reason may be, the problems will be varied and consequently your solutions will also be diverse.

Critical is your flexibility in coming up with solutions. That way, you will be better able to resolve even the trickiest problem that gets dumped in your lap. A few general approaches on being flexible are:

1. Always consider carefully every alternative for solving a problem. The most obvious and simplest solution may not be the best one for any number of reasons which aren't immediately apparent. Only by carefully considering alternatives and their consequences can the right choice be made.

2. Be willing to change course in dealing with workplace problems. If one solution isn't working out, be ready to shift focus rather than adamantly sticking with your initial decision on how to handle the matter.

3. Don't be secretive about your desire for assistance. Let people know you have a problem and ask for advice on how to handle it.

4. Accept suggestions for solving workplace problems from any and all sources. Don't discount ideas based upon the source. For example, the suggestion for a solution from a recent hire may not be given any credence. Yet the very fact that this person hasn't been on the scene very long may give him or her the vision to see something from a less hidebound perspective.

5. Work closely with other supervisors in coming up with joint answers for common problems.

6. Keep your sense of humor. When you're trying to make a decision on a complex problem, it's easy to get tense and snap at people. This solves nothing and only aggravates the situation. Always remember that when you're looking for solutions you need allies—not enemies.

7. Don't be afraid to ask your boss for assistance. There's a natural reluctance to take problems to a boss. For one thing there's the ego factor to overcome in not wanting to look bad by having to ask for assistance. This is a foolish notion unless you don't have the best of bosses. For the most part, a boss welcomes it when you ask for guidance. Another reason for reluctance to approach a boss is the notion that the boss couldn't contribute any constructive ideas for dealing with the dilemma. Even if this is true, there is still an advantage in bringing the problem to the boss's attention, because it serves notice should the problem escalate into something serious, which draws the attention of upper levels of management. If you haven't briefed your boss, the first thing you will hear is, "Why didn't you tell me about this?" You obviously can't say, "Because you're an empty suit," so you're left stammering over some half-hearted alibi such as, "I just overlooked it." To avoid these situations, it's best to get the boss involved, even when you know it's of little value.

8. Always establish priorities when workplace problems are brought to your attention. It's easy to treat every issue as the crisis of the moment. Yet some workplace problems are more significant than others. Be willing to focus your efforts on those that are most significant, even though they may be the hardest to deal with.

THE RIGHT WAY TO SAY "NO" IN SENSITIVE SITUATIONS

There will be occasions when, no matter how much you would like to approve an employee's request, it will be necessary to say "No." Actually rejecting a request, as difficult as it may be, isn't the hardest part. What can be tricky, though, is doing it in such a way that the rejected employee understands the basis for the rejection. That isn't to say that this will necessarily make an employee happy. That isn't the purpose at all. What you want to accomplish is to leave the employee with a feeling that you were fair in what you did, and offered a valid reason for doing so. Everyone gets rejections, but how they are handled is what determines whether or not there are after-effects.

Avoid Favoritism

First and foremost, in dealing with various employee requests, avoid favoritism in any form or fashion. This appears to be something that is a given and doesn't even merit any discussion. The problem is that even though most supervisors attempt to be fair there's a natural tendency to favor certain people. You can unconsciously grant requests for some employees which would be denied if they were made by someone else.

Perhaps Jamie, a top producer, wants to leave early one day and her supervisor approves the request. The following week Joanna, the constant complainer, makes a similar request and it's rejected. In the boss's mind, perhaps there was too much work on the day that Joanna made her request. On the other hand, maybe it was subconscious bias based upon the respective performance of the two individuals. Then again, someone might make the argument that a top performer deserves special considerations. Whether that's valid or not, the rewards shouldn't include being arbitrary about which employee requests are granted and which are refused. One very practical reason is that co-workers witnessing one person's request granted and a similar request turned down will perceive it as favoritism.

Be Considerate in Rejecting Requests

A second critical element in turning down employee requests is to avoid being abrupt. Saying something such as, "As you can see we're too busy to let you go early," may be factual but how this is conveyed to someone makes a great deal of difference. Take the time to learn why the employee is making the request, the importance of the request being granted, and to explain why you must refuse it. Be sincere and explain that you would like to help but circumstances don't permit you to do so. Nevertheless, avoid getting caught in the trap of debating whether or not you should grant the request. If an employee persists in trying to persuade you to change your mind, cut the discussion short in as casual a manner as you can.

Know When to Put the Employee First

Although you want to be generally consistent about granting or rejecting requests, from time to time employees will come to you with emergency requests. These will cover everything from sudden illness to accidents or any of the numerous other misfortunes that befall people without prior notice. Family emergencies are just that and should be handled with dispatch. Grant the request and worry later about covering the employee's assignments.

If the situation warrants it then you should go beyond approving the person's request to leave right away and offer any assistance that might be needed. For example, transportation might be a problem if someone is car-pooling or is otherwise tied to a set schedule for transportation to and from work. In these situations you might want to see if another employee would be willing to drive.

Be Careful When Approvals Are Conditional

There are times when you may be willing to grant an employee's request if he or she meets some prior condition. For example, taking a Friday or Monday off to make a long weekend may be conditioned on the employee's workload being completed. When you use conditions such as this, make sure they are specific and that both you and the employee agree on what they are. Furthermore, make sure the conditions are fulfilled before the employee receives final approval.

Be Practical

For the most part, it's of little consequence when an employee makes a request to leave a few minutes early. Nevertheless, even minor deviations from normal working hours should receive your prior approval. If not, before you know it a few people will start coming and going at their leisure and you will have to take corrective action. Of course, if your company uses some form of flextime, this sort of situation can be avoided.

Another practical issue you can't avoid is the need to be detached about saying "no" when it's necessary to reject a request. Don't let your emotions get in the way. Your desire to accommodate a reasonable request can have you granting approval when the proper course of action would be a refusal.

Today's modern workplace is one where working hours have a lot more flexibility built in to meet the needs of a diverse workforce. In many instances technology allows people to do their work from home or at some other site removed from their place of business. All in all, this makes it easier to work around employee needs for time off to attend to personal problems. Nevertheless, there are and will continue to be plenty of jobs requiring people to be present and working at a fixed site. This means there will be occasions when requests for time off have to be turned down. That shouldn't be a problem for you as a supervisor as long as you are perceived as being fair in your decisions.

GOING BEYOND PREACHING TO PRACTICING WHEN PROMOTING TEAMWORK

How effective teamwork is within your group is influenced somewhat by factors beyond your control. If top management within your company doesn't insist upon teamwork from top to bottom throughout the organization, then the level of support you will get in promoting teamwork may be nil. Even where top management does issue policy statements encouraging teamwork, sometimes there is little follow-up, and as a consequence managers throughout the company pay little more than lip service to the concept.

Although it's certainly easier for you when the company as a whole embraces the concept, even lacking that you can forge ahead and make teamwork a viable practice within your own group. However, as with any other difficult endeavor, a lot more than talk is required.

Cooperate with Your Peers

One fundamental step in encouraging teamwork is to practice it yourself in your dealings with other managers. If your subordinates see you work closely with other supervisors on problems of joint interest, they have first-hand evidence of your belief in teamwork. On the other hand, if you are frequently engaged in disputes with your peers, then teamwork doesn't come across as one of your strong suits. This doesn't mean, of course, that you always have to be in agreement with every course of action that another supervisor wants to take. However, disagreements should be based upon a thorough airing of your respective positions and a respect for the other person. For this reason, other supervisors shouldn't be openly criticized by you to subordinates.

As indicated, teamwork doesn't mean everyone has to be in agreement on everything or reach a unanimous decision on every action. This is a misconception that's sometimes implied, especially if someone doesn't agree with something. Next, someone will say directly or indirectly that the individual isn't a team player. What it does mean is a willingness to work toward the group's objective even though you may not totally agree with the approach. In short, people should have a chance to express themselves and every effort should be made to agree on goals and objectives. But once the discussions have ended it's time for everyone to put their oars in the water and row together.

Several Factors Foster Teamwork

Incidentally, promoting the concept of teamwork within your group goes beyond a "show and tell" process where you show employees you practice teamwork and then tell them they should, too. First of all, you have to get employees actively involved in making suggestions as to how the work should be done. If you don't, then they won't feel they are part of a team. In fact, they may think your preaching about teamwork is nothing other than a gimmick to keep them from raising valid objections to work-related problems. This is where trust comes into play. If you have established a solid level of trust with your employees, they will be more willing to accept your crusade for teamwork as genuinely in their interests.

Remember that it's also necessary to address the self-interest of employees in working together as a team. To do this effectively, you have to demonstrate your willingness to work toward the best interests of the team, which involves several factors. One is to battle for the necessary resources employees need to do their jobs. Aside from the practical aspects, it demonstrates that you as the team leader will work hard to make it successful. It's also important to show your appreciation for team efforts, which can range from praise for worthwhile efforts to occasional social get-togethers to celebrate the accomplishment of team goals. All in all, what you're trying to achieve is the sort of camaraderie that will inspire the efforts of your team to work together cohesively.

Recognize Both Individual and Team Performance

One of the quandaries in the area of teamwork is to differentiate team accomplishments from individual performance. This is a serious matter, especially in the minds of top performers within a work group. They may resent the emphasis on teamwork which downplays their individual contributions. They may develop an attitude which is characterized by thoughts such as, "Why should I be working my butt off to make John look good?" where the named individual is a less than stellar performer. The end result is that hard workers may slack off if they feel they are being used to carry the load of their less competent co-workers.

This isn't an insurmountable obstacle, and teams will have members with varying abilities. The trick is in recognizing this and not blindly assuming everyone should perform to the same level. Be ready to recognize performance differences and to reward standout performers individually as well as for group achievements. As long as the best performers are recognized for their achievements, they won't balk at working with their peers in a spirit of teamwork.

Knowing Different Jobs Promotes Teamwork

In an environment of teamwork, every worker should know the relationship of his or her job to that of other co-workers. This may be more or less obvious, depending upon the nature of the work within a group. In some instances everyone may be doing essentially the same type of work, while in other groups the individual responsibilities may differ. Where they do vary, it's beneficial for every worker to understand how his or her job impacts upon other jobs. Workers will thus become aware of how their actions can help or hinder co-workers in performing related tasks.

Where teamwork is emphasized it's also easier to train workers in doing other jobs. This form of cross-training benefits both supervisors and workers. It gives the employee the chance to learn different jobs, acquire valuable skills, and relieve boredom. For you, it provides a pool of people ready and able to fill in on other jobs during absences or other times of need.

SEVEN MEASURES FOR SELLING TEAMWORK TO WORKERS

With the inherent difficulty involved in instilling teamwork within your group, there is a very real need for you to do a bit of a selling job to convince workers that working together is to their individual benefit. If you work in a company that has historically had an "everyone for himself" mode of operation, promoting teamwork won't be an easy task.

Even under circumstances where teamwork has been and continues to be encouraged, it's an on-going effort that must be sustained to keep individual employees from going it alone to the detriment of the group. Although every individual situation presents specific opportunities for demonstrating the value of teamwork, here are seven broad measures you can use:

1. Appeal to the self-interest of workers by pointing out the personal advantages of teamwork. A few representative responses here point out its benefits to skeptical workers:

   Worker: "I've got too much work to do. I don't have time to waste in discussions with Sam and Sally."

   Supervisor: "Teamwork will give you a chance to learn other skills by working closely with other people. That certainly improves your future chances for promotion, Juan."

   Worker: "Why should I waste my time showing someone else how to do this job?"

   Supervisor: "For one thing, Nate, teamwork and cooperation are now performance evaluation factors. So working well with others is essential for anyone to obtain a superior performance evaluation rating. And as you know, Nate, those ratings come into play when people are considered for promotion."

   Worker: "There's no benefit for me in wasting time in group meetings and having job discussions with other people. All it does is slow me down in doing my work."

   Supervisor: "Carlos, we've discussed in the past your potential for future advancement to a supervisory position. Remember, if you're ever going to get a shot at a supervisory slot, you're going to have to be able to demonstrate your ability to work closely with other people. You can see how I have to coordinate with other managers all of the time. One good way for you to prove your ability to cooperate with other people is being an avid team member within the group."

Worker: "What's the big deal with all of this teamwork stuff? It just seems like another way to waste more time in meetings."

Supervisor: "Everyone contributes to the company, so what other people think is important to all of us. Besides, we can always pick up valuable tips from other people, so it's a good way to improve your knowledge of what goes on both within the department and within the company. Beyond that, close cooperation will improve everyone's ability to do their job. That should help increase profits and provide greater job security for everyone."

2. Communicate on a personal as well as business basis with employees. Spend some time in general chit-chat and get to know people on an individual basis. This sort of familiarity makes it easier for everyone to work closely together as a team.

3. Encourage people to pitch in and help out others when needed. How do you do this? By volunteering yourself in certain situations. When employees see their boss willing to help out when needed, it sets the tone for them to do likewise.

4. Be willing to listen to what employees have to say. Workers will be more likely to look kindly on the notion of teamwork if they feel like valued members of the group.

5. Make a conscious effort to recognize and reward teamwork when you see it.

6. Don't avoid taking disciplinary action because you think it will discourage teamwork. To the contrary, workers who are trying to cooperate in the interests of getting the job done have little respect for co-workers who are disruptive or otherwise aren't performing up to minimal standards. Therefore, any action you take will improve the ability of the remaining workers to work cooperatively on joint endeavors.

7. Take the time to spell out why teamwork works to the ultimate benefit of everyone. For example, explain how learning different jobs enables people to fill in for co-workers who may need time off

to deal with a personal emergency. Let workers know that this flexibility benefits them individually.

HOW TO MAKE TEAMS ACCOUNTABLE WITHOUT MAKING THEM PARANOID

Aside from fostering a general spirit of teamwork and cooperation within your department, you may have the opportunity to use formal teams on a regular or occasional basis. One of the most difficult hurdles to overcome when teams are used is to provide for oversight, making teams accountable for their performance without making them apprehensive about being blamed for failure. If not done properly, team members may feel that they are being used as scapegoats.

Once teams develop a fear of failure in the performance of their duties they will soon become reluctant to take any chances in doing their assigned tasks. The end result will be the inability to forge teams that will work well together toward a common goal. Individual team members will instead concentrate on protecting their own self-interest and little or no effective work will be forthcoming from the team. Consequently, it's extremely important to provide for accountability for teams and at the same time reassure people that they aren't being set up to fail. Explain that mistakes may happen in the performance of their duties but they won't be used as the basis for criticizing the team.

The starting point in establishing accountability is to clearly define the task that is to be performed by the team. This is where problems frequently occur because of a failure to be specific enough about what the team's goal is and what the schedule for completing the work will be. Be certain that the team understands these criteria so there won't be any future complaints such as, "We didn't know you wanted us to do that."

Team Leader Characteristics

If you're not going to be the team leader yourself, then appoint someone who will be responsible for coordinating team efforts. In selecting the appropriate individual you want to consider the following factors:

a. Does the person have patience? A team leader should be patient enough to be able to listen to the varied views of a number of different people.

b. Is the person a good listener? Being a good listener isn't quite as easy as most people think. Some people listen half-heartedly, while others can't let more than a sentence go by without saying something themselves. The individual appointed as team leader has to be able to listen and absorb the thoughts of a variety of people.

c. Can the person communicate clearly? As the team leader the person selected will be responsible for making certain everyone knows what other team members are doing. This may require the ability to interpret technical jargon for certain team members, especially if the team consists of people from a variety of functions with a broad diversity of skills. Everyone may not know what a particular member is talking about in a technical area. It's the responsibility of the team leader to clarify what is being said.

d. Does the person have the temperament for the assignment? The team leader must not only be able to get along with group members, but may also be required to interact with people from other departments, or perhaps even with customers and/or suppliers. Therefore, the person should have the political instincts to deal appropriately with a variety of different people with different business interests.

e. Does the person have the skills/experience to command the respect of team members? A team leader may have to deal with some team members who have big egos. For this reason it's wise to select a leader who will command the respect of others on the team. This will minimize the opportunity for bickering to break out and for people to challenge the team leader's authority.

f. Does the person want the assignment? Being a team leader is a daunting task, requiring a good deal of diplomacy; not everyone relishes such an assignment. Therefore, it's important to consider as team leader only those people who truly want to serve in such a capacity. A person's willingness to assume such a role should be discussed with the individual before the person is appointed. Be careful to point out the negatives of the job so someone doesn't accept the role under erroneous assumptions. That will help avoid future problems for you, the individual appointed, and the team.

Of course, what characteristics you favor most heavily in appointing a team leader will reflect the nature of the task to be performed and the composition of the team. For example, if your team will have little or no interaction outside of your department, the ability of the person to interact with others outside of your group won't be important. The fundamental point is to exercise great care in selecting a team leader who can serve as a coach and facilitator without being so obtrusive as to dominate the working relationships of the team as a whole.

Establish Reporting Guidelines

If the project assigned to a team is one that will take a substantial period of time to complete, you should establish reporting guidelines so you can assess the progress of the team in meeting its goals. Depending upon the circumstances, you can provide for periodic briefings in whatever format best suits your needs. These can be formal or informal as the need and your management style dictate. One major requirement to keep in mind is that you must be apprised of any potential problems that may impact the team. In addition, you want to know what the team is doing to resolve the problem. You should also ensure that you are briefed on any needs the team may have that will require your intervention.

For the most part, you want to limit any team oversight to the minimum necessary to be certain that satisfactory progress is being made. If your supervision is too heavy-handed, it may impede the team in doing its work because of excessive reporting requirements. It may also discourage team decisions from being made without your prior approval. In essence, monitoring the progress of teams requires a delicate balance between a level of supervision that ensures performance and one that is inclined to impede progress.

HOW TO DEAL WITH TURF BATTLES WHEN TEAMWORK IS EMPHASIZED

Teamwork, of course, sometimes requires individuals to work toward team goals when doing so may not be in their own self-interest. At times such as this, resentment and even open hostility may erupt if a worker feels that other workers are intruding on his or her turf in the guise of teamwork. This may or may not be true, but that isn't as important as the negative reaction of individuals who feel they are being imposed upon.

Not all people work well in formal teams, or even in practicing teamwork or cooperation in a more general way. Every workplace has loners who come to work, do their job, and go home without having more than a minimal amount of interaction with anyone else. In fact, some of these people are very hard workers and excel at what they do. The problem is that these people don't want anything to do with teams and they certainly don't want team members telling them how they should or shouldn't do their jobs.

Hostility can erupt when individuals object to teams intruding into what the individual considers to be his or her work. The best way to handle this is to practice prevention beforehand. There's a wide range of personality types within any group and it pays to know the quirks of those who work for you. By doing this you can avoid as much as possible the placement of loners into formal teams where they will contribute nothing more than animosity to the group.

On the other hand, you can't arbitrarily disrupt the smooth functioning of the operation to pander to people who are out and out uncooperative. In some circumstances it may be possible to tolerate people who don't interact well with others, for example in jobs where there is little or no need for someone to deal with other people on a regular basis. Aside from these, however, the need to work closely with co-workers calls for teamwork in getting the job done. So you want to avoid having people work for you who like to go it alone. The starting point for doing this is in your hiring. Don't neglect to carefully assess the ability of job candidates to work well with other people when you do any hiring. This can save you a lot of grief further down the road.

Of course, future hiring doesn't help you much in working with the hand you have already been dealt. If you have people within your group who don't work well with others, you have to work around this handicap. Aside from loners, you may also have employees who are more intent on competing with each other for promotions than on cooperating in team endeavors. These individuals aren't about to do anything that will help a peer look good. In fact, at their worst these people may go out of their way to make co-workers look bad.

How to Weed Out Candidates for Teams

Whatever the individual motive may be for being a foe of cooperative endeavors, there are several factors which pinpoint employees who aren't good candidates for either formal teams or any activity requiring teamwork. They include:

- employees who don't get along well with others
- co-workers who constantly disagree with one another
- those who constantly bicker over job assignments
- employees who jockey for promotions
- employees who exhibit a failure to coordinate work with other people
- people with strong biases or thinly disguised prejudices
- empire builders interested in increasing the status of their jobs
- argumentative individuals
- super-ego types who have all the answers
- those who zealously guard their knowledge and refuse to answer questions

Although the traits listed indicate those that aren't conducive to teamwork and cooperation, they don't prevent insurmountable obstacles to working in a group. Aside from a few really severe cases of individuals who channel their competitive energies in the wrong direction, most employees will adapt to a teamwork-focused system if they see it to be in their best interests.

The best way to encourage them to see the light is to emphasize the importance of teamwork within your group. Those who tend to lag in their cooperative efforts should be counseled individually. Let these people know that a failure to work well in cooperation with their peers is a handicap that will hinder their future with the company. Nothing can make this point more clearly than promoting an employee who is known for working well with others.

RECOGNIZING AND DEALING WITH THE PITFALLS OF TEAMS

No matter what the particular management concept may be, there are always advocates touting it as the cure-all for everything that's wrong. The hard truth, however, is that any individual technique is at best only a tool that has practical uses and is limited in scope. Any one concept is no cure-all for everything, and as long as you recognize this you can never go wrong. So it is with teams. Just as they have practical advantages and applications, so too do they have pitfalls which have to be recognized and dealt with. The failure to do so can render teams useless even in situations where they should be an asset.

Teams are often used in situations where cross-disciplinary functions are required on a project. These individuals may come from different groups and are assembled to work together to achieve a specific purpose. Upon the completion of the assignment the group disbands. In other instances, teams are organized on a more or less permanent basis. Sometimes teams are organized with little or no distinction from a traditional operating unit. These represent lip service to a concept; calling a group a team and the supervisor a team leader doesn't do much for anyone—except the consultants who were handsomely rewarded for recommending the concept.

It's Teamwork—Not Team Structure—That Counts

This leads to the first pitfall of teams, which is to recognize that they are not the cure-all for anything and shouldn't be adopted as the fad of the moment. The organization of teams isn't as important as the amount of teamwork that takes place. Remember that there are teams without too much teamwork, while there is teamwork without any formal recognition of a team. Names and nomenclature do not make for cooperative endeavors. It's the willingness of people to work together for a common cause that does the trick. When it comes to selecting team members, along with any specific skills required, the general attributes to avoid were discussed in the previous section. Of course, since in your supervisory capacity you are limited in the people you have to pick and choose from in organizing a team, you have to be flexible about your requirements.

Another hazard to overcome in organizing teams is the selection of an appropriate team leader. The key requirement is someone who can keep everything on course while remaining in the background, not assuming complete control. What you want is someone who can provide guidance when needed, but who will let the team operate without undue interference. The pitfall to avoid is appointing someone who assumes control and operates essentially in a supervisor/subordinate relationship. This totally destroys the prospects for the cooperation you sought which was the basis for establishing the team in the first place.

One potential problem with teams is that they sometimes take on a life of their own and continue in existence long after the initial purpose for their creation ceases to exist. This isn't unlike what happens with other types of organizations where, once the structure is in place, the participants don't want to relinquish their roles. To avoid being disbanded, the team may take on "make work" projects to justify the team's continuing existence. Another alternative consists of doing a legitimate project for which the team is ill-suited, one perhaps better suited for a team whose members have a different variety of job skills.

Another danger to avoid is that of a manager who may see a team as a means of expanding his or her power base. For example, when individuals from different departments are assembled into a team, its manager may try to permanently absorb the team members into his or her department under the guise of continuing the team's mandate to work on other assignments. Avoiding these types of bureaucratic power plays requires that a team's charter be clearly established when it's created. If it is being assembled for one specific purpose, that should be so stated at the time.

Don't Ignore Individual Achievements

The accomplishments of outstanding individuals on the team can be easily overlooked. It's meaningful to emphasize cooperation and teamwork, but it's equally important to recognize individual accomplishments. Some employees are better at what they do than certain of their co-workers. They fully expect their skills and hard work to be recognized whether they are in a formal team structure or not. Just as great sports teams may have individual stars who are recognized as such, so too should work teams. The deliberate failure to recognize individual accomplishment can discourage the best and brightest workers from performing to the best of their abilities. This not only reduces the productivity of these people but it also hinders team performance.

PRODUCTIVE TECHNIQUES THAT ENCOURAGE WORKER COOPERATION

You can encourage cooperation from the people who work for you in a number of subtle ways. In some individual instances it may be harder, but on an overall basis the use of some practical strategies should help you maximize cooperation from your people. Of course, you have to recognize that what you get and how hard you have to work to obtain it are influenced by factors beyond your control.

For instance, if your company has low overall morale and perhaps has gone through one or more rounds of layoffs, workers aren't likely to be particularly cooperative. On the other hand, this can be dealt with as long as you're able to channel their efforts toward you as opposed to the company. The better you're able to do this, the greater cooperation you'll get if the overall work environment isn't too positive.

If you want people to do something, then the obvious way is to offer them some benefit for doing what you want. That, of course, isn't always either possible or practical, and encouraging your workers to cooperate with one another shouldn't require bribery. Nevertheless, it never hurts to provide whatever incentives are feasible to nudge workers toward positive goals. In line with this there are several easy ways to reward workers for being cooperative in their efforts, whether within the group, interacting with other departments, or dealing with customers or suppliers.

Offer Praise for Cooperative Efforts

The first place to start is in communicating your expectations to those who work for you. Let everyone know how highly you value teamwork and get in the habit of consistently praising group accomplishments. Emphasize the group aspect whenever you're talking about departmental goals or achievements. For example, saying something such as, "If we work together, we won't have any trouble meeting our deadlines" is preferable to "Everyone has to meet their deadlines."

People are by nature competitive, so another way to encourage cooperation is by letting your employees know how they did compared to other groups. Being told how good they are makes people feel better so this is actually a form of psychic reward. For example:

"Our department had the fewest quality defects in the company."

"Mac D. (the corporate executive vice-president) says we're the best department in the plant."

It's, of course, not always possible to compare one department or group with another, but even here comparative yardsticks are useful. Always try to identify several standards by which your group's performance can be measured. Then set goals for beating the standards and hold periodic meetings to let everyone know the progress. This sort of competitive challenge gives workers something to shoot for. If the goals are beaten you may even want to provide some form of reward recognizing the achievement. It doesn't have to be anything significant as long as it's something that shows recognition and appreciation for what was accomplished.

If your group deals with outsiders such as customers and suppliers be certain to relay positive comments to employees. This is particularly significant in the area of customer service where businesses are always striving to motivate workers to furnish better service. One of the easiest ways to accomplish that is to recognize and publicize it when a customer makes favorable comments about an employee. Praise employees before the group so that not only does the worker know you appreciate the stellar performance, but coworkers are also made aware as well.

One of the better means of encouraging cooperation is some form of monetary incentive that rewards group achievement, such as a bonus to teams that meet certain goals. Both the availability and structure of such incentive pay systems are determined at the corporate level, so as a supervisor there's little you can do if your company doesn't have such a plan. Even so, you can still provide your own informal incentives through higher pay raises and promotions for those employees who best practice teamwork and cooperation. Encouraging employee cooperation doesn't have to be difficult, but it does require on-going emphasis of its importance.

LEARNING THE RIGHT WAY TO DEAL WITH MISTAKES

Blunders are made all the time that you can easily recognize as being part of the job. Nothing is or should be said of these routine errors. Then, of course, there are the mistakes that shouldn't have been made but result from carelessness, nonchalance, or just plain negligence on the part of a worker. These can get your blood boiling quickly and, unless you're extraordinarily good at controlling your temper, someone is going to incur your wrath. Unfortunately, like it or not, even when dumb mistakes are made, losing your cool isn't the answer.

Whatever the nature of an error, getting angry is not part of the solution. This isn't to say it won't happen, since some situations may trigger the temper of even the calmest of the calm. Other supervisors may just have a short fuse which they aren't always able to control. Whatever the case may be, if you do happen to lose your temper when a mistake is made, always try to apologize when you cool down. When you do so, however, be certain you apologize only for getting angry, not for complaining about the mistake. What you don't want to do is convey the impression that you're condoning the error.

The practical approach in most instances where mistakes are made is to identify why they were made and what can be done to prevent their repetition. In some instances, it may well be that, given the circumstances, the mistakes were to be expected. For example, perhaps your group is working long hours of overtime because of a shortage of people. Mistakes increase because people are tired and overworked. Assuming you have done everything possible to secure additional help without success, there's little you can do to rectify the situation. Under these conditions, reassure workers that you understand the pressures they face and that you recognize an increase in errors is inevitable.

Incidentally, in a circumstance such as this, it helps to be able to correlate increases in errors with increases in workload. This type of data comes in handy when you're arguing for additional help. It also serves to counter any criticism that may surface from on high about quality of work deteriorating. You want to be in a position to show that the lower quality of output is the direct result of not being able to sufficiently staff your department to meet the workload.

Don't Unfairly Assess Blame

It's essential to identify the reason for a mistake. Otherwise, it may reoccur. Furthermore, if the cause isn't identified, blame may be incorrectly assessed. For example, a worker may make an error which on the surface appears to be his or her fault. Yet, after looking into the matter, you may find that the error resulted from a cause beyond the worker's control. Perhaps the worker was led astray by a poorly written procedure. If the error had been taken at face value, the worker may have been admonished to work more carefully. Then you would have had a resentful worker who felt unfairly blamed. In addition, the flawed procedure would have led to further errors by other workers. For these reasons, the cause of a mistake should be clearly pinpointed.

The Learning Process Includes Making Mistakes

Whenever new technology and procedures are introduced, it's inevitable that mistakes will be made as employees learn a new approach to doing their work. The significant aspect of these errors is that they should be caught and corrected as soon as possible to prevent workers from becoming conditioned to doing something the wrong way. As long as they're corrected, this type of error will gradually decrease as employees become more adept at working with new equipment.

There may be rare instances when the error rate doesn't decrease, which may signal some significant flaw. It could be a training error where workers were incorrectly shown how to do something. On the other hand, perhaps the training was accurate but it was done in haste and was misinterpreted by those learning the process. Whatever the cause, it should be sought out and rectified. Otherwise, workers will continue to make the same mistakes without even realizing they are doing something wrong. In a few situations it may be that the new equipment itself is at fault and that some modification or replacement of the equipment is in order.

Faulty Communications Can Cause Blunders

The failure to communicate clearly is a fairly common basis for errors. Always be certain you don't give vague assignments. Incidentally, there may be occasions where you are convinced you were perfectly clear about what you wanted to be done. The employee who made the mistake may be equally convinced that you said something other than what you did say. This kind of misunderstanding happens because communications are a two-way street. Both parties should be participating fully in expressing their own thoughts, as well as listening to what the other person is saying. It may be that you correctly stated what you wanted, but the employee may not have been doing a good job of listening to what you had to say. To prevent this, always confirm that the employee knows precisely what you want done. Ask if there are any questions. By doing this you will significantly reduce the number of mistakes that are made which result from miscommunication—at least between you and subordinates.

Beware of False Accusations of Mistakes

Once in a while people try to use others as scapegoats when something goes wrong. Someone can be accused of a mistake he or she didn't make. The most common example of this is when people outside your department allege that some form of mistake was made by your group. For example, a deadline is missed for some reason and someone points the finger at your group. When you investigate, it turns out that your employees disagree with the claim that's being made. Unfortunately, unless there is documentation or third party corroboration, it boils down to one person's word against another.

How best to cope with this dilemma is to practice a bit of prevention. If false accusations occur frequently, or some work of special significance is being done for another department, confirm in writing what is to be done, as well as any deadline dates. This way you will have written evidence of what was agreed to, which will leave no margin for false accusations if something goes wrong at a later date. Incidentally, the documentation doesn't have to be anything too formal. The important point is to make the agreement a matter of record.

5 Solving Personnel Issues the Enlightened Way

With change continuing in the workplace, one of the keys to keeping worker skills current is the need for constant training. As a supervisor, you have to be alert for the training needs most appropriate for your group. Not only must it reflect the actual needs of individual workers, but also the approaches used must vary to reflect workplace realities. After all, everything can't just grind to a halt while training takes place. This chapter discusses various alternatives for conducting training, as well as specific methods that best meet the needs of individual workers.

Beyond the many and varied training-related problems you have to deal with, there are other issues that impact upon employee retention and development. These include dealing with job stress and worker burnout, as well as providing opportunities for employees to learn new jobs and improve their skills. And as unpleasant as it is, there may be times when you have to overcome workers' insecurity about their jobs, and in a worst case scenario cope with the varied problems associated with layoffs. Finally, because changes in the workplace are often viewed by employees as laying the groundwork for job cutbacks, you, as a supervisor, have one of the toughest tasks in encouraging workers to participate fully in implementing changes. So let's start by looking at ways to make workers more receptive to change.

ENCOURAGING WORKER PARTICIPATION IN RECOMMENDING CHANGES

As mentioned earlier, many changes within the workplace aren't exactly welcomed with open arms by workers. Therefore, it's not an easy task to encourage them to be active participants in recommending changes. However, the more you're able to convince workers to collaborate in making changes, the greater the chances for success. There's no mystery about this, since folks are obviously going to be more receptive to changes they think up themselves. To be a successful agent of change, you should first convince your group to initiate change rather than wait for it to filter down from above. That way, both you and your group have greater control over what changes take place.

There are two main approaches to convincing workers of the benefits of participating in making workplace changes. The first is to be able to show how particular changes will benefit the workers themselves, while the second approach relies on the argument that any changes made by the group will be preferable to those imposed from on high. This is the old "Let's do something about this before someone else does, since it will be less painful if we do it ourselves."

Showing people how they can benefit is a good way to interest workers in recommending revisions in how they do their work. After all, it's unrealistic to expect people to expend time and energy in thinking about how to revamp their jobs if doing so offers them nothing in return. Although the strategy is simple enough to state, it's not quite as easy to come up with ideas as to how job revisions will benefit workers. Furthermore, employees aren't going to jump through hoops based upon generalizations such as, "What's good for the company is good for you." The fact is that most employees won't buy such an argument, and certainly not to the extent that they will try and revamp their jobs to become more productive. Actually, in some companies where extensive layoffs have taken place in the past, workers will be rightly suspicious of any attempts to realign how their work is performed. They may quite rightly feel that job revisions are the first step toward abolishing more jobs.

Set an Example for Recommending Changes

One possibility for increasing worker participation in suggesting changes is to encourage workplace adjustments that make life easier for employees. A common example of such a change at the corporate level might be the adoption of flextime with flexible working and quitting times for employees. Of course, these kinds of changes are beyond your immediate control. However, even when it comes to potential changes that require decision-making at higher levels, you can win points with your people by lobbying for them. If you, as the supervisor, recommend and support broad-based changes, then this will encourage your subordinates to be active participants in making suggestions about the way they do their work. The point is that if you suggest changes to your bosses that benefit your subordinates, they are likely to follow your lead and make suggestions of their own. And since individual employees best know the nuances of their own jobs, who else is better positioned to know what adjustments can be made to make tasks easier to do?

Sell the Benefits of Making Suggestions for Change

As you know, many of the more dramatic changes in the workplace are those that are decided upon at executive levels and filter down from top management. These would include all kinds of reorganizations, layoffs, and similar trauma-inducing changes. However, even those of a lesser magnitude are often put in place without prior consultation with those at the operating levels. New equipment and workplace logistics decisions are typical of changes which, while not as dramatic as large-scale layoffs, still have a significant impact on the people involved.

For example, if your boss decides that moving your workplace location is beneficial, then such a change may be enacted even though it's not in the best interests of either you or your group. Many times changes like these can be preempted if you and your group see it coming and make a prior recommendation that better serves the group's interest. Even without making any recommendation for change, a sense of awareness of the possibilities and readiness with counter arguments can sometimes work to avoid unwelcome changes. For instance, if your group is aware of a piece of machinery being considered for purchase that won't be suitable, you can be prepared to argue this issue in the planning stages before a purchase is made.

In still other instances, there may be situations where your own people will come out ahead by making a recommendation for a particular innovation before a planned change is implemented by higher management. Perhaps your group's work has declined significantly and, as a consequence, a realignment of the work structure is inevitable. This could, of course, mean a reassignment of work, the abolishment of your department, the combining of your department with another, or perhaps even layoffs. To avoid the more unpleasant of alternatives, you and your people might be able to brainstorm a recommendation for change that keeps the group pretty much intact. Perhaps, for example, you could recommend that some additional work that fits well with the skills of your department be reassigned to your group. Whatever the specifics might be, the important point is that by making suggestions before any action is taken, your group may be able to steer the end results toward a reasonable solution. This sort of recommendation can have a high success rate if it's well thought out, since it solves what may be a difficult dilemma for higher management in determining what action to take. By providing the solution, you have solved their problem as well as your own.

Other times, you may be able to foresee changes that are likely to be made in the interests of efficiency—at least as seen by top management. By making your own changes within the department beforehand, you can be the one who determines what is done. This is the sort of reasoning you want to instill in your employees, that by making suggestions for change, the group will be better able to control its own destiny.

ADAPTING TRAINING NEEDS TO WORKPLACE REALITIES

Training is an area where a great deal of money is spent with sometimes less than satisfactory results. One problem is where the money is spent. Frequently, extensive funding is committed for middle manager and technical training, with little or nothing done for the working level. A second recurring problem is the priority given to training. Courses often are scheduled and then hastily abandoned due to changing workload commitments. Another headache is the seemingly constant need to update the skills of workers as new technology comes on stream at a faster and faster pace, leaving recently learned skills to be quickly outdated. This particular problem is of greater severity in those industries where changing technology assumes a dominant role.

Naturally, in the general scheme of things you could probably care less about the broad overview of training. What you are undoubtedly concerned with is the need for training of people under your supervision. Requirements here will vary with the specifics of the type of work performed by people in your department. The best way in which to focus on training is to be realistic. That means that first of all, any training such as outside courses has to be justified in your training budget.

Outsmarting the Budget Cutters

To begin with, don't overdo it in submitting training requests that aren't easily substantiated. Otherwise you will find a red pencil being taken to your training requests and there may be little attempt to determine any priority attached to those you have already made. Therefore, if the training is necessary, justify it. If it isn't essential to improving the operation of your unit, don't include it in any request for funding.

You may have to request funding for different types of training. If they all have roughly the same priority, then it will make little difference which ones may be eliminated during the approval cycle. If you do have priorities attached, the question to be dealt with is whether or not you should highlight this in your request. Although it would appear to be practical to do this, what's practical isn't always the wisest course of action. For one thing, if you prioritize your request, it's easier for a budget cutter to automatically eliminate the lower priority items. If there are no priorities listed, then perhaps either no cuts will be made, or you will be contacted to determine which items should be cut. At that point, you can prioritize. Even if you don't prioritize your request and your most important training priority is cut, you can go back and negotiate the restoration of the priority training item in exchange for eliminating others to produce the same amount of savings in the budget. Therefore, on balance, the wiser choice may be not to attach priorities in your budget request.

On the other hand, as part of your training budget request it may be a requirement to rank training needs according to priority. This, of course, makes life easier for those at staff and operations management levels who are involved in reviewing and approving training budgets. If cuts need to be made, then the lower priority items have already been identified by you and that's where the cuts will be targeted. If this is the type of procedure you have to follow, be careful how you handle it. For one thing, don't arbitrarily give high priority to the most expensive training needs and low priority to the least expensive, assuming the lower priority items will be cut and the expensive training needs will survive. Budget cutters are looking to save money and will cut until they get it, so they might then zero in on a single high priority training need that gives them the dollar reductions they need.

One way around this dilemma is to list a couple of lower priority training requests that are relatively expensive. The odds are that any cuts will then be focused on these items. Naturally, don't be obvious about this and always make certain that the training has some relevance toward your unit's operations. It's one thing to be cute about something, but it's quite another thing to be caught at it.

Do Your Training When It's Doable

For a number of reasons you may find yourself increasingly frustrated with the amount of training required for people within your department. Your needs may range from basic skills training for new hires to retraining for veteran workers when new technology is introduced. Aside from funding, perhaps the biggest hurdle most supervisors face is finding the time for training to be conducted. Heavy workloads don't leave much in the way of downtime for training needs, and no supervisor wants to be in the position of telling a boss that production goals weren't met due to time spent in training employees. All in all, the fundamental question becomes "When can training be done?"

To a large extent, finding time to conduct training means balancing training needs against the realities of a heavy workload. Some types can be done with a minimum amount of productive time lost. Concentrating your efforts in this area will yield the best results. There are also practical approaches that will minimize the loss of productive time. For example, if you want to teach a new technique to ten people, do you instruct them as a group or on an individual basis? There are arguments to be made for either approach. Training all ten people at once obviously saves you time, while training people individually makes allowance for the differences in how quickly people learn. A few workers may ask questions, while other workers may be hesitant to ask even the most basic questions. An additional consideration, and the primary one in many situations, is whether or not it's feasible to train the whole group at once. Perhaps the nature of your work operation is such that everyone can't leave work unattended at the same time. For this reason alone, this method may be impractical.

There are other considerations in finding time to train employees. If you're lucky your workload may be cyclical enough to provide significant periods of downtime to use for training purposes. Alternatively, you may be able to schedule workloads to factor in time to train one or two employees on an intensive basis if such training is required.

Not to be overlooked as a time-saver is who does the training. For example, if you are going to delegate the teaching of a new work process to one of your subordinates, the person you select will have an impact on how long it takes to teach other workers. Someone who has the inborn ability to teach others will be far more efficient than someone who can't communicate well.

Certain types of training may be provided on a voluntary basis after working hours. Courses such as English and math can be offered if the company workforce has a sufficient number of workers lacking in these basic skills. Programs such as these will, for the most part, be handled by your company's training staff, so you will have little input. You may, of course, recommend such courses be established, since these needs are usually recognized first by supervisors at the working level. And naturally, you will be the one best positioned to encourage your workers to attend.

In summary, there's little doubt that finding the time to conduct necessary training will be an on-going problem. There will be no single solution, but by using a variety of techniques you should be able to cobble together the necessary time to meet training needs.

EFFICIENT APPROACHES FOR RETRAINING WORKERS

With the rapid pace of technological change, many workers' skills rapidly become outdated. Therefore, in order to maintain peak efficiency, it's necessary to constantly update employee technical skills, since all the new technology in the world won't do much for your department if people aren't trained to use it properly. On the other hand, one of the biggest wastes of time is retraining workers who don't need it. This is done more often than is recognized or admitted. In fact, there are those who would argue that even though an employee may not be using updated equipment that has been recently procured, it's still beneficial for the worker to know how to operate it. This argument can be made on both a specific and generic basis.

From a specific standpoint, the employee who is a potential future user of the equipment should certainly be trained. The general argument might be made that even though the employee won't be using the equipment, it's always useful to increase one's knowledge. That argument is fine in theory, but in reality it's a waste of company resources in time and money to train employees where it has no relevance to their job. With the heavy training burden imposed by rapid technological change, productivity can be hampered by the time lost by workers in training sessions. Therefore the first step in efficiently retraining workers is not to train those who don't need it.

Retrain Displaced Workers

Aside from retraining workers to update their skills, there will be occasions in many companies when jobs are phased out either through obsolescence, reorganization, or some other business reason. Concurrently, there may be job opportunities within other parts of the company for which some or all of the phased-out workers can qualify with minimal retraining.

There's a distinct advantage in retraining displaced workers for other jobs within the organization. The obvious benefit accrues to the individuals involved, but the advantages extend far beyond this. There is a positive impact on overall morale within a company, since workers view these reassignments as positive steps to keep people on the payroll. Beyond this, even though retraining may be required, the new position will be filled by someone who is a known quantity within the company. This is better than taking the chance that a new hire with existing skills may turn out to be a less than satisfactory employee.

Offer Encouragement to Employees

As the unit supervisor, your most difficult problem when it comes to retraining workers may be to convince them of its benefits. Some workers welcome all the training they can get. Others have an almost knee-jerk reaction to any kind of training. Many will actively resist any at all; others will reluctantly participate without really attempting to learn anything. For some of these people, attending the training session may be of little more benefit than not going at all.

Given these problems, what are you to do as a supervisor? The obvious answer is to motivate employees to accept retraining. How do you do that? The answer is relatively simple. Let employees know that the retraining is necessary to save their jobs. You don't have to be an alarmist in getting this point across, but don't waste a lot of time on the general virtues of learning something new. Many workers—as you know from experience—couldn't care less about increasing their learning opportunities. For this reason, you're better off sticking with the basic reality of the situation: as technology changes, workers have to update their skills if they want to retain their jobs.

Although with some employees the retraining itself may be a hard sell, there are steps you can take to make it more palatable. For one thing, try to adapt the training to each individual's needs. While formal group instruction may work well for most people, you may have a few workers who need one-on-one instruction. Some folks learn more quickly than others, so provide for additional training for those who need it. The important point is to recognize and adapt to the variations in worker abilities to absorb training. Making it as user-friendly as possible will eliminate much of the fear and frustration some people experience in learning anything new. Naturally, there are limits to what you can do, but being aware of individual employee needs can help in doing what you can to overcome the pitfalls associated with this process.

USE OF ONE-ON-ONE COACHING TECHNIQUES TO IMPROVE PERFORMANCE

Whether it's training a new employee or teaching new skills to an experienced worker, one-on-one coaching techniques are an excellent way to improve skills. The hardest task you have is selecting the appropriate person to do the coaching. Try to avoid assuming this function yourself. For one thing, it's very time-consuming and can seriously impact upon your other supervisory duties. You will be interrupting the training so frequently to attend to other matters that it will take much longer and be less effective than might otherwise be the case.

Trainer Selection Is Crucial

Even though you shouldn't be conducting the training yourself, it's not a job that should be arbitrarily parceled out. There are four essential guidelines to follow in selecting one of your subordinates to become an instructor. First, the person selected should be knowledgeable about the subject matter of the training. Second, he or she should have the communication skills to conduct the training. Third, it is critical that the chosen employee has the respect of others within the unit to be trained. Fourth, there has to be a willingness to assume the assignment.

It's worthwhile to discuss these factors in greater detail. It's obvious that people have to be knowledgeable about a subject to teach it to others, but what gets frequently overlooked is an ability to communicate this knowledge. Often the worker with the best skills is routinely selected as the person to conduct one-on-one coaching, despite the fact that he or she may be totally incapable of teaching these skills to anyone else. For this reason, you need to compromise between selecting the person with superior skills or someone who is perhaps less proficient but a far better communicator.

Incidentally, you may want to select different people for one-on-one coaching assignments based upon their area of interest. For example, someone in your group may be both knowledgeable and enthusiastic about anything having to do with technology, while another is equally proficient in working with administrative procedures. Naturally, their coaching assignments should reflect these interests.

Also, consider the factors of willingness to handle the assignment as well as the relationship of the individual with other workers. If someone is unwilling to assume the role of acting as a one-on-one coach, it's not a good idea to force the issue. A reluctant instructor will not do a thorough job of teaching, and may convey negative thoughts to the person being trained. This isn't particularly helpful especially if the trainee is a new hire. Finally, a person may possess the competency and willingness to train others but have a personality that doesn't fit the role. Someone who is impatient, brusque, or generally disliked by others falls into this category.

The primary advantage of one-on-one coaching techniques is that there's always a ready mentor available whenever someone experiences problems. It's impossible to expect 100% retention of what is learned, and the availability of someone to answer the inevitable questions that arise is invaluable to the learning process. For this reason it's often useful to appoint someone as the "go to" person whenever new equipment is introduced into the workplace. This way you always have an on-hand expert long after any technical assistance training provided by a vendor is long forgotten. It's also the type of training that can be pretty much done without any sort of formality. This appeals to many workers who shun training courses that require various forms of student participation as well as testing.

Use One-on-One with New Hires

One-on-one coaching works particularly well with new hires. It gives them a mentor as a resource even after they have learned the basics of the job. This close working relationship also allows for a faster assimilation of new hires into the group. Frequently a supervisor will advise a new employee to check back with any problems or questions. However, even where such a supervisor is willing and able, there are disadvantages to doing so. For one thing, a newly hired employee is less likely to ask questions of a boss because of timidity and the natural fear of being seen as not having sufficient knowledge of the job. This handicap doesn't exist when the employee is assigned to a co-worker. In fact one of the first questions new employees want answered is what kind of a boss they have, and a co-worker is the only place they will get that answer.

Be cautious, however, when appointing one-on-one coaches. Their importance can't be overemphasized, because they will be teaching techniques that their co-workers use on the job every day. The students will take this training seriously, since they can see its immediate application. This is doubly true with new hires who are thirsting for knowledge about all aspects of their job. Contrast this type of hands-on instruction of motivated students with many general training courses and seminars which may not have a specific job relationship for the student. These latter courses don't always work out well because the students see no immediate relevance of the training to their jobs. Given, therefore, the importance of one-on-one training, it's essential that only the best people be selected. Another cautionary note: anyone appointed to these assignments will find them to be time-intensive, particularly if they involve working with new employees. This should be considered before selecting someone, and the person should be made aware of the time constraints.

HOW TO PROVIDE OPPORTUNITIES FOR EMPLOYEE SELF-IMPROVEMENT

Many supervisors have people working for them who are essentially in dead-end positions where there is little or no hope for advancement. This isn't an impediment to all workers since some people aren't looking for a position with career advancement opportunities. For others, though, the opportunity to increase their knowledge and skills is a real concern. Unfortunately, this isn't easy to do in many jobs whether they are in the service industry or on a manufacturing line.

As an enlightened supervisor, you can provide the opportunity for self-improvement which is one of the best motivational tools for ambitious workers who are looking to better themselves. If you are successful in doing this, you will find workers to be more productive and motivated since they now have future goals. How you go about providing these opportunities will vary according to both the specifics of your work operation and the educational and training policies of your employer.

Encourage the Use of Educational Benefits

If your employer has a wide-ranging program of educational benefits, then one of the techniques you can use is to actively communicate the possibilities available to those who work for you. This is more significant than it may appear, since employees aren't always alert to the opportunities that may be available with their employer. In fact, some may generally know about the programs but be hesitant to inquire about them for fear you will think they are looking for a job somewhere else. Therefore, your active encouragement and involvement in promoting educational opportunities will be welcomed.

Aside from formal educational programs, there are a number of measures you can take within your own group to increase the skills of those who work for you. Cross-train your workers to do other jobs within the unit. This has additional benefits beyond employee self-improvement, as will be discussed in the following section. Suffice it to mention here, this is one area that is truly a win-win situation for both you and the employee. The employee improves his or her skills while you have someone trained in doing more than one job within the unit.

Give individual workers new and more challenging assignments to broaden their skills. Be careful, though, not to overdo it in giving projects to workers which may be beyond their current abilities. The danger in doing this is that it can set workers up for failure and can result in discouraging them from further efforts to improve their skills. In these situations you want to have a balance between giving the employee enough independence to gain valuable experience and exercising enough supervision to keep employees from coming up short and getting discouraged. A good way to do this is to agree on progress checkpoints beforehand where the employee will get together with you to assess how the assignment is progressing.

Help Employees Establish Goals

Although you may want to help every worker to take advantage of opportunities for self-improvement, you have to recognize that not all will have the same motivational levels to succeed. Good rapport and one-on-one communication with workers will give you the opportunity to assess employee career goals. Naturally, formal job evaluations include discussions of training needs and so forth, but furthering career advancement for workers is an on-going duty that doesn't begin or end with a single meeting or a yearly performance evaluation.

To be truly successful in steering your workers toward self-improvement, you should spend enough time informally discussing an employee's future goals so you have a good handle on what he or she wants to do in the near and long-term. You also want to help redirect an employee who is focusing on impractical goals or has no particular objectives in mind.

It also helps to reassure employees that by taking on more challenging assignments, they won't be subjected to ridicule or criticism if they fail. This reassurance is critical for many employees who would otherwise have an overwhelming fear of failure. After all, employees don't want to take on anything new that they may not be able to handle if their failure may anger the boss or even cause them to lose their jobs. Although that may seem foolish to you, don't forget that how people feel about something that is often dictated by the position they're in at that particular time. Let's look at how you can go about accomplishing this.

Background   Alice, a supervisor in the purchasing department of a consumer products manufacturer, has decided to give Francine, a purchasing clerk, the opportunity to train as a junior buyer. This is the first rung in the career ladder for professional buyers within the company. She calls Francine into her office and, after concluding informalities, the following discussion takes place:

The discussion

Alice: "Francine, I have good news for you. Your work has been excellent and I think you have all the qualifications necessary to become a junior buyer. I'd like to start giving you a few assignments to train you in this area. After you learn the ropes, I will process the paperwork to make the promotion official. Naturally, at that time you will also get a raise in pay. I assume you're interested?"

Francine: "Well, the money sounds good, but I don't know if I could handle the additional responsibility. Maybe it would be better to wait another six months."

Alice: "Believe me, Francine, I've seen people come and go here for years, and you certainly have the ability to do the job. There wouldn't be much sense in waiting. Besides, I have to fill a junior buyer vacancy so I can't just leave the position open indefinitely."

Francine: "What happens if I can't do the job? After all, I've never dealt with suppliers before."

Alice: "I have no worries about you not being able to do the job. Furthermore, once you formally become a junior buyer, you will be working with a senior buyer who will be able to give you all of the guidance you need."

Francine: "I guess you have me convinced. I hope I haven't seemed ungrateful or anything. I'm thrilled about getting the opportunity, but I just worry about not being able to do the job, and letting you down after you gave me the opportunity."

Alice: "I understand, Francine. We all are nervous when it comes to starting anything new. Please feel free whenever you have any doubts or difficulties that aren't getting resolved to come to me and discuss the problem. That, after all, is why I'm here in the first place."

Comments

Notice how Alice went to great lengths to reassure Francine not to worry about failure. This encouragement is often useful, since many competent employees may not be risk-takers. If they perceive any risk to be associated with taking on new and more difficult assignments, they will avoid them at any cost. Incidentally, when it comes to promotional opportunities, not every worker will welcome the chance to move up a rung on the career ladder. For any number of reasons, some people want nothing more than to continue doing the job they are presently doing. This includes some of the people who may be the best candidates for promotion. If you should encounter someone who truly wants to remain in a current position, don't prod him or her to accept an unwanted promotion. In the same vein, if someone is promoted into a position and subsequently wants to return to the former job, try to accommodate if it's at all possible. This also applies when someone isn't working out in the higher level job.

HOW TO USE ROTATING ASSIGNMENTS TO INCREASE WORKER FLEXIBILITY

You may supervise workers who do routine and repetitive tasks on a continuing basis. Naturally this can lead to tedium, can cause carelessness, and can result in lowered productivity. Although it's beneficial to make tasks diverse enough to avoid such results, this isn't always possible. Another approach to coping with this problem is to rotate worker assignments periodically to prevent boredom. This technique trains your workers to do a variety of jobs within the department, which is invaluable when you need someone to fill a position on short notice because of an unscheduled absence.

Aside from relieving boredom, this also allows workers to increase their job skills and broaden their experience. Admittedly, in some situations the nature of the different jobs may not be such that a great deal of learning will take place. Nevertheless, no matter how minimal the skill level is required for a position, the experience of actually doing the job in and of itself has value.

There is, however, much more to be gained from rotating assignments than simply relieving the boredom of workers who are doing routine tasks. Cross-training workers in a variety of different positions can benefit both the individuals involved and the company. From the worker's standpoint, the ability to do other jobs increases job security, and workers who know they are of value to the company in more than one capacity get a boost in morale.

Another major benefit of rotating assignments is that it provides opportunities for workers not only to learn other jobs within the department, but also to get to know their co-workers better. It gives them a solid understanding of the different jobs within the department and how they relate to one another. This furthers the cause of teamwork within the group, since the efforts of the group are channeled toward working together rather than separately as individuals.

Learn How to Counter Worker Resistance

You may not have wholehearted worker endorsement when you first start to rotate assignments within your department. For one thing, some workers may be perfectly satisfied doing the one job they know best. They may also want to zealously guard the knowledge that surrounds the particular job they do. A few workers may think that teaching someone else their job is the first step toward easing them out the door, or at least to a less desirable job.

You may, on occasion, also find worker resistance based upon the dislike of two workers for each other. Putting them in the position of trainer/trainee and having them work together for a period of time can lead to an emotional eruption. The easy way out of this type of dilemma might be to assign these two people to other workers who do similar jobs when you're rotating assignments. However, this approach to problem avoidance isn't always possible. Furthermore, when people in your group don't get along to the point where it affects their work, it's time to do something about it anyway. So the inability for them to get along while they are trained for a rotating assignment gives you a perfect reason to tell them to get their acts together. Here's how such an exchange might go:

Background Waldo and Miguel have long disliked each other, and after Elaine, the supervisor, assigns Miguel to learn Waldo's job, the two loudly argue within fifteen minutes. It's a situation which Elaine has tolerated in the past because both have worked independently of one another; there has been no observable impact on their work. Lately, however, the company is placing emphasis on teamwork, which is one of the reasons everyone is rotating assignments to learn other jobs. Elaine decides it's time to straighten this situation out, since it could lead to dissension throughout the group. She calls the two of them into her office.

Confrontation

Elaine: "Look, the company is looking for team players to help us stay competitive in the marketplace. You two may not like each other, but you better put it aside and not let it affect your jobs. Your arguing won't help you learn each other's jobs. In fact, if it gets out of hand, it could cost you your jobs."

Miguel: "But this stupid—" [at which point Elaine interrupts]

Elaine: "Look you two. I'm not here to referee your bickering and I'm not interested in listening to you two call each other names. Go back to your old jobs for the rest of the day. Tomorrow morning, I want each of you in my office before work to let me know whether or not you are willing to work together. If not, I'll have to take some other alternative. That's all for now."

Comments

The specifics of handling such a situation may vary with the individuals involved. Sometimes it might be better to talk to each person individually. Other times, as here, it's preferable to tell them together. Doing it together doesn't allow for either to think the other person is being favored—or has been told something different. This is important in this situation, since Waldo and Miguel have to work together until Miguel learns Waldo's job. Given their argumentative nature, if Elaine didn't have a joint meeting, they would probably argue over what she had said to each of them.

It's also worth pointing out that Elaine interrupted right away when she saw that the two were about to trade accusations. There was nothing to be gained by letting the two workers engage in verbal combat. In fact, what was said would only serve to worsen the matter. This is quite different from a situation where you as the supervisor may be doing some fact gathering to discover what is causing a problem. In this situation it's an obvious dislike for one another which has been on-going. The whys and wherefores are irrelevant. Elaine's job isn't to get the two people to learn to like one another. It's to try and get them to tolerate each other enough to work together.

By giving the two workers until the following morning to decide whether they could work together, she is giving them time to cool down, discuss the situation outside of work, and make a calmer decision in the morning. It's also worth noting that Elaine said she would have to take some other alternative if they couldn't work together. This leaves her options open for the time being, but it also implies that one or both of the workers could be transferred or even lose their jobs. In fact, when these situations get so that it interferes with work, then termination or transfer may be the only viable alternative.

A final problem you may encounter in the area of rotating assignments is when one or more of the jobs within your group is relatively undesirable. Someone rotated to these positions will generally object to having to learn the position. All you have to do here is point out that the goal is to learn how to do every job in the group, not just the ones that everyone prefers to learn. As long as everyone receives rotation assignments fairly, this complaint will quickly subside.

As your workers wend their way through learning the different jobs within the group, you will be able to identify those who are most adept at doing particular ones. Everyone's skills and interests vary, so even where the jobs aren't significantly different, you may find a variance in how efficient different individuals are in their performance. You will have valuable input to use in making future assignments of individuals filling in on jobs for whatever reason.

STRATEGIES TO PREVENT WORKER BURNOUT

One of the inevitable results of too much work being done by too few people is worker burnout. As employees are pressured day after day to handle a workload that never decreases, it's inevitable that sooner or later something will have to give. The end result may be workers quitting to go to work elsewhere where the pace may be a bit slower—or at least workers think that will be the situation. For other workers, burnout may manifest itself in careless mistakes, a drop-off in output, or perhaps on-the-job accidents as safety lapses occur.

Whatever its specific manifestations may be, the end result isn't good for either the individual or your department. For these reasons it's imperative that you develop strategies to prevent worker burnout within your unit. The most practical way to do this is to keep your department's workload within reasonable limits. Easier said than done, especially if the workload continues to increase with no opportunity to hire additional help. There are, however, measures you can take that can help alleviate the situation.

Learn How to Avoid Additional Assignments

First and foremost is to resist attempts to overload your department with work. This can be tricky since it pretty much consists of having to convince your boss and other higher level management types not to assign additional work to your unit. Needless to say, this has to be done carefully if you want to maintain the good graces of those who control your destiny within the company.

For starters, you have to convince your boss that your group is overloaded with work. Don't wait to do this until the boss decides to assign additional work to your group. If so, your claim may be looked upon as a mere dodge to avoid the new assignment. Instead, period-ically mention during casual conversations with your boss about how overworked your people are. Don't overdo it to the point of aggra-vation, but make sure your point is subtly made. Without a doubt, the boss's response will be some expression of generalized sympathy with no promise of specific relief. That's to be expected and isn't a real problem, since all you will be doing is laying the groundwork for that time in the future when the boss tries to pawn more work off on your group.

It also pays to prepare yourself to defend against the next wave of work headed for your group. Play the numbers game. It's hard to argue with numbers, especially if they are grounded in recent work history rather than rough estimates which aren't very convincing to anyone. Try to assemble numbers that show how much additional work has been accomplished without a corresponding increase in the number of employees. Assemble overtime figures and other data which will support your contention that your group is stretched to the limit. It also helps to have comparable figures showing your department's output versus other groups doing similar work. This isn't always possible since there may not be other groups doing similar work, but if there are, and you can make valid comparisons, have these figures prepared. Incidentally, if the occasion should arise when you want to show these figures to your boss, don't be too blatant about it. The figures will speak for themselves, so don't ad lib with comments such as, "Wilson's group doesn't have much to do. Why don't you give the job to them?" Doing this will serve no purpose other than raising your boss's blood pressure. No boss, yourself included, enjoys having a subordinate tell him or her what decision to make. So don't lose sight of the political possibilities in protesting against assignments of additional work.

Incidentally, a great way to shunt aside additional work is to present your boss with unacceptable alternatives. If you do this right, then you won't even be suspected of deliberately trying to avoid additional work. Let's look at how a supervisor can play this angle with a boss.

Background   Allen M., plant manager for a mid-size manufacturer, is having a one-on-one meeting with Bob J., a direct report, who supervises one of the seven units engaged in sub-assembly operations. The purpose of the meeting is to assign additional work to Bob J.'s group.

The discussion

Allen M.:   "Bob, I hate to do this to you since I know how busy your group is, but I need this rush order worked on for Dismal Distributors. You know they're one of our best customers."

Bob J.:   *(looking at the delivery dates on the order)* "There's an impossible conflict here, Allen, since we're presently working on the SXS order which is also a priority. As you know, with our present complement of people it would be impossible to meet both dates. If we try doing both, the end result is that we may not finish either one on time. Of course, if you can find someone else to take over the SXS order, then we could do this one. The other alternative would be to find someone else to do the Dismal order. Which one do you want us to do?"

Allen M.: "Are you sure you couldn't handle both jobs, Bob?"

Bob J.: "I'd be leading you astray if I promised that. Look at these figures which show our output per worker. Even with maximum overtime we've never even come close to matching the numbers that would be required to do both orders at once. In fact, that would require the addition of 7 to 10 more people depending upon their experience levels."

Allen M.: "All right, Bob, just stick with what you're doing. I'll try and find another group to handle this assignment."

The result

Bob succeeded in avoiding the additional assignment by presenting his boss with a choice of alternatives: namely, do you want me to finish what I'm working on? Or do I take that assignment instead? He also was prepared to support his arguments with figures showing the capacity output for his group.

Of course, in a worse-case situation, Allen M. could have said something such as, "Go ahead and work on both. Use as much overtime as necessary and do the best you can." This would have dumped the additional work in Bob's lap, but if one or both jobs weren't finished on time then Bob would have had a valid excuse. Incidentally, in such a situation where work is assigned after the boss has been advised it can't be done within the desired time frame, it's always good to document such discussions. After all, if something goes wrong down the line, the boss's memory may need to be jogged. Do any documenting in a casual fashion either as part of a regular written report, or a memo outlining how you intend to proceed based on the discussions that were held. In any of these work overload situations, it's a good practice to send regular progress reports so no one can later allege an ignorance of any problems.

Look for Ways to Adjust Individual Workloads

Some people are able to handle heavy workloads better than others, so even when your group as a whole is overworked, you may still have individuals who can pick up the slack. So you may be able to temporarily reassign work from someone who is struggling to keep up. Be careful here, though, since your best workers shouldn't be expected to do the "heavy lifting" for their less capable or less willing co-workers.

The first step then, if you're contemplating the reassignment of work, is to be certain that the person being relieved of some duties is operating up to maximum ability level and not just slacking off. It's also advisable to talk with the person who will be assuming the duties and solicit their assistance in helping out. Asking gets a lot more accomplished than telling. Hard workers may be quite willing to help out, especially if their assistance is solicited rather than demanded. In the latter case, a top performer may become embittered about being asked to do what is considered someone else's work. Use this method of coping with an increased workload only: (1) as a temporary fix, and (2) when the workers asked to pick up the slack can be rewarded somehow at a later date.

Aside from avoiding additional work or temporary reassignments of workload as a coping manuever, there are other individual measures which you may be able to use from time to time. Look for nonessential work that can be eliminated or at least temporarily postponed. A lot of reports and routine paperwork fall into this category. You should also be on the alert for ways that technology can be used to increase the productivity of your group. It helps to do your own research in this area whenever possible. As you know, funds are always scarce, or so upper management will always proclaim, so if you're the first one to find a new piece of equipment that will increase productivity, you will be the first to include it in your budget. That should make it easier to gain approval, especially if it's an item that would have widespread use throughout your company. Once the word gets out and every manager is looking to make a purchase is when the red pencil starts going through budget requests.

There is one more important step to take beyond the types of action outlined above to reduce or prevent worker burnout. Always offer encouragement to your workers. Let them know that you realize they can only do so much. Furthermore, don't let one or two workaholics burn themselves out. If you notice someone pushing too hard, urge a day or two off to relax. Be solicitous of your workers' concerns and reassure them that workload or no workload they have to retain some balance in their lives. Of course, this same policy applies to you, so do what you can with an overload of work but don't let it overwhelm you.

HOW TO COMBAT CHANGE-RELATED JOB STRESS

Aside from the stress and burnout associated with an overload of work, one of the most common stress generators in the workplace is that associated with change. This is especially true in the case of major changes that come with reorganizations and/or layoffs. Naturally fear of the unknown, and the real or perceived threat of job loss will create stress. Under these circumstances, you may find yourself spending a lot of time communicating and counseling workers. Don't view this as unproductive time, since the sooner workers get over change-related stress the quicker operations will get back to normal.

Informed Workers Adapt Better to Change

The starting point for minimizing change-related job stress is to keep workers informed about potential changes on a continuing basis. Surprise from a sudden change is obviously going to create a good deal of worry and concern on the part of workers. Avoiding this sort of climate is best done if you have a corporate environment where change is promoted on a continuing basis as a way for the company to remain competitive and provide job security for its workers. When they are expected and discussed beforehand, they are easier to adapt to. Furthermore, if workers are solicited for input on prospective changes, they will feel they have some control over the process. This negates the feeling of helplessness which can lead to stress.

Naturally, the amount of change-related information that flows from top to bottom within the company isn't within your control. But even if corporate communications aren't the best in the world, this shouldn't deter you from doing your best to keep your workers informed. Employees will also take their cues from you in how they react. If you pretty much take changes in stride, then those who work for you will tend to adopt a similar attitude.

Take it Slow When Making Changes

Another useful device for minimizing the stress related to change is not to overdo it by making all kinds of major changes either simultaneously or consecutively. People need time to adapt and learn how to function in a different way after a change takes place. Until they learn how to settle into this new pattern, they are vulnerable to stress if still further changes are forthcoming. Here again, if the changes originate with upper management you may have little control over their frequency. However, for those changes over which you can exercise control, try not to overdo it in pushing several changes through within a short period of time.

Get Bad News Out Early

Sometimes when changes aren't of a positive nature, you want to avoid discussing them with employees. This hesitance accomplishes nothing, because if employees aren't given valid reasons as to why a change is taking place, they will supply their own answers. More often than not, the assumptions made are far worse than reality. Therefore, whether it's layoffs or job transfers, getting the news out and stating the reasons for the action are far preferable over the long haul.

Admittedly, anyone receiving a layoff notice may suffer from stress, but when layoff rumors circulate for a long period of time before the actual event takes place, stress is placed on everyone throughout the organization. This promotes a situation in which hundreds of employees may be concerned about being laid off, when actually only a fraction of that number is being let go. A related example is where repeated layoffs take place so that a sense of insecurity is always in the air. This not only places on-going stress on a work force, but it encourages workers to look for jobs elsewhere. And so unfortunately a business loses employees it wanted to retain.

Rather than foster false hope, it's far better to get layoffs over with at one time and as quickly as possible. This approach will at least minimize the stress of those who remain on the payroll. That, combined with a generous severance payout and effective outplacement assistance, will help alleviate stress even for those who are losing their jobs. Of course, at lower supervisory levels, there's little you can do to control the timing and magnitude of layoffs. You can, however, be as supportive as possible to anyone in your group who is affected. You can also provide encouragement and reassurance for remaining workers. Most of all, keep your own morale up, since workers will see that as a positive sign of better times in the future.

The Daily Stress Producers

Even minor changes may create unforeseen stress producers that can cause real problems if not spotted and corrected. These are sometimes associated with a change such as a reorganization or shift in work. Problems may occur when two workers who don't get along are placed in circumstances where they have to work closely together. This can cause a good deal of stress, not only for the two individuals, but also for any co-workers who have to cope with the resulting tension. It's easy enough to say that it's the responsibility of individuals to do their jobs whether or not they like the person they are working with. Nevertheless, personality conflicts are a reality of life and in work situations where you as the supervisor can adjust assignments to avoid these problems, doing so will alleviate unnecessary stress.

Another common stress producer is when individuals are reassigned to jobs they either don't like or can't master. This is always a tricky problem to deal with, since some assignments are basically undesirable, yet someone has to do them. Workers can't be allowed to arbitrarily beg off just because they don't like what they are doing. There are a number of tactics you can use to cope with this stress-producing problem. First of all, be certain the complaining employee has received adequate training to handle the new assignment. This alone can resolve many of these types of problems. Another approach is to see if the job can be redefined to eliminate or reduce some of the undesirable characteristics. Finally, if it's feasible to do so, you may actually decide to reassign someone who is a bad fit for a particular job. Everyone has different talents and a worker who excels at one job may not do well in a different assignment. Although you certainly don't want to let workers dictate which assignments they will or won't work at, you want to maximize their strengths by putting them in positions where they can perform at their best. After all, in the final analysis a worker under stress in a job for which he or she is ill-suited won't be performing at peak proficiency. Such a worker may ultimately look for employment elsewhere, leaving a vacancy to be filled with all of the hiring headaches that go along with it.

HOW TO AVOID WORKER INSECURITY ABOUT FUTURE JOB LOSS

One of the frustrating problems you may have to deal with is workers' insecurity about their jobs. This is particularly true if your company has had recent layoffs, or business is slow and layoff rumors are rampant. Serious worker insecurity can severely affect productivity as people spend more time chatting than churning out the work. How well you handle this problem will dictate how much work gets done during such insecure periods.

As a supervisor, there is only so much you can do to alleviate worker insecurity about future job loss. In fact, circumstances may be such that you are just as worried as those who work for you. Yet, to a large extent, much of the worry about job loss is based on rumors which develop a life of their own as they pass from one person to the next. Most of this scuttlebutt never comes true, and even when layoffs do occur, they generally aren't of the drastic magnitude that was predicted by the rumor mill.

Knock Down Rumors

The primary weapon to dispel workers' fears of losing their jobs is to quickly quell rumors. If you have clear lines of communication with your subordinates, you will be made aware of any rumors at their infancy. Always put these rumors to rest at an early stage, since if left unchecked they can take on a life of their own. In fact, your failure to act quickly may be used as justification to support the rumor. For example, someone spreading gossip may make statements such as, "You know this is fact when the boss hasn't denied it." Your very silence is seen as confirming the scuttlebutt that's being circulated.

Rather than waiting for rumors to appear before taking action, use a little preventive medicine. You can do this by periodically reminding workers to come to you with any questions they may have on anything they hear through the rumor mill. It accomplishes little, however, when employees do approach you for confirmation or denial of a rumor, if you barely acknowledge what they tell you and do nothing else. If you don't have sufficient information to confirm or deny a rumor, assure the workers you will follow up and get back to them.

Assuming that top management within your organization supports a policy of keeping employees informed, you should have little trouble in ferreting out the facts relative to the rumor. There are, however, circumstances where either the company doesn't believe in open communications, or for strategic reasons is withholding certain information. In these situations you may not be able to obtain sufficient information to either confirm or deny the rumor.

When circumstances are such that you can't determine whether or not a particular rumor has any validity, don't hesitate to make that fact known to your employees. Be careful how you phrase your statement so as not to add fuel to the speculation. First of all, don't criticize top management if they were less than forthcoming about your inquiry. There are times when, for strategic reasons, even the most progressive companies in terms of employee relations have to be closemouthed. For instance, on-going secret merger talks may preclude making any statement relative to layoffs. Even if your company's top management is just reluctant to share information with workers, this is no justification for a supervisor to be openly critical of such a policy in front of employees.

In this latter situation, you won't lose stature with workers by not being critical of top management for its failure to supply information on a timely basis. If companies are notorious for failing to openly communicate with their employees, this characteristic is no secret with workers. They won't hold you responsible for keeping them in the dark as long as they know you always make an honest effort to get the facts. All you need to say is something such as, "I wasn't able to learn anything that either supports or rejects the rumor about layoffs." Naturally this may not end the discussion since a logical follow-up question is likely to be, "What do you think, boss?"

When you're asked to speculate, the golden rule is to avoid doing so. Reply to a question such as this by saying something such as, "I really don't have information to make a guess one way or the other." You might also want to point out the futility of trying to speculate since, without knowing all the facts, it would be impossible to draw any conclusions. This may help to deflect the impact of the rumor on at least some of your workers. Incidentally, once you have done everything possible to track down a rumor, don't be overly concerned about worker reactions. Some workers will always take their cue from you and pay little credence to rumors. Others will welcome each and every rumor as a diversion to the drudgery of their day-to-day activities.

Don't Keep Good News a Secret

One of the least recognized ways to prevent worker insecurity is to keep workers informed about good news. A reason for this is the assumption that, with things going good for the company, there's no reason for anyone to be insecure about losing their job. First of all, that may be true in a given situation, but more than one company with hefty profits has had layoffs for one reason or another. It may also be that even though a company is experiencing rapid growth, the overall economy might not be faring so well. This also can cause insecurity.

Beyond these general reasons, the rumor mill can turn unrelated events into the basis for speculation of bad things to come. For example, suppose your company does a small piece of business with another company. The other company makes news by announcing substantial cutbacks. The rumor mill within your company might then start to circulate a rumor of pending layoffs due to a loss of business with the other company. None of this may have any foundation in fact, but it can take on an existence of its own until it is soundly denied by management. For these reasons, as well as for the positive impact on morale, it pays to make the extra effort at all management levels to let employees know the good news about company progress.

THE MOST EFFECTIVE WAYS TO MANAGE LAYOFFS

There may be a time when everyone's worst fear comes to fruition and layoffs take place. This will present a major challenge as you attempt to keep your operation functioning smoothly in the face of a reduction in payroll numbers. The extent of the impact will, of course, be dictated by whether or not your group itself actually lost people. If your unit was fortunate enough to survive intact, then the after-effects may be minimal. Even here, though, there may be changes in work patterns if departments you work closely with had significant reductions in personnel. Therefore, even without losing people from your own department, you may have to make adjustments in the way you work with other groups.

Sound Layoff Policies Can Minimize Morale Problems

On the other hand, if your group has people who are losing their jobs, the results of the layoff will be up close and personal. Some effective ways to manage layoffs are beyond your control. For example, when a company has policies that provide substantial severance benefits and outplacement assistance to employees, this helps lift survivor morale. After all, it's reassuring to know that not only did you survive a layoff, but also that your co-workers not so fortunate were treated with dignity and respect. It also helps if top management makes an effort to reassure remaining employees about future company prospects.

Management's efforts along these lines are more than just the right thing to do. They also contribute to retaining employees the company doesn't want to lose. After all, the best and the brightest of those retained after a layoff are the ones better positioned to secure jobs elsewhere. If these employees see others treated shabbily, then they are more likely to jump ship in the expectation they may receive similar treatment in the future.

Supervisory Tactics to Reassure Workers

Irrespective of what measures top management takes, there are several actions you should take to stabilize morale within your own department. First and foremost is to be readily available to talk with workers immediately preceding, during, and after a layoff. It's a time of understandable nervousness and, more than anything else, what workers need is someone willing to listen to their concerns. Try to be as reassuring as possible, but under no circumstances should you make promises that can't be kept. A layoff may appear to be the final one for the foreseeable future, but it's unfair to inspire such an outlook when you aren't in a position to guarantee such an outcome.

You will find that layoffs engender different emotional reactions among individual workers. Some will be silent and depressed while others will openly voice their anger over the cutbacks. Whatever you do, try to remain calm and composed as you try to ease your group back toward normality. As unfair as it may seem, you can be the object for criticism of the company. This shouldn't be unexpected since you are the direct conduit toward upper levels of management. Even though workers may fully understand a layoff wasn't of your doing, their emotional fervor won't allow them to distinguish between you and the managers at the decision-making level.

Take Advantage of Opportunities

Although layoffs aren't the brightest moments of anyone's lifetime, they do present opportunities that might not otherwise occur. From the standpoint of the people who work for you, the survivors of a layoff have expanded opportunities in terms of their duties and responsibilities. Try to reassign work to give everyone a chance to broaden their experience and learn new skills. Discuss openly with workers how best to realign jobs to accomplish the department's mission. Being a part of determining their duties will give people a vested interest in making the downsized department a success.

From a more general perspective, layoffs present a golden opportunity to realign not only who does the work but also how it is done. As you may have experienced, it's not always easy to make procedural changes in a company which has done everything the same way for years. This reluctance to break with tradition can make it difficult to get approval for even the most minor change in work procedures.

With layoffs, and the resultant necessity to do more with fewer people, you can make changes that you see fit in how the work is done. You're unlikely to meet with a great deal of resistance from your boss and other managers, who just want to get the work done, if you assure them that your changes will increase productivity. Something such as, "The only way I can get the work out now is if we..." puts your boss, or anyone else who may object, in the position of opposing a means to accomplish the existing workload with fewer people.

Over the long-term, one of the better things you can do to protect your employees from layoffs to is have them learn as many skills as possible. The more valuable and versatile an employee is, the less likely an employer will be to let that worker go. Even in the event such a worker is terminated from employment, the mastery of a variety of skills will make it far easier to secure employment elsewhere. It doesn't hurt to point this fact out to workers, many of whom are often reluctant to undergo any type of training. After surviving a layoff, they may be more willing to listen to your argument that the best job protection is being able to do a number of jobs well.

WAYS TO PRESERVE EMPLOYEE LOYALTY DURING UNCERTAIN TIMES

Layoffs, a reorganization, a sale or merger of the company, or a slowdown in the company's business can cause a downturn in employee loyalty. Lower morale, of course, doesn't bode well on a company-wide basis, and from a supervisory standpoint it makes it much harder to motivate workers to give their best efforts. However, if you establish the proper rapport with your subordinates, then you may be able to maintain loyalty toward the department even though there is resentment and anger toward the company.

Earn Loyalty by Being Loyal

If you expect workers to remain loyal and productive through thick or thin, then the starting point for establishing such an attitude is for you to earn it. Attempts to inspire loyalty that come about when layoffs take place are too late. Workers will have long since determined how much or how little extra effort they will put forth for their boss. This may not always show when business is booming, but it becomes evident when tough times strike.

A supervisor who routinely stands up for and is considerate of employees will be the one who engenders loyalty when times get tough. Let's look at a few examples of supervisory behavior, and decide for yourself how much loyalty it will produce.

Belinda and Bertha are both supervisors of similar customer service departments for a large food retailer. Look at their reactions to similar situations:

Incident

A senior manager complains about a mistake made by the department.

Belinda's Response:	"I'm really sorry about that. I've got a couple of losers working for me who I have to watch every minute."
Bertha's Response:	"That's my fault. I should have double-checked that information before it was released."

Incident

A senior manager complains about a particular individual within the department.

Belinda's Response:	"I'll have to talk to him about that. He should know better than to do something like that."
Bertha's Response:	"That really surprises me since he is one of my best workers. I'll have to see what happened since I'm sure there must be some valid explanation."

Incident

An employee approaches her supervisor about leaving an hour early the next day to attend a son's soccer game.

Belinda's Response:	"There's no way I can give you time off. You know that I don't make any exceptions about that policy."
Bertha's Response:	"I don't have any problem with that, Harriet, as long as your work is wrapped up. You've always pitched in when I needed some extra help on Saturdays. Just let me know when you're leaving tomorrow afternoon."

Incident

An employee asks about getting a new piece of equipment to replace one that is always breaking down.

Belinda's Response:	"There's no money in the budget for that. Try being a little more careful and perhaps the machine won't malfunction all of the time."
Bertha's Response:	"I'll see what I can do, although I can't make any promises because of the budgetary situation. Let me get back to you after I talk to the boss. You certainly can't be expected to operate with defective equipment."

Comment

It's obvious that Bertha is far more responsive in terms of defending her employees against accusations and in meeting their requests. This is the general supervisory demeanor that can inspire loyalty even when times are tough. In contrast, attitudes such as Belinda's aren't likely to motivate workers to perform at their best in either good times or bad.

A supervisor who is considerate of employee concerns and strives to be flexible in responding to employee requests will earn the appreciation of subordinates. This can pay dividends on a daily basis, since workers are far more likely to expend extra effort for a boss they like and respect. It's even more beneficial when uncertain times strike. For example, when a company reduces its employee count, it hopes to retain its most valued workers. However, these employees are usually the ones who are best able to obtain employment elsewhere. As a result, when layoffs occur, sometimes workers who are secure in their positions choose instead to go job hunting elsewhere. The end result is the loss of valued employees.

On the other hand, if employees work for a supervisor they know and trust, there's less of a likelihood they will bail out unexpectedly. Workers will also be more willing to listen to assurances about their jobs not being in jeopardy if they hear this from a boss they trust. All in all, the amount of loyalty an employee has to a company or an individual boss will be predicated on how much loyalty has been earned over a period of time.

Beyond all else, the degree of loyalty of employees will be largely influenced by the company's stability and growth. Being a conscientious and supportive boss will help maintain loyalty, but it can't completely overcome a work environment that consistently faces job reductions. Even under these conditions, however, if you do your best to be supportive of your workers, then they will give you their best effort while they work in your department.

SEVERAL TACTICS TO HELP WORKERS ADAPT TO THE NEW WORKPLACE

When we talk about the new workplace, this, of course, refers to the ever-changing workplace which sees new management practices, technological change, and even differences in the means used by companies to compete with one another in the marketplace. What this means to individual workers will vary from time to time and company to company. Some businesses are leaders, while others are laggards in the area of change. The same holds true for managers at every level from first-line supervisors to top management. Whether a company or a manager is first or last out of the gate in adapting to change, over the long haul it will be necessary to adjust to a changing workplace and a changing world.

Just as it isn't always easy for companies or their managers to adjust to change, so too is it difficult for workers. Therefore, one of your supervisory responsibilities is to help workers adapt to any and all changes that affect them in their jobs. By doing this effectively, you will minimize the unproductive time spent in adapting to new technology, techniques, and workplace practices.

First, it's important to be ready to consult with and reassure workers when changes take place. They will have little clue as to what the outcome of any change will be and will look to you as their key source of information. Be prepared to answer a multitude of questions, some of which may not always be sensible and many of which will be repetitive. Your patience may well be tested at times, but don't forget that helping your employees adjust will make it easier when future changes take place.

Be Accessible

With things being done differently whenever there is change in the workplace, the anxiety level of workers can run high. They have questions large and small that need answering about how any given change will affect them. The one source they have for reliable information is their supervisor. This means you as their boss have to be accessible at all times.

This can be disruptive since accessibility won't always give you the quiet time you need to perform some of your tasks. If you encounter this problem, you may want to come in a little early or leave a little late to give yourself an uninterrupted period to do chores that require concentration. Another way around this is to work through what would normally be your lunch break. Then take your lunch later when everyone else returns to work.

Explain the Basis for Changes

The information employees need to adapt to change in the workplace will, of course, depend upon the nature of the change. With layoffs and reorganizations the questions quite naturally will concern job security. In changes that are directly work-related, the needs of employees will vary with the type of change. Some changes may just be procedural and will require little more than an explanation of the change. At other times, the introduction of new equipment and technology will require instruction of a formal or informal nature.

One of the keys to adopting anything new in the workplace is to ensure that employees are thoroughly schooled in how to use the new equipment. The failure to do so can negate the very purpose of installing the equipment in the first place. It's not unheard of for situations to develop where new equipment and technology resulted in problems so serious that productivity was lower than before the equipment was installed. These headaches can be avoided by training certain employees to use new technology when it's introduced.

Don't Undermine Top Management Changes by Being Critical

The most common question you will have to face from subordinates about any sort of change will probably be "Why are we doing this?" Frequently, the answer is not difficult, but there are occasions when you might not have the answer yourself. This is particularly true with reorganizations—with or without layoffs—which are instituted by top management with little or no input from lower levels of management. This can put you in the somewhat uncomfortable position of trying to defend something that you had nothing to do with, which you don't understand, or don't agree with even if you do.

The bottom line in dealing with questions pertaining to actions taken by top management is to be as forthright as possible without conveying a negative attitude. In other words, you want to finesse your answer to avoid being critical of upper management, even though you think they didn't handle the situation in the right way. You have the right to take your complaint up the line if you want to put your career at risk, but you shouldn't undermine any change by criticizing it before those who work for you. In these situations, it's best to say something such as, "I don't have any details on why this change is being made, but I'm certain it's for a valid reason. Let's do our best to make it work."

Show Results

One of the best ways to encourage a positive attitude toward change is to be able to show results after a change is implemented. A lot of effort goes into implementing changes but once everything is running smoothly it's on to something else. This is, of course, as it should be, but it's equally important to place emphasis on the positive aspects of the change.

By being able to point out the positive results of changes, you make it easier to convince employees to accept other changes in the future. This is especially true when workers were highly skeptical about a change before it took place. If you're able to say something such as, "See, Joe, I told you that new equipment would make your life a lot easier," this may help encourage Joe to be more receptive the next time a new piece of equipment is introduced. Another tactic is to refer to a successful change when you're meeting resistance with introducing something new. For example, you might help overcome resistance by saying, "This should work just as well as the new equipment we introduced last year."

Perhaps the key ingredient for helping workers adapt to a changing workplace is to be a good listener. More than anything else, if employees are able to voice their concerns to someone who they know and who will at least listen to what they have to say, then they will overcome resistance to change. It may not be the most enjoyable of your duties, but it goes with the territory.

IMPLEMENTING IDEAS THAT ALLOW EMPLOYEES TO GROW WITH THE JOB

Changes within the workplace may not mean much to workers unless the change affects them directly. Even then, more often than not, the initial reaction of workers to change may be negative. This is obvious if a change involves layoffs or some other adjustment that offers no apparent benefit to workers. Yet it is important to implement new ideas that employees can benefit from, since they have little motivation to stay with a company that doesn't provide interesting jobs and the opportunity to learn new skills. In fact, challenging assignments are essential to retain skilled workers, since there is declining loyalty in a job environment where long-term job security isn't guaranteed.

As a supervisor, you may not be a contributor to major changes such as corporate reorganizations which are planned at the executive level. However, when it comes to implementing working level changes that will help your employees improve their skills and work more efficiently, you are the person in control. One of your on-going strategies should be to continually search for ideas on how to broaden the skills of those who work for you. This will not only benefit the individuals themselves, but it will also be of value to your department as a whole.

Advantages of Increasing Worker Skills

From the employee's viewpoint increasing skills will allow him or her to perform a wider variety of jobs, thereby providing a greater opportunity for internal advancement as well as a measure of job security. It also improves employee qualifications for jobs outside of the company. This isn't always seen as beneficial to the present employer, but it offers a couple of advantages. First of all, when people are given the opportunity to learn new skills they are less likely to become bored and start to look for greener pastures. The skills that are learned also benefit the company in terms of increasing the productivity levels of individual workers. In addition, work force efficiency is increased since people are available to fill in on other jobs during absences or workload fluctuations. In the event a company does have layoffs in the future, the training workers have received will position them for job opportunities they otherwise wouldn't have had. Workers can then have confidence that if a business downturn were to occur in the future they would be able to find other jobs. This is a morale builder that bodes well for an employer in both good times and bad.

Convincing Workers of the Benefits of Job Revisions

How do you go about looking for ways to improve how workers do their jobs, and how they learn additional skills? The fundamental way to make this tactic work is to openly discuss possible ways to change with employees. Point out the advantages of simplifying jobs as well as the benefits of learning new skills. One of the reasons workers resist new job techniques is that they don't see the personal benefit. In fact, they usually see job revisions as a negative factor solely designed to squeeze more work out of them, or perhaps even to eliminate jobs. For these reasons, it's not surprising that workers don't always embrace even the simplest change in how their jobs are done. If you can get beyond this hurdle by pointing out the benefits of learning how to do other jobs, and training to learn new skills, then you will find workers cooperating by coming up with suggestions of their own.

Probably the most difficult question to answer from skeptical workers is "Why should I simplify how I do my job, since it will just mean I'll have more work to do?" This is a very basic concern which is at the bottom of all worker resistance to job simplification. Responses like "It will improve productivity and profits and provide jobs over the long-term" don't carry much weight. They are often viewed by workers as nothing more than a shallow excuse to justify cutting jobs. On the other hand, if you let them know that coming up with ways to be more efficient in doing their jobs will provide time for learning new skills, you are able to identify a direct benefit for the worker.

Naturally, not every worker will see learning how to do new jobs, or doing their own job more effectively, as in their best interest. However, once the majority of people working for you adopts the habit of participating in on-the-job training and refining how their work is done, then the laggards will have peer pressure to keep up. Incidentally, those who don't want to change their ways may learn that your theory about learning new skills to help save your job is correct if a future layoff takes place. Unfortunately, the laggards will learn the hard way as they will likely be the recipients of the layoff notices.

Managing Empowered Employees on a Daily Basis

Encouraging workers to readily accept certain aspects of change in the workplace can present a real challenge. It requires you to be not only a master motivator, but also an amateur psychologist. After all, enlisting employees in such matters as planning ways to increase productivity isn't easy to do. This is particularly true when workers sense that new procedures may ultimately lead to the elimination of their jobs.

But even basic aspects of change, such as motivating workers to make suggestions, isn't always as effortless as it might appear to be. So even though you may work in an environment where employees are actively encouraged to practice teamwork, as well as empowered to control their own work practices, these attitudes must be constantly reinforced to be successful over the long haul. The thrust of this chapter is to discuss what you as a supervisor can do on a day-to-day basis to encourage workers to participate as partners in getting the job done.

PRACTICAL GUIDELINES FOR INTRODUCING
NEW OPERATING TECHNIQUES

The previous chapter concluded with a discussion on how to get workers to accept new ways of doing their jobs. That topic focused on revisions in the way individual workers perform their tasks, as well as on the benefits of employees learning how to do other jobs. Here, the emphasis is on revising the working procedures for your department or unit as a whole. This typically comes about after a reorganization or substantial downsizing which calls for significant realignment in how the work is done, as well as who does what.

Workers are generally suspect of new operating techniques for no better reason than they are content in doing the work they are presently assigned. When a supervisor comes along with a whole new set of operating procedures, it's understandable that employees will be suspicious about any of their proclaimed benefits. Most of this reluctance will evaporate with the passage of time, especially if the new procedures have been carefully planned beforehand.

The first step in introducing any new procedure should take place long before it is formally introduced. If your group is empowered to maximize its ability to make job decisions, then its input should have contributed to the preparation of the new procedures. Needless to say, if your workers were participants in preparing the procedures, they aren't likely to voice substantive objections to their introduction. Unfortunately, worker input into any substantive form of reorganization is generally minimal at best. In most instances where a reorganization of the unit is to take place you will be dealing with a situation where it was imposed without prior input at the working level.

Consult with Workers for Input on Implementing New Procedures

With or without prior worker input, the first step to take when changes in operating practices are to take place is to hold consultation meetings with workers to iron out the pros and cons of what will be changed and how it will be accomplished. How much or how little cooperation you get in assigning who does what job, as well as the procedures to be followed, will depend to a large extent on the magnitude of the changes. If the organizational changes are to be minimal, you will likely encounter little resistance.

On the other hand, when substantial adjustments of the workload are called for, either because the department lost people in a layoff, or acquired additional work due to a reorganization, worker resistance may be stiff. This is especially true where workers will have to learn new jobs, assume additional duties, or find themselves suddenly burdened with unpleasant tasks formerly done by someone else. You will thus never be able to get a consensus from the group as to the best way to realign duties to deal with the new reality of the organization.

Even though it's futile to expect consensus in such a situation, you should still allow employees to have their say. Some contributions will be of value and, even though everything isn't resolved, it's useful for workers to express their concerns. You may have to exercise restraint in responding to some of the more vehement protests you hear, especially from those who perceive themselves as coming out poorly in the reorganization. After all, if a worker has been given more work of a less desirable nature with no increase in salary, there's little reason to expect anything other than dissatisfaction. However, if you have been fair in reassigning the workload, then after a period of time all but the chronic complainers will have adjusted to the necessary changes.

One of the most important elements in gaining worker acceptance of a reorganization is how they view your reaction. If you fought long and hard to preserve jobs in your unit and to keep your department from being overloaded with additional work, then workers are more likely to respond favorably to your requests. Conversely, if workers conclude you didn't argue the cause in their best interests, they may do their utmost to make the reorganization fail.

Be Fair to Your Best Workers When Making New Assignments

In deciding how to realign jobs and redistribute workload after a reorganization or layoffs, try to do so in an equitable way. Sometimes there's a tendency to overload the best performers to the detriment of those who are less capable. This can have adverse side effects, one of which is to send your best performers out looking for jobs else-where. Generally these dedicated workers will accept additional duties without complaint if they perceive it is being done on a fair and impartial basis. However, if they view themselves as being scape-goats forced to carry the load for co-workers who are slackers, they may well decide to take their talents elsewhere. For this reason, whenever necessary, put pressure on people who aren't carrying their share of the workload. At the same time, go out of your way to express your appreciation for those who are doing more than their fair share. Rewarding these people for their efforts should be a top priority.

Take Advantage of the Opportunity to Dump Marginal Tasks

The best chance for success in juggling duties and workload during a downsizing or other necessity for reorganizing is to be able to come up with ways to eliminate chores and make the remaining tasks eas-ier to do. Sometimes this can come about if new technology is being introduced to the workplace. But even in the absence of labor-saving devices, unnecessary work can be eliminated and difficult tasks can be simplified. Frequently, the best source of how this can be done is the people doing the work. In fact, they may have long since con-cluded there are easier ways to perform their duties, but have kept that information to themselves. After all, many a worker sees job simplification as nothing more than the opportunity for manage-ment to bestow more work on the individual. When the workload is realigned, however, workers may be more amenable to sharing their thoughts on easier ways to get the job done. They are the ones with the additional work to perform and it becomes practical for them to adopt all of the short cuts they can.

Don't be shy about shucking off tasks if a reorganization finds you burdened with an overload of work. There comes a time when priorities dictate what gets done and what doesn't, so when necessi-ty forces the issue, place priorities on everything, and those with the lowest ranking should receive the least attention. There will be occa-sions when you will need approval from your boss and others to dis-card certain duties. It should be much easier to get this approval when you face an overload of work from a large-scale layoff or a combining of groups. So rather than try to slog along doing everything, use this opportunity to dump chores you have long considered to be unnecessary, such as many of the mindless reports topside that have always been a waste of time. Get agreement on dumping them while you can, as this sort of opportunity may not present itself again for a long time.

THE SENSIBLE WAY TO FOLLOW UP WHEN ANYTHING NEW IS INTRODUCED

More often than anyone would want in the fast pace of the modern workplace, new procedures or practices are introduced and quickly forgotten. This is particularly true if the change was relatively minor and perhaps has only affected one or two workers. Unfortunately, this failure to follow up can be the cause of both short and long-term problems. It also can create worker resentment if employees feel that changes are just thrust upon them with no regard for whether or not they experience any difficulty in dealing with them.

Follow-Up Prevents Problems Large and Small

All sorts of unforeseen difficulties can arise if you don't follow up closely after anything new is introduced. Some of these problems will be small, others more serious. Frequently, they can arise from nothing more important than a misunderstanding at the time a change was initially introduced. Perhaps the worker misunderstood what was said and consequently performs a task differently from what was planned. A few of the more common causes and consequences of a failure to follow up would include the following:

a. *A worker misinterprets directions given at the time a change was introduced.* The impact of this sort of blunder can vary. In fact, if it causes a major problem, it will probably be detected and corrected in short order. But when this type of error doesn't have any immediately noticeable impact, it can go undetected for long periods of time. For example, perhaps an employee is using a new machine in such a way that satisfactory performance results, but this falls short of the productivity levels that could be achieved if the equipment was used as directed. Since there is no unsatisfactory performance, such an oversight might never be detected. In fact, minor errors like these that can only be detected with effective follow-up can have a serious cumulative effect on performance over the long-term.

b. A worker who has been given new procedures for doing his or her job lapses back into the old method of performance. Old habits die hard, and when workers are given new instructions on how to perform certain aspects of their jobs, it's easy to lapse back into the old way. Sometimes this results from the employee having difficulty learning the new techniques, while at other times it's almost a reflex action. In other instances the worker who is learning how to do something differently may see going back to the old way as necessary to maintain productivity.

Carefully following up when new procedures are introduced will prevent this from happening. A caution here: avoid expressing anger or dissatisfaction with a worker who backslides into the old way of working. This isn't always intentional on the part of the employee and even when it is, the worker may feel it is justified to get the job done.

What you want to do in these situations is to reassure the worker that it will take time to learn the new procedure and not to worry about being slowed down while learning the new practice. You have to use your judgment here, though, since with the wrong worker this is an invitation to goof off. Let the employee know you should be contacted if satisfactory progress isn't made over a reasonable period of time. This is more to reassure the employee of your availability than anything else, since you will want to closely monitor the situation to be certain the employee is gradually mastering the new task. Of course, if it appears that additional training is needed, see that it is scheduled.

Ironically, it sometimes turns out there are valid reasons for employees reverting to the tried and true methods of old. Perhaps a new work procedure needs some adjustment to make it work effectively. Whatever the kinks may be, if you follow up closely, you will be able to take remedial action at the earliest possible time.

c. A new piece of equipment doesn't perform as planned. There are plenty of occasions where new equipment doesn't work as well in practice as it did during a demonstration. While workers will sometimes bring these problems to your attention, at other times they won't for any number of reasons. These include:

1. The employee doesn't know the machine's capabilities and assumes it is performing as planned. This can happen when performance is adequate, although perhaps well below accepted standards for output, quality, or some other parameter. By following up you will be able to verify that new equipment meets the standards expected of it.

2. Employees see the new technology as a threat to their jobs. When labor-saving equipment or technology is introduced into the workplace, workers aren't going to be enthusiastic about seeing it meet with success. Consequently, they may not go out of their way to alert you to problems that develop. Follow-up is especially important anytime equipment or technology is introduced that workers are opposed to for one reason or another.

3. Employees are having trouble learning how to use the new technology, but don't bring this fact to your attention, since they don't want to look like they can't handle the situation themselves. When new equipment is introduced, the training is frequently inadequate. Workers not wanting to look stupid will struggle through and learn how to use the equipment by trial or error rather than by bringing the problem to your attention. A close follow-up will enable you to provide additional training, where required, to speed up the learning process.

Whatever the reasons may be for difficulties with new equipment, close follow-up is crucial. This will allow for action to be taken which can vary from early contact with vendors to correct problems, to additional training, or perhaps even to the replacement of the equipment.

Follow-up Techniques

In terms of follow-up technique there are a few considerations that shouldn't be overlooked. First of all, your personal approach can impact greatly on how much you learn. You will be far more successful if you act like an interested observer rather than as a boss who is on a mission to find something wrong. Nevertheless, don't be vague in asking questions about the new procedures or equipment. Don't blindly accept assurances such as, "Everything's fine, boss," if you have reason to believe otherwise. Ask pointed questions that pin down any potential problems. Otherwise, you can be led astray by the typical initial answer someone may give who really doesn't want to discuss a problem.

After your initial follow-up visit, when something new is introduced, learn to balance the amount of follow-up with the needs of individual workers. Some people will need more assistance than others. You also have to take individual personalities into account. Some will be more sensitive than others to your visits. What you want to avoid is putting workers in the position of thinking you are questioning their capabilities. Whatever you do, avoid criticism if there are problems. If you don't, you will find employees reluctant to discuss any difficulties with you.

PROMOTING FEEDBACK ON NEW WORKPLACE PROCEDURES

There's always an adjustment period for the kinks to get ironed out whenever significant revisions are made in workplace procedures. No matter how much planning takes place beforehand, changing the way people do their work is bound to turn up unforeseen problems. Most will quickly come to light and be corrected without causing too much difficulty in getting the work done.

But sometimes problems won't readily surface for a couple of reasons. One, workers don't want to be the ones who bring bad news to the forefront. This is especially true when elaborate new equipment may have been introduced with much management fanfare. Needless to say, a worker doesn't want to be the one to come to you and say, " Boss, that new equipment isn't functioning the way it is supposed to." A second reason problems may not be quickly discovered is that workers may not even recognize one exists. Whether it's new machinery or a revised method of doing the work, any given worker may not even realize that a certain function is supposed to be performed in a certain manner. After all, the entire process is different from what it used to be. Therefore, if new equipment is added, which has numerous new capabilities, workers may not notice if one or more of these new functions isn't being utilized.

Even when new equipment or processes appear to be working fairly well, there may be unrevealed difficulties which you aren't aware of. For example, some workers may be having trouble adjusting to the new methods. In fact, some may surreptitiously be performing their tasks in the old familiar way without your knowledge.

The key to smoothing over the transition to new workplace procedures is in encouraging workers to provide you with feedback on how things are working out. For the reasons just mentioned this isn't always easy to do. Actually it takes time to build a sufficient foundation of trust so that people who report to you are willing to provide you with the feedback you need to resolve minor difficulties before they escalate into something more serious.

Avoid Blame When Things Go Wrong

One of the best ways to build this sort of trust is to refrain from blaming the messenger when bad news comes your way. Sometimes this is unintentional and is a general release of built-up tension rather than anger directed at the person bearing the bad news. That person, of course, doesn't know that and is likely to vow never to bring you bad news again. If this happens once or twice, your entire contingent of direct reports will quickly decide that it's not a good idea to let you know when something goes wrong. The end result will be a breakdown in communications which prevents early intervention to resolve problems.

It's admittedly easy to advise maintaining a calm demeanor, whatever happens. But when you have been told that this week's production quota just got ruined because of a workplace foul-up, it's quite another thing to keep cool. Nevertheless, the right way to handle things is to attack the problem, not the bearer of the bad news. If you tend to be hot-tempered, you may well engage in an emotional outburst, perhaps aimed at no one in particular. If you know this happens to be one of your tendencies, try and control it as best you can.

On those occasions when you do lose your temper, apologize to those who witnessed your outburst as soon as you calm down. When you do this, employees will recognize that your temper runs short and there is no personal animosity involved in your outbursts. After all, everyone experiences problems dealing with anger, so it isn't an unforgivable calamity if you occasionally lose your cool.

Effective Feedback Is Essential with Off-Site Employees

Incidentally, when it comes to obtaining feedback, it's especially important to maintain effective contact with off-site workers, including telecommuters and employees who operate from locations apart from your primary place of business. Feedback here is not only important when anything new is being introduced, but is essential on a continuing basis. This will not only keep you informed as to what the employee is doing, but also keep the employee posted on what's happening at the office.

To maintain close communications it's wise, when practical, to have telecommuters and other off-site personnel spend at least one day a week at the home base. This allows them to not only catch up with business scuttlebutt, but also to partake of the general office gossip. Then these employees will feel as if they are part of the social life of the enterprise and an integral part of the team, rather than a home-based freelancer.

One-on-one conversations with telecommuters also gives you a greater opportunity to discuss any problems the employees may be having. This is particularly true with equipment snafus and the like. Sometimes in these situations a telecommuter struggles to resolve equipment problems that would be quickly referred to a technician if they occurred in the office. So it pays to reassure yourself that the employee isn't having problems you're unaware of.

On-site time has another aspect of feedback for off-site workers. It gives them an opportunity for direct discussions with people they may communicate with regularly in doing their work. Being able to have periodic face-to-face meetings adds a personal touch to these working relationships which improves their effectiveness. In the absence of direct encounters the possibility exists for on-site employees to ignore or give only second-rate service to their off-site counterparts.

As for feedback procedures themselves, make an effort to closely observe what's going on whenever new equipment or practices are put in place. Visit regularly with employees at their workplaces and inquire as to how everything is working out. Do this in a nonchalant manner so as not to indicate to a worker that you don't have confidence in his or her abilities. Incidentally, just because a worker isn't able to handle new equipment or techniques as quickly as others doesn't necessarily mean there is a problem. Some people learn faster than others, so don't jump the gun if it appears you have one or two people taking more time to learn the ropes.

Feedback is a two-way street, which means you should make an effort to praise workers as they go about learning new procedures. It's not only good for the employee, but it's good for you, too. After all, it's nice to be able to compliment people rather than just wander around searching for problems.

HOW TO RUMMAGE THROUGH THE RUMOR MILL FOR NEGATIVE FEEDBACK

Apart from the feedback you want to generate on the operations of the workplace, there is another type—negative feedback—that you can use pertaining to a wide variety of matters. It may concern employee unhappiness over certain company policies, or even negative reaction to your own performance and that of other managers. Whatever its basis, negative feedback isn't likely to come your way directly, especially if it involves criticism in some way of you in your role as a boss. However, there is a little used approach you can take advantage of to keep abreast of this aspect of what's going on behind the scenes. Here the rumor mill which, although it's not always reliable, can furnish some useful information if you learn how to filter out the nonsense.

Probably the biggest hurdle in obtaining information from the rumor mill is being able to separate fact from fiction. Those who spread rumors have little or no regard for the truth, and in some instances they may start rumors to serve their own cause. For example, an employee trying to outflank a co-worker in jockeying for your favor may spread rumors that the co-worker was making unfavorable remarks about you. This is, of course, done with the full knowledge that this will get back to you through the rumor mill. The person making the assertions will be certain not to repeat them to you, but will instead plant them with one or two of the office gossips.

Keeping People Informed Minimizes Criticism

Naturally, the best way to prevent damaging rumors when changes are about to be made is to keep employees informed about what is going to happen. This is especially important in terms of substantive matters such as layoffs, reorganizations, or any other issues bound to be of significance to employees. Although it's impossible to completely eliminate the rumor mill, a company that keeps employees well informed about important matters leaves only the insignificant trivia to be bandied about by rumor spreaders. Unfortunately, open communication of this nature is a corporate matter so, as a supervisor, you are captive to the type of culture your company cultivates.

Negative feedback is at its peak whenever anything new is introduced into the workplace. Change of any sort is unsettling and so objections to it will be common. The magnitude of the unhappiness will, of course, vary with the circumstances, but being able to ferret it out will provide you with an opportunity to take any necessary action to correct misunderstandings. This is important since many changes can have a significant negative impact on morale. By the way, if any of the criticism involves your own actions as a supervisor, then it will give you a chance to reassess your method of dealing with certain topics or individuals.

When to—and When Not to—React to Criticism

When you do hear criticism through the rumor mill it's not always necessary to react to it. Anything new introduced into the workplace will generally provoke minimal grumbling from those who like to preserve the status quo. So unless criticism is totally erroneous and serious enough to be damaging to morale, let it slide for what it is, which is nothing more than routine gossip.

When you do stumble upon serious falsehoods being circulated throughout the rumor mill, deal with them directly. Hold a meeting with your group and discuss the rumor and point out why it isn't true. Let employees know that they should come to you anytime they hear a rumor and want to verify its validity. This, of course, means you will spend some time tracking down rumors in response to inquiries, but it's a small price to pay for being kept in the rumor mill loop.

You may want to talk separately with the originator of the rumor if you can definitely identify the culprit. Let him or her know that you find it to be unacceptable to spread damaging rumors. Point out the potential harm and advise the worker that you don't expect to hear about him or her spreading falsehoods in the future. This message should convince all but the most blatant gossips not to spread rumors—at least not of the type that are likely to arouse your ire.

Don't Be Too Sensitive

Probably one of the hardest problems to contend with is hearing criticism of your own performance through the grapevine. This will likely come to you second-hand with comments such as, "A few of the people in the group think you don't listen to them," or "I know it's tough to get anything approved, boss, but a couple of people have said you don't even try to get us the resources we need." More often than not, these kinds of comments will come to you from other supervisors or people in other departments.

You generally want to ignore these remarks in terms of direct response. First of all, in most cases you don't know where they originated. Second, being criticized goes with the territory of being a boss. Sometimes, however, you may want to give some serious thought to what you hear. For example, if you are getting a lot of negative feedback about being willing to listen to employees, then you may want to think about sharpening your listening skills. In the hectic pace of business, it's easy to lapse into bad habits. Use the negative feedback from the grapevine as information that can keep you from falling into such traps.

You won't be able to eliminate all rumors and criticism, but you can control it to keep it to a relatively harmless level. If your employees feel at ease in discussing their concerns with you, then they aren't likely to pay attention to the one or two chronic gossips that every group seems to have.

HOW TO USE MOTIVATION TO ACHIEVE QUALITY IMPROVEMENTS

There are always on-going programs of one form or another geared toward fostering higher levels of quality in the workplace. Some of these are effective, others less so. Beyond the impact of these programs is one constant which is essential to inspire workers toward improving the quality of their work, and this is motivation. You, in your supervisory role, are on the front lines of providing the necessary motivation to encourage employees to manufacture better products or provide better service. How can this be achieved?

Personal Pride Can't Be Programmed

First of all, it's necessary to consider what will motivate workers to do their best. How much or how little people care about their jobs involves a wide array of factors. Many of these are job-related such as good pay and benefits, fair treatment, job security, and the like. Work relationships also come into play, such as worker attitudes toward their boss and co-workers. Beyond this are the personal attributes of each individual worker. One such attribute is personal pride in doing the best job one can. This isn't something that can be instilled in workers by the use of canned quality programs.

There are people who will strive to do the best job they can irrespective of circumstances, while others will put forth only the minimum amount of effort even under ideal conditions. Some workers will respond favorably if you appeal to their competitive nature, while others will show interest only in a paycheck and no urge to prove their superiority in producing more and better output than their co-workers. Then too, the diversity of work attitudes will find people who relish the team approach, while other individuals prefer to work on their own.

Put Buzzword Solutions in Perspective

Given all of these variables, it's little wonder that, despite all the emphasis on acronym-laden programs designed to maximize quality, most of them don't pan out well. The bottom line reason is that there's no simple solution in terms of a set program that will solve any company's quality problems. Instead, attention to a host of details on a continuing basis is what will best serve as a motivator.

As a supervisor, getting the most out of your people starts with recognizing that there's no magic bullet to improve performance. Unfortunately, you may never be able to convince your top management of that, and as a result periodic programs will continue to funnel down from topside designed to conquer the so-called quality problem. In fact, being unwilling to accept a single formula as the answer for quality performance is the first step in improving the performance of your department. What you have to do is play to the strengths that you have to work with. If your company is worker-friendly, then you have a sound basis to start from in motivating your people to do their best. This is, of course, something beyond your control but other factors are within your ability to influence.

For example, workers can become frustrated if the tools and resources they need to do their jobs aren't adequate. This can encourage an attitude of "If management doesn't care, why should I?" Therefore, one necessity in the formula to inspire employees to improve quality is to make certain workers have the resources needed to do their jobs to the best of their abilities.

Don't Neglect the Working Environment

Such things as clean and well-lighted working areas are just as important as updated equipment. In the modern workplace emphasis is placed on using the latest in technology, which in and of itself is a positive development. However, the urge to be on the forefront in the bells and whistles battle may see less glamorous items such as plant and office maintenance being ignored.

Another contributor to this neglect is the pressure-filled pace of most workplaces. This can lead to comments by supervisors such as, "Heck, I've got a lot more to worry about than clean floors. I'll look into that when I get a chance." The complaint from a worker, which generated this response, may have seemed trivial in comparison to the other burdens facing the supervisor at the moment. However, if the worker almost slipped and fell due to a spill that was not cleaned up, then for that worker, at least, clean floors are important. After being waved off by the boss when a complaint was registered, the worker may well decide that the boss couldn't care less about his or her well-being. If this happens, then you know you aren't going to be successful in getting top quality performance out of this employee. Suffice it to say, the routine maintenance of the work environment is just one of the many factors that can contribute to employee attitudes about their work.

Fight for Your Share of Resources

As you know, resources are sometimes hard to come by, so you may have to scramble to ensure that your workers have what they need to do their jobs the best way possible. Reality being what it is, it's obvious that there will be times when you're not able to secure the latest and best in technology for your workers. This, in itself, doesn't mean that the quality of the output of your group has to be sub-par. It may be less than what could be achieved with newer technology, but it still can be outstanding based on the resources your group has to work with.

You may well think that employees will be discouraged by a failure to provide them with the latest bells and whistles version of their equipment, and that this will impact upon their performance. But it's not equipment that inspires excellence, but rather a supervisor who is looking out for the best interests of his or her workers. Whether or not you're able to obtain the latest in equipment isn't as important in the eyes of subordinates as your efforts to do so. As long as workers see their boss fighting to get them the necessary resources they will put forth their best efforts even if the boss is unsuccessful.

Worker Cooperation is Essential

Teamwork is another integral part of any quality improvement effort within your group. A unit that is close-knit, where people work well together, will do wonders for quality. On the other hand, if your employees are engaged in buck-passing and other competitive tactics designed to make themselves look good at the expense of co-workers, then unit pride and performance are bound to suffer.

How much or how little teamwork there is will depend to some extent on the nature of the work within your unit. Some work is best done in a team-oriented environment while other tasks are geared toward individual efforts. Recognizing this will avoid forcing a team approach in working together when it isn't necessarily the way to go. Another point to consider is the personalities of the individuals who work for you. Some will work better independently while others will work better in a group. As long as it's feasible for those who prefer to work alone to do so, don't try and force them into a team concept.

The important angle here is to ensure that everyone is cooperative when it is necessary as a function of their job. The better your people are at cooperating with others, both within and outside the unit, the better the chance of improving their performance. It's sometimes easy to overlook the fact that anyone's work output can be influenced by people external to the group. For this reason, the greater the dependence on outsiders, the greater the need for employees to be able to work well with others.

In summary, there are many factors that will all contribute toward motivating workers to improve the quality of their work. A short list would include:

- Favorable corporate employee policies
- Ready availability of resources
- A good working environment
- A cooperative attitude
- Solid supervisory support

The better a company is in addressing these needs, the greater the likelihood of improving the quality of the goods and services the company provides. You as the immediate supervisor have the daunting task of coordinating these efforts to motivate your employees to excel.

MOTIVATING WORKERS TO MAKE SUGGESTIONS

A frustration of many a supervisor is having to cope with an outdated suggestion system that hasn't kept pace with those workplace changes encouraging workers to have a greater say in how their work is done. If upper management is pushing for greater participation in the employee suggestion system, and both you and those you supervise know that the formal system is ineffective, you have yourself a problem. Many outmoded suggestion systems require too much paperwork, have excessive levels of review and approval, and allow too much time to elapse between the making of the suggestion and the completion of the review. As a result, most workers don't pay much attention to formal suggestion systems.

With today's emphasis on teamwork and cooperation, the use of a formal suggestion system tends to conflict with the notion that employees are working together to seek ways to improve performance, without the need for a suggestion system as a supposed motivator. Historically, in fact, formal suggestion systems seldom served as effective motivational tools.

In the modern workplace environment, it's the function of the supervisor to encourage subordinates to continually work both alone and together as a group to come up with suggestions for improving all aspects of the work and the workplace. Here are a number of tactics you can use.

Listen and Learn

First of all, you have to learn how to encourage workers to make suggestions, which goes beyond merely asking people if they have any good ideas for improvements. What is required is to be a good listener. Some people have difficulty in expressing their ideas and if you get frustrated and cut them short they will refrain from making further suggestions. For this reason you may have to endure extended conversations discussing ideas which may not even make any sense. Not every suggestion will be feasible, but even people who routinely bore you with nonsense may once in a while make a positive suggestion.

Look for the Little Things That Can Be Implemented

The easiest way to discourage workers from making suggestions is to routinely reject every idea they come up with. It's to be expected that many suggestions will be impractical for one reason or another; nevertheless, some are casually rejected because they weren't thoroughly considered. This is especially true when a worker may suggest something that doesn't appear to have any significant payoff in terms of saving time or money. For example, making the water cooler more accessible by moving it to a central location may be helpful for a few workers but yield nothing productive from a business standpoint. Therefore, unless several workers have been clamoring for the change, it might well be shrugged off as not worth the effort when an employee suggests the idea to the boss.

Continually doing this creates an atmosphere of rejection for the workers. Besides that, some of these seemingly insignificant ideas are of great importance to the one making the suggestion. It's important, therefore, to take the time to think through any suggestions that are made. Discuss them with the employee so you fully understand their significance to the worker. Whenever possible, if it involves little or no expense, give approval for implementing suggestions even though they are of little or limited value. The benefit in terms of worker morale will in itself be sufficient justification.

Be Objective in Your Viewpoint Toward Employee Suggestions

Everyone has a viewpoint on how things should be done and some of us are more willing than others to consider other people's thoughts on a given subject. As the ultimate arbiter of what flies and what dies in terms of suggestions made by subordinates, you have to be open-minded in listening to what people have to say. You may have the right intent but you have to be on the alert to not reject something simply because you don't agree with it.

Whenever possible, it helps to kick suggestions around with others in a brainstorming session. This allows for the cross-fertilization of ideas and gives voice to opinions which may not coincide with your own. Group sessions with your subordinates will also allow for a general consensus on the practicality of implementing a particular idea. This is useful if the idea is something that will impact the work of people beyond the person making the initial suggestion. It gives everyone a chance to voice thoughts on the subject, and prevents the sort of resentment that can lead to later criticism of the idea.

Some suggestions made by employees will require approvals or other actions to be taken beyond the confines of your department. Always work diligently to secure these approvals and keep workers apprised of any progress. Of course, not every idea will make it through the approval cycle; for those that don't, let the employee know why.

The most effective motivation for workers to contribute their knowledge in how things can be done better will come from an environment where workers are treated with respect and dignity. Employees who feel secure as part of a team working to continually improve their performance will need little encouragement to make suggestions on a wide variety of work-related subjects.

WAYS TO ENCOURAGE EMPLOYEES TO PARTICIPATE IN JOINT DECISION-MAKING

There's much to be said for encouraging employees to participate in the decision-making process regarding their work. It's easy to assume that workers will welcome opportunities to make decisions in conjunction with their peers. This is, of course, the essence of teamwork. However, there are plenty of pitfalls in getting workers involved. For one thing, not everyone wants to make decisions. Some workers are more than happy to come to work and have a boss tell them what to do. Furthermore, when they encounter a problem they want a boss available to answer their questions. Other people are by their very nature indecisive and experience a great deal of difficulty in making even minor decisions. These people would also prefer to defer to someone else when a decision is required. So getting workers to participate in this process isn't as simple as it seems.

A good first step in encouraging greater decision-making is to reassure workers that they won't be criticized for making the wrong one. It's this fear of failure that often causes hesitancy on the part of people to commit themselves to a plan of action. Furthermore, when decisions are to be made by the group, certain individuals who are very sensitive about criticism may feel uncomfortable about sharing their thoughts with their peers. You, of course, as their supervisor may be well aware of this, but members of your group may not be. As a result, they may inadvertently criticize someone who takes it personally. Sometimes, depending upon the magnitude of the criticism, as well as the sensitivity of the individual, this can have serious repercussions.

Take It Slow

When you want to encourage people under your supervision to work together in making joint decisions, you have to be careful about not forcing the issue. This is especially true if subordinates have traditionally done jobs that required little or no interaction with most of their co-workers. In this sort of a situation, some workers may not know others in their group that well, even though they are in the same department. This tendency is even more pronounced if you have a number of people who work off-site, either in jobs requiring extensive travel or as telecommuters.

Under these circumstances, before you start looking for your group to work well together at making joint decisions, you should first encourage them to be more cooperative in less demanding situations. Hold regular on-site meetings to discuss departmental business and be certain that any telecommuters or off-site personnel attend. This makes them feel more like part of the group, and it also gives people a chance to get to know one another. This is a basic beginning in forming the sort of familiarity you want to encourage, since it's a lot easier to get people to work together in reaching decisions if they know each other.

Beyond the basics of regular meetings, use any one of a number of ways that are most feasible to encourage cooperation. These will vary with the specifics of your department. For example, under some circumstances cross-training employees in other jobs is a good way to have people get to know each other. Aside from the standard benefits, it also brings about familiarity with the individuals doing the work.

Assigning projects to be worked on jointly is another way to encourage sharing of decision-making responsibility. In this manner, employees learn to make decisions with one other person in the course of completing a dual assignment. It promotes cooperation on a limited basis before taking it on a broader scale with the entire department involved. These limited assignments can be gradually expanded to include more people until you feel confident that everyone has a good feel for how to cooperate in group decision-making.

Encourage People to Work Together

There are sound reasons why you should pay attention to promoting the concept of working together and achieving at least a basic level of familiarity with co-workers before you start to institute joint decision-making. Joint decisions on how to do certain aspects of the department's work will sometimes require detailed discussion, as well as some negotiation and compromise on the part of workers. The better they know co-workers, the more willing they will be to make the sort of compromises that may be needed to reach final decisions.

On a more personal level, if people are familiar with the personality traits of those they work with, they are less likely to react negatively to what might be perceived as a slight. For example, an individual may appear to be negative about everything by always raising questions. Yet those who know the person will be aware that this is a personality trait that shouldn't be taken as offensive. It merely represents the individual's manner of resolving matters which essentially involves thinking out loud. Along the same lines, a brusque individual may be much more friendly than first appearances indicate, and, understanding this, someone is less likely to take offense. Just knowing other people better can make it easier to work together when groups are making joint decisions on work-related matters. This is especially true with those who tend to be shy and sensitive in group environments.

In terms of individual employees, not everyone will be an active participant in making decisions. Some people will sit in meetings and contribute little or nothing. This is essentially a personality trait with some folks and there's little or nothing you can do to change this. With a little bit of nurturing you can draw out some of those who are initially reluctant to speak out, but there may be one or two people who choose to keep their thoughts pretty much to themselves. This is to be expected so don't invest a great deal of time and energy in trying to get these people to open up. All in all, most of your group will be more than willing to decide how things should be done, perhaps even to the extent that you have to rein them in at times.

HOW TO NOURISH WORKER SELF-DIRECTION

You may recall times past when workers complained that they weren't even allowed to think. "Just do it the way you are told" summed up the prevalent limits within which employees were allowed to operate. Now, of course, employees are encouraged to make independent decisions. However, there's still a good deal of worker hesitancy to exercise this freedom. As a result, you may find yourself actively involved in getting some of your workers to make more decisions on their own. This is to be expected because not all employees will have the same degree of confidence when it comes to directing their own job efforts. Some would prefer the security of talking things over and getting suggestions and direction from their boss. This is fine to a point. After all, not all employees have the same experience, skill levels, and training. As a consequence, some workers are better able to operate independently than others. For this reason, you have to learn how to gradually boost the confidence of those who experience difficulty in working without a lot of guidance.

Teach Workers How to Make Decisions on Their Own

It helps in this regard to walk people through the decision-making process. Show them how to use a process of elimination to come up with the best way to proceed in what they are working on. For example, if an employee has trouble making decisions on the priority of different projects he or she is working on, go through the process of how such a choice can be arrived at.

When you're trying to encourage employees to exercise more independent judgment, gradually delegate projects of increasing responsibility to them. You will find that some workers are better able to work on their own than others; therefore, try to assign projects with this in mind.

One of the hardest tasks for any supervisor is performing the balancing act that's required when you encourage workers to assume more responsibility. On the one hand you don't want to leave them scratching their heads in trying to figure out what to do next. Nevertheless, you don't want to handhold since this will discourage them from learning to act independently. You still want to be available to assist, but you don't want to step in to make decisions unless it's necessary to do so. The trick here essentially involves steering the worker in the right direction without doing the work yourself. Let's look at a typical example of how this can be done:

Background   Jody M. is the supervisor of several buyers for an electronics company. Procedures have recently been revised so that each buyer can independently select supply sources without securing final approval from Jody. Of the five buyers reporting to Jody, three have readily adapted to making their own decisions. The other two have been unsure of themselves for different reasons. One is relatively inexperienced, and Jody knows and expects this person to need more hands-on assistance. The other buyer whose name is Kate has several years of experience but is indecisive and continually comes to Jody looking for assistance. Jody is determined to encourage Kate to learn to make decisions on her own. This is how she handles one such encounter.

The discussion

Kate: "Say, Jody, what do you think I should do here? I have two sources, both of whom meet all of the requirements. One offers a slightly better price but we've never dealt with that one before. The other vendor has done business with us in the past. Which one should I give the purchase order to?"

Jody: "What do you think you should do here, Kate?"

Kate: "I don't know, which is why I'm asking you, Jody."

Jody: "You have the facts, not me, Kate, so it should be easier for you to make the choice. I'll certainly be supportive of whatever decision you make. What seems to be the problem in making a choice?"

Kate: "Well, it's essentially the trade-off between taking the lower price or going with someone we have experience with."

Jody: "Let me ask you this. Is the price differential significant?"

Kate: "No, it really doesn't amount to much at all."

Jody: "Have we had problems with the other vendor in the past?"

Kate: "That I don't really know."

Jody: "Well, perhaps you ought to check that out with the engineering department. Then you should be in a better position to make a decision."

Comments

Notice that Jody refused to make the selection, but she did try to assist Kate with the thought process involved in making the decision. She also steered Kate toward getting information that was necessary as part of the decision-making process. Notice also that Jody reassured Kate that she would support whatever decision was made. This is something that can't be emphasized enough when you're dealing with insecure workers who are struggling with making decisions on their own. Knowing you will stand behind whatever decisions they make will go a long way toward giving them the courage to bite the bullet.

When employees are having problems making decisions on their own and they come to you, ask them questions that will put them on the right track to reaching their own decision. What you want to avoid is making the decision for them. For once you do that, then there will be no reason for them to make decisions in the future, since you are there for them to rely on.

Off-Site Workers Need Special Attention

By the very nature of their assignment, off-site workers such as telecommuters need even greater ability to operate independently than those employees who have ready access to you for consultations. Naturally, telecommuters have the telephone, e-mail, and perhaps videoconferencing to communicate with you. However, since they're out of sight, they may feel compelled to struggle with working through problems for a long period of time without contacting you. Strangely, you may have a double-sided problem: with on-site employees you may have to get people to make decisions instead of coming to you, while telecommuters may ignore the problem altogether. The rationale is that they will resolve it tomorrow, which of course doesn't happen. Then, when you finally get wind of it, you may have a much bigger problem to resolve than was formerly the case.

The best prevention here is twofold. First of all, always try to have regular on-site time scheduled for telecommuters. This gives you an opportunity to go over in detail any problems they may be having. Second, and most important, is to exercise care in selecting people for telecommuting assignments. Those you choose should be able to operate independently and have the ability to know when to make decisions on their own. For this reason, don't give anyone who is indecisive a telecommuting assignment unless you intend to spend a great deal of time on the telephone.

WORKABLE WAYS TO BE FLEXIBLE IN MEETING EMPLOYEE WORK REQUESTS

The bigger the voice employees have in making decisions related to their work, the greater the number and variety of requests they are likely to make covering different situations. Examples include new tools and equipment, modification of their workspace, and other matters that often involve funding and higher-level approval. How you deal with these requests can influence whether or not workers feel they really have a voice in how things are done.

Luckily, consistent rejections don't have to make workers feel that their participation in decision-making is only being given lip service. The trick is that you have to take the time to explain the details of why requests can't be approved. This is important because at least early on in the process relatively inexperienced workers will be turned down frequently. This will generally be due to budget constraints which don't allow for financing of every request that's made. Since workers—especially younger ones—aren't familiar with the budgetary exercises every department has to go through, they won't understand that you can't arbitrarily approve every request that is made—even if it's otherwise justified.

Painstakingly explaining disapproval of requests is time consuming, but it's beneficial to the type of teamwork you want to generate within your group. It also has the added benefit of training employees in some of the administrative aspects of corporate life. As a bonus, they may show a better appreciation for some of the problems you have to deal with, as they learn the difficulties inherent in gaining approvals for anything—especially if expenditures are involved.

You may find that on occasion an employee's request that would ordinarily have to be turned down can be met by some alternative means. Being flexible about coming up with options will cut down on the number of rejections you will have to make. It also may provide for a less expensive means to meet the employee's request. When you suggest an alternative, try to convince the worker to buy into the decision process. Otherwise, workers are likely to feel you are just thrusting your choice of what to do upon them. Let's look at an example of how this can be done:

Background Marcia is the supervisor of the office services department which provides administrative support to service and sales personnel at a branch office of a large corporation.

The request

Debbie, who reports to Marcia, says that she needs approval to buy a couple of pieces of office equipment. She states that this will allow her to work much more quickly and efficiently. In reviewing Debbie's idea, Marcia agrees that it makes sense. The problem is that there is insufficient funding in the budget. Marcia sees that one of the two pieces of equipment can be bought now and the other one in the next budget cycle. She doesn't come right out and say this to Debbie, since she wants Debbie to feel she is a participant in coming up with a solution. The conversation goes something like this:

Marcia: "Look here, Debbie, we don't have enough money to buy these two items right now. They would cost about $1600 and there's only $900 left in that account until January. Can you think of any way around this?"

Debbie: *(looks at the prices of the two items, thinks for a minute and then says)* "What if we bought one now and the other in the next budget period? That would increase my efficiency somewhat without waiting three months."

Marcia: "That's a great idea, Debbie. It also will give you time to acclimate yourself to one piece of equipment at a time. Let's do it."

Aftermath

Debbie is happy since she feels it was her decision to buy one item now and another later. Marcia could have (1) turned the request down completely on the basis of insufficient funds, (2) suggested the alternative to Debbie, which may or may not have satisfied her, since she wouldn't have viewed it as her idea. By letting Debbie come up with the solution, she made her a partner in the idea. In fact, from Debbie's perspective it was her idea.

Obviously, every such situation isn't as easy to handle this way as this one was. The important point is that you should always look for alternative solutions and, if possible, get the worker involved in proposing the solution.

The other major area of difficulty is in turning down requests that simply aren't practical for one reason or another. You have to exercise care in this area so that the worker doesn't get the impression you are being arbitrary. Take as much time as necessary to discuss why the request can't be honored, and explore the possibility of options that might meet the worker's needs. Don't forget that when workers make the effort to improve the way they do their work, their requests to help them accomplish these goals shouldn't be treated casually. Otherwise, they will quickly decide that management isn't interested in what they have to say. If that happens, possibilities for the kind of cooperation and teamwork that's essential for peak performance of your group will be eroded.

Individual employees will vary greatly in taking the initiative to come up with ways to change the way they do their work. Some will always be looking for a better way to do things, while others will be quite content with things as they are at present. This will be pretty much in line with the personalities of the individuals who work for you. Although you may want to encourage the most reticent people to do some thinking and decision-making, don't be too pushy. Although it sounds great in theory for every employee to be an active participant in determining how their job is done, some workers would prefer someone else do the thinking for them.

Don't expect a constant stream of requests from workers for approval to revise some aspect of their job, whether by purchasing equipment, redesigning the work area, or changing some of the processes of how the work is performed. The ideas and requests will be sporadic at best, since once workers feel they have pretty much exhausted their thoughts on how best to do the job they will fall into a routine they are comfortable with. However, despite the infrequent nature of requests in this area, their importance in fostering a sense of teamwork requires that they be given your priority attention when they are made.

LEARNING HOW TO LET WORKERS CONTROL THEIR OWN WORK PRACTICES

It's not an easy task to let workers do their own jobs in the way they decide is the best way. On one side of the coin is the argument "Who knows better how to do the job than the person doing it?" Like so many other broad-brush clichés, this statement has its share of holes in it. For starters, some people doing a job really haven't the slightest idea as to the best way to do it. They were shown how to do it by someone when they started, and they haven't thought about it since.

Furthermore, "the jobholder knows best" argument ignores matters such as experience and training. Someone who did a job for several years and received extensive training along the way may not work at that job anymore. Yet they may know far more about the best way to do the job than someone who does the job now. All of which means that in fact, you as the supervisor may have more knowledge and experience as to how to do specific jobs than the subordinates who are doing them.

Another problem in this area is that by necessity there are limits imposed on how much freedom workers can have in controlling their own work practices. Many jobs, both on and off assembly lines, are contingent upon other jobs being done a certain way. Therefore, there are fundamental limits on how much change individual workers can introduce into their jobs.

Recognize Contributions Workers Can Make

All of these arguments having been made, enlisting workers as active participants in how their jobs are done has validity. Many times the person in a particular job knows better ways to do something, steps that can be eliminated, or ways to speed up the process that aren't readily discernible or just haven't been noticed by management. Some tasks may be outmoded, and no one but the person whose job it is to do the task even notices.

Encouraging workers to design the best way to do their jobs makes them feel like valid contributors to the company, rather than like someone who is a hired hand with nothing worthwhile to contribute other than the physical labor required. This has a significant payoff in increased morale and improved productivity. So on balance, despite the difficulty some supervisors may feel over relinquishing control, giving workers greater freedom in controlling their own work practices is a plus.

There are pitfalls to be avoided, and overall supervision and guidance is required so that workers don't run amok in revising the way their work is done. Since you as the supervisor see the big picture of your group as a whole, you are in a position to ensure that any changes made by one worker mesh well with the work done by others. Aside from these general caveats, your biggest challenge will be learning how to let go and let workers assume control over how they do their work.

Learn to Delegate

How this is best done is essentially an exercise in delegation. If you're essentially good at delegating work to people, then you shouldn't have any trouble in this area. If not, then you have to train yourself to delegate more and second-guess less. In terms of some of the practical steps to become an effective delegator, probably the first one is to learn to let go. You may think that you can do a better job on something than a subordinate. You may even be right, but that isn't the important point. The crucial element is to recognize that the more you delegate to subordinates, the greater their opportunity to improve their skills in various areas. Even more important, giving them greater control over decisions related to their jobs will make them willing partners in making changes that improve the means by which the work is done.

In so doing, however, there are a few considerations that shouldn't be ignored. For example, certain areas delegated will require employees to interact with people outside of the department. You must clue workers in on some of the quirks of the people they will be dealing with as well as the overall implication of organizational politics. Recognize also that, since not all employees will want to make decisions about the best way to do their jobs, you will have to approach them differently in terms of how much or how little independence they have. Some employees will welcome the opportunity, while others will have no interest whatsoever in doing anything other than what they have always been doing or are directed to do.

Knowing When to Assert Yourself

Just as there are limits on your own job, so too are there limits on how far employees can go in determining how their jobs are done. Generally, this isn't a problem since there will be considerable back-and-forth communication both between yourself and individual employees and with other members of the group. There may be occasions, however, when you have to pull in the reins on a worker who is getting out of whack with the overall functioning of the group. Just as there are individuals who won't want to make any decisions on their own, so too are there people who, given the opportunity, will start to operate as individual entrepreneurs.

While this shouldn't be any particular problem, the one thing to avoid is giving any impression that you aren't sincere in accepting employee ideas on how work is to be done. Be diplomatic in explaining to an employee that even though he or she may find something to be practical, it won't fit into the general scheme of things. If handled with tact, there shouldn't be any problem. In the unusual case where you may be dealing with someone who persists in being unreasonable, you may have to be a little more forceful in making your point known, but there shouldn't be any carry-over in terms of impact on other workers who will be well aware of the character traits of the individual in question.

ENLISTING WORKERS IN PLANNING MORE EFFICIENT WORKING PROCEDURES

One of the hardest motivational tasks you can be forced to confront is getting your subordinates to work together in planning how to make your unit more efficient. When it comes to their individual jobs, workers will be more willing to make changes, especially if the changes make it easier to do their work. The old self-interest argument comes into play here, where people will recommend ways to improve their job if it benefits them directly.

On the other hand, changes in overall working procedures to make the group more efficient may not benefit any one worker directly. In fact, they may not even give the appearance of being a benefit to the group as a whole. These changes are often viewed by employees as ways to speed up the work, which may improve company profits, but not necessarily in their own best interests. So you can have a difficult time in trying to motivate workers to help you plan in this area.

Overcome Worker Doubts

How you go about convincing workers of the benefits of greater unit efficiency isn't as important as first being able to overcome their inevitable doubts. If you can overcome the hesitance, it then becomes relatively easy to convince employees of the benefits of being an active participant. The commonplace misgivings workers have in this area include (1) a fear that greater efficiency means job losses when fewer people are needed to do the work, (2) suspicions that improving efficiency means more work for the same pay, and (3) general resentment that they are being used as pawns to help the company.

Workers will be more willing to help plan efficient ways to do their work if the company is worker friendly and has always done everything it could to preserve jobs and treat workers fairly. If you have this type of employer, your job in convincing workers to help make things more efficient to improve the company's competitive edge will find a receptive audience. If this is not the case, you will have a tough time in getting anything other than superficial cooperation.

The argument that surrounds all of these doubts is essentially one of "Why should I help management make things worse for me?" So your first assignment is to convince people that not only are their doubts unfounded, but that just the opposite is true, and the changes are beneficial. It's like teaching kids that all of those foods they don't like are good for them, except that it's probably an easier sell to convince a youngster to eat his or her broccoli.

The basics of overcoming worker doubts about more efficient working practices start with trust. If you have built up trust with your employees over time, then it is much easier to convince them that a change in procedures will benefit them. The key to convincing someone is to first have valid reasons to support your claim, and second, to have someone who is willing to listen to you. The latter is a lot easier to achieve if you are trusted and respected by your direct reports. If you have a reputation for being honest and are known to level with workers, then they will listen to what you have to say.

Give Reasons to Support the Benefits of a Change

The reasons used to support a claim that a particular change will benefit workers will, of course, vary with the specifics. In some situations the benefits will be obvious, for example, the introduction of job revisions and new equipment that allows workers to produce several variations of a product rather than only the one version currently produced. The argument might go like this: "We increase the number of products we can offer with the new equipment. This will really expand sales which means not only greater job security, but also the chance for you people to pick up some money working over-time."

At other times the reasoning may be more general in terms of its benefit to the workers. For example, suppose you're asking work-ers to come up with suggestions to increase the quantity of an item that is produced. Here the argument would be much harder, since employees might think that increased production per worker means fewer workers will be needed. The contention in support of making such changes might go something such like this: "It will help reduce unit costs which will make the company more competitive and pre-serve jobs." This isn't very specific in terms of the individual employee, but it is the sort of logic acceptable from a trusted super-visor.

Of course, sometimes it's a reach to find any sort of convincing argument that some change is to the benefit of the worker. Then you really have to appeal to the sense of trust you have developed with your workers. Admittedly, a "trust me, I know" argument isn't all that convincing, but it can do the trick if you have enough goodwill built up with your subordinates.

Adapting to New Technology

If you have been in a supervisory role for any length of time you have undoubtedly experienced many of the pitfalls associated with the introduction of new machinery and equipment. Generally, new technology ultimately makes a positive contribution to the workplace once the kinks get ironed out. But during the initial break-in period there are more than a few problems you may have the misfortune to deal with.

One of your first concerns will be the varied reactions of the people you supervise. These will range from a natural resistance to anything new, to a reluctance to learn how to use the new equipment. Varied forms of training will, of course, help overcome these hurdles.

There are, however, other problems that go along with the introduction of new technology. One potential headache you may have to deal with is how to discourage the introduction of new equipment which you know is ill-suited for the intended purpose. This isn't always easy to do, especially if the brainstorm for the new technology came from top management. This can put you in the middle of a dilemma: on the one hand, objecting to the equipment may be a poor political decision, while on the other hand accepting something that won't work will cause working woes. How to successfully hurdle this problem is discussed in this chapter, along with all of the other positive and negative aspects related to the introduction of new technology within the unit you supervise.

PROVEN WAYS TO INTRODUCE NEW EQUIPMENT

Many a supervisor has experienced the frustration of fighting long and hard to get new equipment that would allow for more efficient operation of his or her department. Both the technical and budgetary considerations often involve detailed proposals and persuasive arguments with upper levels of management. However, even if you endure these pangs of progress and see new equipment arrive on the scene, you may discover that your headaches have just begun.

For one thing, your workers may not be quite as enthusiastic as you are about the new equipment. Their concerns can be varied and might include any of the following factors:

- Fear the equipment will eliminate jobs.
- Don't like having to be trained on the new equipment.
- Are convinced the present way of doing things can't be improved.
- Don't think the equipment will work properly.
- Think increased efficiency of the new equipment may cause them to lose their overtime pay.
- Are resentful they weren't consulted about the new equipment before it was bought.

These are, of course, just a few of the concerns workers may have. Many complaints will vary depending upon the nature of the work and the complexity of the machinery being introduced. Furthermore, not every worker will react in the same fashion. Just as some employees will always resist attempts to introduce new technology, others will openly welcome it. Whatever the individual attitudes may be, the majority of workers will ultimately adjust to the use of new technology, particularly if you can show them how they will benefit from using the equipment. Nevertheless, whenever you encounter employee reluctance, the sooner you overcome it the quicker the benefits of the equipment will be realized.

Employee Input Encourages Acceptance

The starting point for garnering employee acceptance of new equipment occurs long before it arrives on the scene. Employees should be active participants in the planning stages for the procurement of any new technology or equipment. They are the ones who will be using it and are best positioned to know the detailed elements of doing particular tasks. During the planning stage, employee suggestions should be solicited and actively discussed.

Particular attention should be paid to questions raised as to how the new equipment can perform certain tasks. If these questions can't be satisfactorily answered, they should raise a red flag as to the feasibility of investing in the new technology. Unfortunately, even when employees get the opportunity to voice their concerns, their opinions go unheeded. The salespeople pushing the equipment manage to convince upper level managers that the efficiencies, cost savings, or whatever other benefits are being touted vastly outweigh any minor doubts expressed at the working level. Later on when the initial doubts become reality, everyone who made the decision to buy the equipment has instant amnesia. The outcome is that you are stuck trying to work around the liabilities of new equipment your people said wouldn't work in the first place.

In the end, whether or not there was employee input before new equipment was procured, there will still be a break-in period during which your employees will learn the ins and outs of effectively operating the new equipment. Obviously, if employee input was sought prior to buying the equipment, there may be greater initial acceptance. Aside from that, there are a number of common measures that will assist in the introduction of new equipment.

Practice Patience When Introducing Equipment

Your first and foremost requirement when new equipment or technology is introduced is to exercise patience. Expectations are always high when new equipment arrives on the scene, especially if it involves state-of-the-art technology which is purported to have the capability of greatly increasing output, quality, and so forth. The higher the cost of such equipment and the greater the initial expectations, the more the likelihood of top management interest in how the equipment performs. This can lead to top-down management pressure for immediate results. This, in turn, can result in rushing the introduction of the equipment. The indoctrination period and initial training on the equipment's use will be minimized and every effort will be made to quickly achieve the expected results. Ironically, this may lead to lower-than-expected performance as workers make otherwise avoidable mistakes in using the new technology.

Therefore, to whatever extent possible, always introduce new equipment and technology gradually. Naturally, if it's a high profile topic which has top management interest, you may be pressured to move things along. Within the limits of what's possible without putting your neck on the line, resist attempts to speed the process up. The best way to do this is to enlist your boss and other higher level managers in your cause. The key is to convince others that not rushing the equipment introduction is in their best interests. How can this be done?

First of all, let your boss know that if the new equipment is put into full-scale use too quickly, the workers won't be able to use it effectively. As a result, the initial results will be sub-par. Your boss shouldn't have to be reminded that this won't sit well with senior executives who are expecting top-notch performance from their expensive investment. Give your boss the game plan you have worked up for initial orientation and training, which will allow workers to familiarize themselves with the new equipment before putting it into full-scale use. Assure your boss that this will maximize the chances of the equipment yielding the results that upper level management expects. Hopefully, this will involve him or her in lessening the pressure for immediate results. If there are other intermediate managers involved in the organizational structure, your boss may make the same pitch to them.

Another good source of support will be the person or persons who originally pushed for the new equipment, assuming the idea originated outside of your department. Perhaps a senior executive or someone in another department was responsible for suggesting the equipment be bought. If so, that person has a vested interest in its success, and might listen to a suggestion that rushing things along too fast could bring about less than satisfactory results. If you're able to enlist enough allies this way, then any topside pressure can be minimized.

One of the reasons for exercising patience in putting new equipment on-line is the need to provide adequate orientation and training for those employees who will operate it. Naturally the type and duration of the training will be dictated by factors such as the complexity of the equipment and the existing skill levels of your workers. If the equipment or technology is complex, generally the supplier will provide some form of initial training. What sometimes gets neglected, though, is the need to have someone available to help workers with recurring questions that will arise only after they have been using the equipment for a period of time. Some of what they learn in the initial orientation may be forgotten while other questions may arise as a result of on-the-job experience. Whether this is contracted for with the initial supplier, contracted for elsewhere, or handled internally, will vary from situation to situation. The important matter is to have the expertise available to handle questions.

Although the initial introduction of new equipment is just one of many subjects involved in adapting to new technology, it's the starting point for handling many of the other concerns which are discussed in the balance of this chapter. Therefore, although patience and proper initial training don't seem to be particularly difficult, their importance to the successful introduction of new technology shouldn't be minimized.

SENSIBLE WAYS TO IRON OUT THE KINKS IN ADOPTING NEW EQUIPMENT

Even when extensive planning takes place prior to the introduction of new equipment, there will always be inevitable glitches that occur. Most of these will be easy enough to overcome, although on occasion serious difficulties can occur. Nevertheless, the sooner you conquer any bottlenecks, the less the likelihood of any disruptive impact.

The necessity of rapid response when new equipment problems take place can't be emphasized enough. That's because, in addition to the work-related difficulties caused by the defect, negative worker attitudes can also form. These, in turn, can make it even harder to resolve any difficulties since employees won't have confidence in the equipment. The typical scuttlebutt will include the following types of comments indicative of such attitudes.

"None of this new stuff holds up when it's put to the test."

"All we have around here now is downtime with this new equipment always breaking down."

"I told them this wouldn't work right before they bought it."

"They spend all kinds of money on new equipment that doesn't work, but they can't even give us a decent pay raise."

The longer glitches exist with new equipment, the more of these gripes will make the rounds. Furthermore, anyone who opposed getting the equipment in the first place will be loudly exclaiming "I told you so." Since it's hard enough to get workers to accept new equipment and then learn how to use it, it's important for problems to be corrected. Otherwise, what little confidence they had in the equipment will quickly erode. One of the best ways to get employees enthused about new equipment is to be able to promote its benefits and performance once it arrives. This, obviously, can't be done if you're continually ironing out kinks.

Many of the minor problems that crop up initially are due to employee unfamiliarity with the equipment. In these cases, all that's required is to correct the mistake being made so the employee doesn't repeat it. If you notice, however, more than one employee making the same mistake, you may want to brief everyone on the proper procedure in that area. It may have been something that was glossed over or omitted during the initial training period.

Get Technical Assistance

Incidentally, don't hesitate to call for technical assistance from the equipment supplier once you determine something isn't easily solvable by you or someone else within the company. This is true even though the problem could be solved if enough time was spent to work it out. Call for technical assistance so you will get the matter resolved immediately and avoid extensive downtime.

If you try to work out the problem yourself through a trial or error process, the apparent difficulty of solving the glitch won't be lost on workers. They may think that when anything goes wrong with the equipment it becomes complicated to correct. For these reasons, use the manufacturer's technical assistance representative and save yourself some time and trouble. People often decide to work out the problem themselves in lieu of feeling foolish by asking for assistance. The fact is that if this assistance is something that's already contracted and paid for, then you're wasting company money by spending your own time looking for the solution.

Be Certain Employees Are Using the Equipment to Full Capability

Employees don't always take advantage of all of the capabilities of new equipment. What happens is that they will learn the minimum necessary to accomplish their job, but won't bother to learn any additional functions that will make them more productive. Some may feel the additional functions are too difficult or time consuming to learn. Others may decide that there's no direct benefit for them in learning the complete range of capabilities a new piece of equipment offers. To overcome this reluctance you may want to schedule formal or informal training sessions.

By the way, there's a flip side to the failure of employees to fully learn how to utilize the capabilities of equipment. Some workers have the habit of continually tweaking equipment to see what else it will do aside from the functions it's supposed to perform. Depending on the nature of the equipment, the personality of the individual, and the technical possibilities, workers can spend more time playing with the equipment than doing constructive work.

This actually isn't all bad when equipment is first introduced, since the more workers play around with it, the more they will familiarize themselves with its capabilities. To minimize this downtime after an initial introductory period, however, you should monitor the use of equipment such as computers and various communications devices that offer the greatest opportunity for misuse. Fortunately, in most instances, this ceases to be a problem once its novelty wears off.

Don't Panic if Expectations Aren't Immediately Met

Sometimes what appears to be a problem with new equipment turns out to be nothing more than unreasonable expectations on the part of those most interested in seeing the equipment succeed, usually those who sponsored its purchase in the first place. What happens is that performance projections are worked up to justify the purchase of the equipment. These are supported in whole or in part by the equipment vendor's sales literature. In fact the equipment may be quite capable of performing to these parameters.

The problem arises when these expectations aren't met almost immediately after the equipment is introduced into the workplace. Management starts asking what the problem is. Quite simply, it's that the performance parameters that everyone is relying on are based upon experienced machine operators. Therefore, until a sufficient point on the learning curve has been reached by your workers, the equipment will not meet expectations. All you have to do if you face this sort of situation is to let your boss and others know diplomatically that new equipment performance will pick up as the workers become more experienced in using it.

EASY WAYS TO IDENTIFY PROBLEMS WHEN NEW TECHNOLOGY IS INTRODUCED

Whenever new technology is introduced, problems of one sort or another are to be expected, which may go beyond the initial introductory glitches covered in the prior topic. For example, the equipment itself may not function properly, or it may turn out to be ill-suited for the intended purpose. Other problems may occur with work flow or some other operational matter. And still further difficulties may be anticipated from workers who are either reluctant to accept the new equipment or are having genuine difficulty in using it. Whatever the nature of the problems that may arise, it's important for you to resolve them quickly.

Prior Planning Can Help You to Anticipate Potential Problems

One of the first steps in tackling problems is to anticipate what issues might arise beforehand, so you will be prepared to cope with them should they occur. You can't, of course, predict with any certainty what might happen when the new equipment arrives. Nevertheless, you can sometimes get a good inkling of what to expect from events that have taken place to date. For example, if equipment is being procured without the knowledge and input of the people who will be using it, it's reasonable to assume you will have difficulty gaining initial acceptance of the equipment by your workers. Even if there was extensive worker participation in the procurement decision, perhaps a few workers were vehemently opposed to buying the equipment. If so, then you may reasonably expect problems in getting these people to use it effectively after its arrival.

Incidentally, it isn't uncommon for some people to voice objections to new technology while others are all for it. The most obvious reason is that some workers may benefit from the introduction of new equipment, while others may feel they are negatively impacted. For example, a machine that makes it easier for some employees to perform their tasks will be looked upon favorably by those people. On the other hand, other workers in the group may think they are being placed in a worse position when the new equipment arrives because certain others are now able to increase their output. Other employees who perform subsequent tasks on the same output and have no comparable new equipment to increase their efficiency would now find themselves at a handicap. They would be forced to handle more work than before due to the introduction of the new equipment. Of course, this may not be what ultimately happens, since, if the difference is significant, perhaps more people would be assigned to the functions which aren't as automated. This problem can easily be anticipated and planned for before the new equipment arrives on the scene.

Learn to Cut Your Losses

Nothing can be more disconcerting than new equipment that just doesn't hack it after a reasonable trial period, despite all sorts of efforts to make it function properly. While it doesn't occur that often, there are all kinds of reasons for it. Perhaps technology was pushed by upper level managers who were not familiar with the work environment. It could have resulted from the efforts of an enterprising sales representative who misrepresented the possibilities of the equipment. In most instances, however, there isn't one particular person for the finger of blame to be pointed at. And even if there is, there's little to be gained by doing so.

Once it becomes evident that new equipment won't do the job it was purchased for, there's nothing to be gained by prolonging the agony by trying quick fix after quick fix in the vain hope that the deficiencies can be overcome. In fact, the longer it takes to remove the equipment the greater the chance that you may end up stuck with it. The same people who suggested purchasing it will argue that if given time the glitches can be worked out. Their hope is that if the equipment stays around long enough they will be able to devise some strategy to cover up their mistake. Unfortunately, their only strategy is to leave the equipment in your department on the pretense that correcting a few flaws will cure the problem. You're the one stuck with the equipment and it is disruptive of your entire operation, so this is an option you should discourage from the start. Simply put, if equipment doesn't work, get rid of it and go back to operating the way you were until something better comes along.

Redefine Expectations

On rare occasions, as just discussed, new equipment won't do the job. However, the more likely event is that the equipment works but not up to the expectations of those responsible for its purchase. The reasons for this aren't hard to understand. All too often, everyone succumbs to the wonderful notion that some new technology or updated equipment is the solution to one or more problems. The difficulty lies in the fact that although the technology has promise, it is blown out of proportion by those involved in obtaining it for use. This is partly due to the demanding nature of the approval process for expensive equipment. The extent to which it has to be justified has people extolling virtues to limits which are beyond true belief. The irony is that after doing this a number of times people start being believers.

Therefore, it's often not so much a question of abandoning new technology because it doesn't meet expectations, but rather lowering the expectations to deal with reality. Once you realize you have equipment which performs adequately but not up to the level of prepurchase expectations, go about letting people know the true capabilities of the equipment.

You may find that some of them will still be believers that the equipment will meet their inflated expectations. They will make comments such as, "It will do better once you get your people past the learning curve." There is no reason to challenge these comments since time will ultimately prove you to be right. The important point is to let it be known that no one should expect output to increase to meet the unrealistic expectations originally made for the new equipment.

WEIGHING GAINS AGAINST LOSSES WHEN INTRODUCING NEW TECHNOLOGY

It's all too easy to look at new technology as a panacea for solving all of the problems your unit or department faces. You've undoubtedly heard comments similar to the following from other supervisors in the past:

- "If I could only get this equipment updated, I could increase production twenty percent."
- "I'll be able to operate with the present complement of people if I receive the new machines I've been trying to get for the past two years."
- "Expenses in my department could be reduced if I didn't have to allocate so much money to equipment maintenance."

Unfortunately, new technology doesn't always live up to its expectations. That in itself isn't so bad, but it certainly doesn't make sense to make grandiose claims of accomplishment based on the receipt of new equipment. After all, higher management might take you up on it by including your wish list in the budget. If that happens, you had better be prepared to produce what you promised. The long and the short of it is that although you have to substantiate the need for new equipment, don't do it by making claims that can't be fulfilled. If you do, they may come back to haunt you.

New technology may look promising, whether it's one piece of equipment for the office, or an entire automated production process.

Yet, as with many other things, there are both pluses and minuses when introducing anything new to the workplace. Having the foresight to recognize both the negative as well as the positive will make it easier to deal with the situation if things don't work out quite as well as was initially expected. Chances are they won't, since expectations generally tend to exceed performance. This often isn't the fault of the technology, as we have said, but a function of unrealistic expectations on the part of those who procured it. So the first step in weighing gains and losses from new equipment introductions is to recognize that things can and will go wrong. Accepting this potential will put you in a better position to cope with hassles as they occur.

In addition, there are a number of questions to be considered in order to determine if it's worthwhile to pursue the acquisition of new technology. Even if it's deemed to be beneficial to install new equipment or technology, weighing the various pros and cons beforehand will help deal with problems that may arise. The factors to think about will vary with the specifics of the work and the related technology, but here are some common considerations:

1. *Will the new equipment provide quantitative gains in terms of output?* Perhaps one objective in installing new machinery is that it will supposedly provide for an increase in production volume. This, incidentally, isn't confined strictly to a production line concept of volume, but rather to an increase in whatever it is that the machinery does. For example, it might be technology that increases the amount of information available to a manager or service worker.

   Whatever the individual situation might be, what you have to decide is whether or not additional output will be provided. This determination isn't always as straightforward as it might seem. You have to probe for the facts rather than rely on a vendor's unsubstantiated assertions. All too often, the glitzy appeal of new technology is seized upon without closely examining the true potential behind the fancy show-and-tell presentations. Comparing situations where this technology has done what is claimed are the best predictors of success in your own operation.

   One sometimes overlooked factor is whether or not the additional output provided by new equipment is needed. It certainly doesn't make sense to spend money on equipment that will provide additional output you don't even need. This seems like a no-brainer trap that no one would ever be caught in. Yet it happens all of the time for a couple of reasons. One is the natural seducement of having the latest in new equipment and technology. The other reason is that, when business is booming, expansion plans are made that soon result in overcapacity when business volume returns to a more sedate level. Therefore, a conservative assessment of need should always be made.

There are related questions to address in this area. Will the additional output from this technology impact on other people within your department, or other groups throughout the company? If you are producing an item that goes through a process and is subsequently worked on by others, will they be able to absorb the additional input? If not, what additional resources will they need? Sometimes even the introduction of one new machine can cause various ramifications that haven't been explored beforehand.

2. *Will the new equipment or technology provide qualitative gains?* Sometimes rather than increasing output quantitatively, new technology will be procured to improve the quality of the products or services being produced. Here again, it's necessary to verify that the purchase will produce those gains you're looking for. Furthermore, as with quantitative gains, you have to assess any potential impact on other aspects of the business operation.

3. *What are the costs of the equipment or technology?* Not simply the acquisition cost of what you're buying, these also include directly related expenses such as additional facilities, training, and so forth. You also have to weigh any costs that may be incurred as a result of using such equipment. For example, perhaps additional people may have to be hired in other areas to handle additional output resulting from new equipment added in your group.

The point here is not to overlook other areas of cost impact. All too frequently, assessments are made purely on the basis of the cost of the equipment. In the final determination you have to decide whether the equipment will be cost-effective. This doesn't always mean that the equipment has to produce additional revenues or meet some other quantitative yardstick of financial benefit. It's entirely possible that new technology may produce qualitative or state-of-the art-improvements which far outweigh the financial considerations involved.

4. *What are the people costs involved?* Personnel costs can't be ignored whenever you're weighing the potential gains or losses from adopting new technology. The most obvious is when new equipment is purchased that reduces labor needs. Even here, however, it pays to be cautious in making such assessments. Sometimes the introduction of new equipment may result in eliminating certain jobs, only to require the addition of workers with different skills. This may be positive or negative depending upon the circumstances, but the important thing is that this sort of assessment shouldn't be overlooked. If one of the attractions for buying equipment is its labor saving capacity, be certain this is truly the case before taking such drastic action.

5. *What are the training ramifications?* The complexity of new technology is the major factor in determining how much or how little training will be required. Other determinants include the existing skill level of your workers, the logistics involved in training the required employees, as well as who will do the training. You can't overlook the disruptive aspects of the training on your on-going operation; how much downtime your group will accrue in learning how to use new technology can sometimes be a significant element.

6. *What are worker attitudes toward the introduction of new equipment or technology?* One of the critical elements for the successful introduction of new technology is the willingness of workers to accept and learn new methods of operation. For this reason, it's vital to determine how they feel about new equipment. If you have a team-oriented environment where everyone is attuned toward working together to make the group as effective as possible, then new technology will be welcomed. At the other extreme, if workers perceive technology to be a threat to their jobs, then you can only expect that they won't embrace any suggestion for updating the equipment they use and your supervisory skills will be tested to the limit in trying to convince them of benefits from the new technology.

These are just some of the considerations that have to be made when new equipment or technology is being introduced. It's easy to ignore thinking about these matters, especially if you had little or no say in the decision for its introduction. Even so, you should weigh all of the potential positives and negatives since you and your subordinates will be the ones having to live with the new technology on a daily basis. In addition, if the equipment doesn't live up to the inflated expectations of upper level management, you will want to be in a position to point out exactly why that is so. Otherwise you may be blamed for the failure of others to think things through before they made an expensive and not so practical decision.

HOW TO DISCOURAGE NEW TECHNOLOGY YOU KNOW WON'T WORK

Sometimes in your supervisory role you find yourself caught in a quandary with regard to the introduction of new technology. From your experience at the working level you may know that certain equipment isn't suitable for the work being done by your group. Nevertheless, somewhere at higher levels of management, discussions are taking place about installing this equipment in your department. Perhaps the idea is the brainchild of a top manager, which means you have a touchy political landmine to overcome in order to kill the notion of buying the nonessential equipment.

How you go about dealing with this type of dilemma can be complicated. As a minimum, it requires you to exercise a great deal of diplomacy in making your point known. Naturally, this sort of business decision shouldn't be taking place without prior consultation with you as the supervisor of the unit involved. Unfortunately, as you well know, the real world of business doesn't always operate according to how things should be done. As a result, management decisions on equipment are made without consulting those most affected. It isn't proper and it isn't efficient, but it is done. For this reason alone, you should know how to make yourself heard, or suffer the consequences of having to deal with equipment and technology that don't do the job.

Look for Allies Who Support Your Position

One of the best ways to derail any ideas about installing equipment or technology you don't want is to enlist support from other managers with similar feelings. The higher they are in the organization, the better off you are. You have to do this casually, though, since you can't be seen as deliberately trying to undermine progress—which is exactly what you will be accused of by whoever is touting the new technology. Try to feel people out to see where they stand on the issue.

It's also useful to play to the objections raised by different individuals. For example, managers with financial responsibilities who are fiscally conservative may object to the cost of the new equipment. If possible, give them facts and figures and other information to support their contentions. Perhaps they may be unaware of large-scale training costs that would be required. Perhaps the new equipment would require a significant amount of expensive maintenance. Whatever the specifics may be, what you want to do is feed this sort of information to those who will use it to support their objections—and yours.

Organize Your Opposition

It's of little value, however, to have a number of people opposed to the unwanted technology if there is no organized opposition that will kill the idea of buying the equipment. Putting the potential procurement on ice can be done in a couple of ways. It mainly depends upon the organizational structure where you work and the position of power held by those advocating the equipment versus those opposed to the idea.

What you want to do is either convince those sponsoring the procurement that it is a bad idea and should be dropped, or alternatively have management at higher levels than these people direct that the project be dropped. The nuances of how this is accomplished will vary from case to case, but from a general standpoint your approach can be either specific or indirect.

The specific approach pretty much follows the normal procedures for making your viewpoint known throughout the organization. For example, you can make your thoughts known in a memo to your boss outlining your objections and the detailed reasons for your position. Such a stance may ultimately lead to various meetings of both proponents and opponents. Ultimately the proponents may decide that it isn't worthwhile to pursue the procurement of the new equipment, or top management may be forced to make a decision one way or the other.

Cut into the Support Base of Proponents

A useful tactic when you're rallying support for your cause is to simultaneously weaken the cause of proponents of the new technology by whittling away at their support. For instance, whenever positions are taken on controversial matters, some people are borderline in their enthusiasm. What you want to do is convince marginal supporters that the new technology isn't a good idea. Try to show them why this is so from some aspect that would appeal to them. For example, those with quality control responsibilities could be swayed by convincing them that the new technology could undermine the quality of existing products.

This technique breaks down the support needed to gain final approval for any decision that will require the expenditure of significant sums of money. Without this support top management approval won't be forthcoming. Even when you don't turn people completely around in their thinking, just planting the seeds of doubt can have value. For example, if a senior manager asks someone for an opinion of a proposal to procure new technology, there's a big difference between a respondent saying, "I think it would really improve our competitive position," and a remark such as, "It could be of value but I have some reservations about the idea." The latter comment will lead to follow-up questions which will bring forth the negative aspects you had previously pointed out. Whatever the outcome, planting the seeds of doubt in supporters' minds is a sound way to undermine support for an idea you oppose.

Exercise Caution When Senior Managers Sponsor New Technology

A more indirect approach may be called for if the chief sponsor of the new technology happens to be a senior manager. After all, you can't openly challenge a member of top management if you value your future with the company. In this type of situation it helps to find someone of equal or higher rank who either opposes the idea and is in a position to overturn the project, or who can convince the sponsor that it isn't a sound idea to go ahead. In this situation you want to furnish any information you can to help defeat the proposed acquisition without putting yourself in the spotlight as a detractor. This is especially true if you're unsure of whether or not the procurement will be killed.

Whenever the new equipment or technology is proposed by top management, your best chance of changing that decision is to offer proven alternatives to meet the objectives of those wanting to buy the new technology. For example, if the thrust behind a suggestion to replace machinery in your department is to reduce costs, then you should be prepared to show how costs can be reduced without the added expense of the new equipment. If you're really lucky, then you may be able to make an argument on both a better way to meet the objectives, as well as pointing out that the proposed procurement isn't likely to accomplish its goal in any event.

Naturally you have to deal with reality in these situations and there may be times when equipment or technology is procured where you had little or no input in the decision. It's not right, but it happens, and it can place you in the uncomfortable position of trying to make do with technology that doesn't cut it. All you can do here is work around such problems as best you can and be able to prove that you weren't the one that wanted the new technology in the first place.

SEVEN METHODS FOR TACKLING WORKER CONCERNS ABOUT NEW TECHNOLOGY

As discussed earlier in this chapter, worker concerns about new technology are natural. But they can turn into a real bottleneck if ignored, or be quickly dispensed with if handled properly. A few good methods for dealing with them include the following:

Communicate Early and Often

This may seem like a no-brainer, but it can't be overemphasized. In fact, even when a conscious effort is made to communicate with workers about new technology, frequently it isn't handled properly, which isn't much better than not communicating at all. Hold meetings to answer worker questions and discuss their concerns. Discussions about new technology should begin long before it arrives on the scene and will alleviate some of the anxieties when the equipment is installed. In fact, if you're able to convince workers beforehand as to how they will benefit from the technology, they may be quite receptive to its arrival.

Demystify to Limit Technical Trauma

Try to take as much of the mystery as possible out of new technology. This isn't always as difficult as it may seem. There is frequently a great deal of technical jargon associated with new technology and equipment that can be easily explained by a little translation into easy-to-understand language. Historically, computers provide the best example of unnecessarily complex terminology that only served to delay a user-friendly environment.

The problem here goes beyond semantics. When people are unable to comprehend the language itself, they are far less likely to be receptive to the underlying technology. Furthermore, even in situations where you don't need to know much about the technology, if you can't quite fathom the language that will allow you to use it, then it's reasonable for you to assume there is a good deal of complexity involved.

Solving this problem is simple enough as long as you make the effort to convert confusing terms into language that people can understand. Simplifying descriptions of what technology is and how to use it will make it much more worker-friendly. Of course, it would be so helpful if technology designers and developers did this in the first place, but don't bet the farm on that happening despite what you may hear being preached from these sources. Take matters into your own hands and explain what terms mean in plain language. If feasible, work with manufacturer representatives to learn the functions necessary and how best to explain them in everyday language.

Provide the Proper Training

Various aspects of training have been covered elsewhere in this book (particularly in Chapter Five). The point to be made here is that by making certain employees receive the proper training on new technology and equipment you will help alleviate their concerns.

Overcome Worker Doubts

Workers may harbor various suspicions about new technology in either one or more areas. The key to success here is being able to overcome these reservations. Among the most common suspicions are the following:

- The technology will eliminate jobs.
- It's extremely difficult to learn how to use the equipment.
- I will be required to do more work.
- The equipment always breaks down.
- We're being used as the guinea pigs for the rest of the company.
- They're sprucing up the equipment in order to sell the company.
- We will have to train to use the technology on our own time.

These are just samples of the reasoning why new technology is being introduced into your group. As you know, the rumor mill loves to nurture negative thoughts, and when you have nervous workers apprehensive about change taking place, the ground is fertile for rumors to be planted. You have to move quickly, therefore, to dispel rumors, as well as let people know the actual reasons for implementing new technology.

Incidentally, if worker doubts are valid, don't try and gloss over them since this will only lead to greater suspicion. For example, if it's a foregone conclusion that new technology will eliminate jobs, discuss this in detail. Odds are that the fears are probably exaggerated. New equipment may be more productive, which will eliminate the need for adding people to the payroll rather than laying off existing employees. Alternatively, even though jobs are to be eliminated, the company may plan on doing this through attrition. If that's so, let employees know, since it can substantially alter their attitude about acceptance of new technology.

Give Workers Reasons for Wanting to Use New Equipment

Sometimes getting workers to accept new equipment involves nothing more elaborate than giving them a specific reason for wanting it. The reasoning, of course, can take many forms. Perhaps a new data management program contains information that makes it easier for salespeople to do their job, or production machinery might eliminate a currently unpleasant task that assembly line workers have to perform. Whatever the reason, if you can make it advantageous for workers to use new technology, overcoming their concerns will be much easier.

Explain the Benefits of the Technology

Let people know what the purpose of the new technology is and why it's important. Stating that it will allow the company to become more competitive is a pretty vague statement. Go into detail to explain how it makes that possible. Then take the issue further to explain why it's important to increase the company's competitive position. Do so in terms of things the employee can relate to, such as saving jobs. People will be more receptive to something new if they know there is a valid need for such a change.

Be Understanding

One of the simplest ways to ease employee concerns over the implementation of new technology is to show empathy toward their concerns. Take the time to listen to their laments. This may sometimes start to wear on you, but do your best to maintain your composure because the results can be beneficial. If workers know they have the willing ear of their boss for their complaints, they can overcome their sense of helplessness when they are overwhelmed by new technology. Just being able to vent their frustrations will give them some sense of direction over something they find to be beyond their control.

USING TECHNOLOGY TO HELP GET THE RESOURCES YOU NEED

One problem many supervisors have to contend with is the extreme difficulty in obtaining the resources necessary to run their departments effectively. After all, budgets are tight in any cost-conscious company, and the competition between groups for resources can be harsh. Therefore, those supervisors who succeed in securing approval to purchase additional equipment, or add people to the payroll, will be the ones who are most creative in justifying their needs to top management.

The most common methods of being successful include a mix of office politics and sound proposals that somehow show that the additional resources will result in greater efficiency, lower costs, higher profits, or some other benefit. This, of course, is a common approach any supervisor can use, which means that the better you are at selling the benefits of being given additional resources, the greater are the odds of getting them. It isn't an easy task to make your own pitches for more help, and/or new equipment, stand out from the competition. And shine they must or you will likely hear some form of rejection such as:

"There isn't any money in the budget for new equipment."

"I understand your plight, but the company isn't adding to the payroll this fiscal year."

"Your request makes sense, but funds are tight this year. Why don't you try to replace your outdated machinery in next year's budget cycle?"

Use Technology to Make Presentations

These are just a few of the standardized responses used to shoot down requests for anything that will cost the company more money. "Make do with what you've got" is the universal aim of budget-conscious managers responsible for holding the line on budget-busting requests. Therefore, to defeat this mindset and succeed in getting the resources you need, you have to be creative in using every tool at your disposal. One way to do this is to make better use of existing technology to help you prove your point.

All too often, presentations are made in the same old way, when using newer technology can greatly enhance the presentation. The irony is that sometimes supervisors are requesting technically updated equipment for their departments, but are using outdated flip charts to prove their point. At the same time within that very company, the marketing department and others may use various forms of video and computer-based technology to make glitzy high-tech presentations to potential customers.

This, of course, doesn't mean you have to make a costly and time-consuming presentation justifying your every request for additional resources. However, within reasonable limits, it behooves you to make your proposal pitch as efficient and convincing as possible. In fact, failure to do so can sink your request. For example, a higher level manager might be listening to your presentation for high-tech equipment costing thousands of dollars, with an accompanying inch-thick volume of supporting data that is definitely low-tech. The conclusion might be drawn that here is a supervisor who doesn't use the current technology effectively, so why approve this request for still more? Furthermore, someone in the approval cycle won't relish reading volumes of data in support of a request. No question that a well-thought-out presentation using computer graphics can be more convincing.

Prove the Value of Technology

Aside from having the foresight to use up-to-date methods in making your requests for resources, there are other aspects of technology that you can use effectively. If you're requesting new equipment, strive to show specifically how it will benefit the company. Do enough research to present a case that supports your request. Perhaps you can show where a competitor has recently adopted the equipment in question. Or maybe you can present evidence that the equipment has increased efficiency in other companies which use it to perform functions similar to its intended use within your department.

By taking this approach you are using the technology itself to prove its worth. This isn't insignificant, since the complexity of new technology can be such that it's not readily understood by the managers who have the final say-so on approving the purchase. Therefore, by being able to demonstrate that the technology works elsewhere, much of the mystery of its potential is simplified. And it's a lot easier to get approval of an expensive purchase when the decision-makers can see its value in action. This can be especially helpful if you know the approving authority isn't particularly enthusiastic about high technology.

Use Either/Or Comparisons

Technology can be used for comparative purposes in certain situations. If you want to purchase new equipment and can show where it will be a less expensive alternative to other choices, you have a leg up in getting what you want approved. For instance, if you can show that the alternative to purchasing certain equipment is the hiring of additional people, then your chances for success increase. The flip side of the coin might also work here if you are looking to hire people and can show that it would be more effective than buying updated technology. Whichever approach may be called for, the fundamental point is to furnish evidence in the form of facts and figures to support your position.

Know Friend from Foe When Using Technology

The extent to which you incorporate technology into your proposals for additional resources should be determined by the individuals whose approval you are seeking. There are managers who have an almost congenital distaste for technology in any form. Some will openly admit it, while many keep these tendencies to themselves. If you know that certain managers in the approval cycle fall into this category, then downplay its use in your proposal pitch. Of course, if it happens to be technology itself that you want to buy in the form of new equipment, then minimize the whiz-bang aspect of what the equipment can do. Instead concentrate on the value of buying the equipment in terms of dollars saved by lowering expenses, increasing sales, or whatever other quantitative indicators you can feasibly use.

Commonly proposals for additional resources require several approvals. If what you are seeking is significant in terms of need, or requires significant funding to purchase, you may want to vary your proposal pitch. Emphasize technology here when pitching to staff and management people who are likely to be impressed with this approach, but use more traditional proposal formats with those who may not be technology buffs.

TRAINING EMPLOYEES TO USE THE DATA THAT TECHNOLOGY PROVIDES

As you know, technology has the capacity to churn out data more quickly than it can be absorbed by the end-users. So some people pay scant attention to much of the technology-based information they are bombarded with, whether it's e-mail or computer-generated spreadsheets, while others spend countless hours reading e-mail or analyzing computer reports. Chances are the first group is missing out on some valuable information, while the second group is wasting valuable time on non-essential matters.

The end result of this dual reaction toward available information is often to blame technology for creating the problem. Of course, it's true that technological advances have made more information available more quickly to more people. On the other hand, it's not the fault of technology that a great deal of it is garbage. Back in the era of pens, pencils, and manual typewriters, information that was garbage was still a problem. The only difference was that there was less of it to go around. At least now if an employee gives you a spreadsheet with numbers based on a wrong assumption, it's easy enough to go to the computer and make the proper adjustment.

Train Workers to be Selective in Working with Available Information

In reality, the problem isn't exclusively the quality or the quantity of information being churned out. It's a question of training employees to use data more effectively, both in its preparation and its dissemination. With the wealth of potential information available for use, selectivity is the first step in bringing order out of chaos in using computer-generated data.

The precise details of how you train employees to be selective will vary with the nature of the workload of your department. The key is to use whatever methods best suit the requirements of the job while simultaneously reducing the volume of data to be scrutinized. The better the job you do as a supervisor in this regard, the easier it will be to increase the efficiency of your unit. Doing this will, of course, help to improve the quality and quantity of the information generated within your unit. Beyond that, however, it will also train employees to seek out and use information that they aren't aware is available to them.

Why Technology Isn't Used Effectively

Some employees will use existing technology to its fullest, while others will use it only to the extent they are required to. This can lead to situations where a worker will spend an inordinate amount of time doing computations or assembling information manually that could have been done on a computer in a fraction of the time. When queried about this, the likely response may be, "Gee, I didn't know I could do that." The reality is that some workers aren't about to take any initiative in learning the capabilities of the equipment they have available to them. For this reason alone you should always be quick to point out to workers the specific ways that the available technology can help them do their jobs.

Naturally workers are taught the fundamentals whenever new equipment is introduced. The problem is that sometimes the training ends there. While it certainly may be valid to do this in some instances, in others, once employees have absorbed the fundamentals of handling new technology, it's time to train them to operate at the next level. Just as technology gets updated, so too should the skills of your employees. In this fashion, workers will become more and more expert at maximizing the benefits of technology. This will also contribute to productivity increases which come about only when workers are schooled in maximizing the investment in equipment.

Hold Equipment Usage Forums

From a supervisory standpoint, the best approach to maximizing the use of your available technology is to hold periodic meetings with your group devoted to its use that has been recently introduced into your area. They will provide an appropriate forum for workers to exchange tips on how best to use the equipment and to suggest how new equipment could be added that would enhance the group's operations. All in all, what you want to do is provide for the exchange of ideas which will not only broaden the knowledge of everyone within your group, but also contribute to demystifying the complexities of new technology. These gatherings should be informal with the overriding theme of "How can we make this equipment work best for us?" If you can accomplish that, then you will be well prepared for adapting to new technology as it filters its way into the workplace.

HOW TO CONTROL AN INFORMATION OVERLOAD

When technology first brought computers to the workplace, the crystal ball crowd bravely asserted that the future held forth prospects of a paperless office. That, as you well know, didn't materialize. In fact, it could be argued that computer technology has contributed to an increase in the volume of paper that overflows desks throughout the business world. And, of course, plenty of substitutes for paperwork have been added when you consider the volume of e-mail, electronic data interchange, along with voice mail and other modern day contributions to keeping people overloaded with work. The irony is that most of the technology was touted as being a productivity booster, but in many instances it has actually been a productivity buster.

Communicate As a Group

Your initial action to control information overload is to encourage open and informal communications within your unit or group. You might want to hold a brief daily meeting where anything important is to be brought up. Let employees know that unless something is of such an urgency that it can't wait until the following morning's meeting it shouldn't be brought to your attention during the day. This will alleviate a steady stream of visits and phone calls on relatively inconsequential matters.

You might wonder how instructing people not to bother you unless something is urgent encourages communication. It's group communication that is being encouraged. Many of the one-on-one visits by employees aren't of any great value and some are nothing more than attempts by individuals to score a few points with the boss. Asking for anything important to be brought up at the daily meeting puts it on the table for discussion by the group. This works to encourage the teamwork and group problem solving essential to a cohesive and productive unit.

In this fashion, you have transformed communications into a group endeavor rather than meeting with individuals in your office. Naturally, you want to exclude certain topics such as personnel matters and the like from any group discussions. However, most work-related business should be on the table for discussion. After you hold a few of these meetings you will be able to refine the process to maximize the benefits of group discussion for everyone involved.

Incidentally, one practical advantage of this sort of communication is that it eliminates the back-and-forth of four or five people asking the same questions at different times. It also minimizes the odds of someone getting different answers from different people within the group. There may, of course, be differing opinions given during a meeting, but at least everyone has heard both versions, as well as anyone else's thoughts on the matter.

Business Practices Are a Culprit

Holding a daily group meeting is only one aspect of trying to control information overload, since much of the paperwork and data originate outside of your department. In fact, routine business practices are a major cause of information overload. Excessive reporting procedures, repetitive requests for data on one subject or another, and the need to justify expenditures large and small all contribute to piles of paperwork and electronic correspondence.

Shoddy practices and laziness can also contribute to overload. For instance, requests for information are often responded to with a quantity of data that overwhelms the recipient. The reason may be that the person sending the data finds it easier to send everything on the subject rather than taking the time to pinpoint the most relevant information. On some occasions, the sender thinks that sheer volume alone will be impressive enough to carry the day. There are also times when the blame actually lies with the person requesting the information who may have made a vague request. He or she subsequently pays the price by being buried in a blizzard of information.

Whether you're talking about paper, electronic submissions, or computer-generated data, dealing with it requires you to establish certain priorities. What these are will vary with the nature of your supervisory position. The overriding consideration is that you will find certain patterns in information: that which you can completely ignore, that which you can read at your leisure, and that which truly requires a response. The fortunate part is that the bulk of the information overload you have to deal with comprises material that you don't have to give much credence to. That, of course, doesn't say much for the overall productivity of a business if so much little used information is being generated. That fortunately is someone else's problem to deal with.

USING QUALITY MANAGEMENT TECHNIQUES TO FACILITATE IMPROVEMENTS

If you're a supervisor in an industry or company where quality improvements are constantly being emphasized, you may have had the misfortune to endure a repetitive cycle of buzzword programs supposedly aimed at improving quality. You may also have discovered that most of them didn't produce the accomplishments that their initial fanfare promised. What's new about that? Nothing. Buzzword fixes are a way of life. Some are useless, most have some merit, and a few really succeed in improving operations. As a result, they just can't be ignored, so you have to learn how to separate the wheat from the chaff.

Establish an Informal Quality Program Within Your Department

Aside from any formal quality programs the company may have in place, you can implement your own informal one to improve operations within your department. The starting point is a recognition that a main theme of any quality program is to focus on improving customer service. This is where many groups stray off the path, since a typical response may be something such as "We don't deal directly with customers so this isn't something for us to concentrate on."

Such statements couldn't be further from the truth. When it comes to quality management, it's not only customers in the traditional sense who buy goods and services. The meaning includes all of those groups and individuals we deal with, within or outside of the company. This includes other departments and individuals in staff functions. If your group interacts with them on business, your goal should be to look for ways to improve your service to them.

Naturally, you have to understand how your customers view your group's performance before you can set goals for improving the quality of your department's output. You can obtain this in a relatively informal way by asking various people you do business with if they are experiencing any problems in doing business with your group. Most folks won't be reticent to let you know about any problems once they see you are sincere about hearing their grievances. There will, of course, be occasions when you don't have to ask anyone if something can be improved—when you hear that some aspect of your group's performance was sub-par, at least in the eyes of the complainant.

Your next step is to get your employees involved in working to improve the quality effort of your group. This basically involves empowering workers to make decisions and encouraging them to recommend changes. How to do this has been covered elsewhere within this book so there's no need to repeat those details here. What is important is to make quality improvement something that is emphasized on a regular basis.

Establish a Means of Measurement

Determining measurement yardsticks can be tricky. It's helpful to set specific goals to determine how performance toward meeting these goals will be measured. The nature of the goals will vary significantly according to the nature of the work performed within your group. For instance, in a manufacturing environment, reducing the number of product defects might be used, while in a retail environment the number of customer complaints might be a good yardstick. Whatever the goals and means of measurement are, make sure they are both relevant and achievable.

One of the sometimes overlooked aspects of quality management is that it involves continuous improvement rather than setting a goal and then quitting when it's reached. To be truly successful a quality program should always be striving to reach higher and further in terms of improving the quality of the group's output. This is true whether you're talking about your own department or the company as a whole.

8 Gaining Cooperation from People You Don't Supervise

One of the imperatives for success as a supervisor in the modern workplace is an ability to secure cooperation from a wide range of different people and groups who can influence the success of the unit you manage. These individuals range from co-workers in other departments within your company, to outsiders such as suppliers and customers. How good you are at working with these different constituencies will determine the ease or difficulty of getting your job done.

To a degree, the extent of the cooperation you receive will depend upon your skill at practicing the art of office politics. This isn't always a pleasant task for some supervisors, but like it or not, political skills can come in handy. Of course, gaining and maintaining a high level of cooperation with people isn't just a matter of glad-handing everyone in sight. People have their own agendas and priorities and the ability to recognize and work around these hurdles is a necessity. This chapter will discuss tactics to get the resources you need to do your job, as well as those necessary to gain cooperation from suppliers. Also discussed will be ways to counter critics, as well as how to provide the proper feedback to top management.

HOW TO COPE WITH THE UNCERTAINTIES OF REORGANIZATION

One of the most troublesome problems you may experience is a reorganization that affects the group you supervise. You may recall that dealing with the internal aspects of reorganizations was covered in Chapter One, "Supervising Your Way Through an Organizational Overhaul." Here the emphasis is on helping displaced workers get other jobs and handling external relationships with customers and suppliers.

The impact of a reorganization may be as major as abolishing your group, as minor as a departmental name change, or somewhere in between these two extremes. Whatever the particulars of the reorganization may be, the working relationships you establish with other department heads will help determine the relative ease or difficulty of coping. Naturally, the extent and nature of the reorganization will dictate which departments you deal with. They will either be impacted themselves or be in a position to help you cope.

In addition to assistance from other departments and staff personnel when a reorganization affects your group, outsiders such as customers and suppliers can also help. What can they do, you wonder. The fact is that either of these groups can aid you immeasurably depending upon the nature of the reorganization. For example, if your unit is being reorganized to the extent that there will be some disruption in work flow, customers and suppliers who are understanding will ease your supervisory burden.

A good relationship with customers also makes it easier for you to reassure them that business won't be affected if a large-scale reorganization takes place. This is valuable, since customers can get skittish when they see a company reorganize. They might see it as a sign of financial difficulty or something else that could impact their status as customers. And finally, from a career standpoint, a good working relationship with customers and suppliers can come in handy if a reorganization should realign you out of your job.

Your first and foremost task with any reorganization is to look after the needs of your own employees. Concentrate first upon efforts to guarantee that none of your workers lose their jobs. This isn't always possible, since many reorganizations result in a cutback of employees. Nevertheless, even when certain people in your department are targeted for dismissal, there are actions you can take to decrease the number affected.

For starters, at the first indication that you will lose people from your department, begin to look for ways to minimize the losses. Taking on additional responsibilities is one way to save jobs. This isn't easy to do if reorganization plans are generally known, but if the news hasn't leaked yet, it allows you to buttress the position of your department before any action is taken. Understand that this is also highly unlikely. Once a company has started to formulate plans for a reorganization, even though they aren't generally known, those in power won't want to make any type of interim change since wholesale reorganization is about to take place. Therefore, they will scuttle any attempt on your part to take over additional work from other departments. Nevertheless, it never hurts to volunteer to assume additional duties. If nothing else it marks you and your department as a group that is willing to work hard at being productive.

Help Employees Find Other Positions

A more likely way to save the jobs of employees in your group who otherwise would lose jobs in a reorganization is to get them transfers into departments that aren't affected. If you maintain good contacts with other managers throughout the company, you will be well positioned to make recommendations concerning people who work for you. Incidentally, training your people to do a variety of jobs pays off at times like this, since they have skills that may be transferable to other positions throughout the company.

When a reorganization costs your department people who can't be placed elsewhere within the company, do whatever you can to help them locate jobs elsewhere. If you have particularly well qualified people, then let your contacts in other companies know about their availability. This reaction on your part will be appreciated, not only by those employees who are being laid off, but also by those that remain. Being helpful will be personally fulfilling, as well as boosting respect for you in the eyes of those still in your employ.

Reorganizations are always fertile ground for rumors which tend to magnify what will take place. Under these circumstances it's not hard for the rumor mill to turn a simple departmental name change into massive corporate-wide layoffs. You can't, of course, eliminate the rumors, but you can work to counter the damage they can cause. This is best done by letting your people know what's going on. Unfortunately you're limited in doing this by the amount of information that you receive from higher levels of management. In any event, do your utmost to keep your people informed, since this helps maintain productivity levels that tend to slip when rumors start to fly.

Answer Customer Concerns

One of your major tasks in any sizable reorganization is to answer the concerns of customers and suppliers. They too may have heard rumors, so you may have to overcome a good deal of misinformation that these people picked up from other sources throughout the company. Always do your best to reassure them that the relationships won't be affected by the reorganization—assuming that is true.

On the other hand, if the reorganization brings about any changes in the way in which your department interacts with either suppliers or customers, be certain to clearly establish what the changes are. If they will be dealing with people unfamiliar to them, arrange introductory meetings to break the ice. The importance of trying to keep external relations with customers and suppliers from being impacted by a reorganization can't be emphasized enough. Skittish customers who aren't kept informed will soon give someone else their business. Whatever else the goals of a reorganization were, this wasn't one of them.

PRACTICAL TACTICS TO GET THE RESOURCES YOU NEED TO DO THE JOB

One of the topics covered previously was the use of technology to help justify your need for additional resources. But a first-rate presentation by itself won't be the sole determinant of whether or not you get what you need to do your job. In fact, if you work in a highly politicized company you may discover that certain supervisors have all their needs filled while others get little or nothing. This may be even more surprising if the supervisors who most often win budget approval aren't particularly skilled at using technology to enhance their pitches.

You ignore at your peril the fact that, though companies may be global, and technology may be all-important, who you golf with can carry the day in positioning you to get the resources your department covets. Therefore, you have to learn how to use practical tactics to enhance your success on the job. Paramount is the judicious use of office politics. It's easy to say you don't play that game, but if you're the only one not playing it, then you will automatically be vulnerable. Even though you may find cozying up to upper management most distasteful, you may want to rethink your alternatives. If nothing else, at least practice a few tactics that will allow you to operate successfully—both for your own benefit as well as for those people you supervise.

No matter what your feelings may be on practicing office politics, one basic technique is essential in helping you get the resources you need for your department. That tactic is to always justify your requests for resources in such a way that they benefit your immediate boss, as well as anyone else within the approval cycle. If they can be justified in a way seen as being in someone's career self-interest, they are likely to be approved. How you do this requires an understanding of what's important in the overall scheme of things within your company.

Don't Buck the Trend

A need to increase revenues or decrease expenses is a common ongoing theme with most organizations. Moreover, at any given time top management of a company may emphasize certain aspects of performance more than others. For example, it may concentrate on broad issues such as increasing sales, or specific areas such as reducing travel expenses or eliminating overtime work.

Your boss, along with other managers whose approval you must obtain, will follow these themes in determining whether to approve or disapprove your requests. Therefore, if cutting the payroll is a major corporate objective, your boss won't view it to be in his or her best interest to go along with your request for two additional people in your department. On the other hand, if top management is demanding increases in production, and you can make a strong case that buying a certain piece of expensive equipment will increase output, your boss will likely be supportive. For the same reason, your request would be likely to receive favorable consideration from others in the approval process.

In addition to the operating policy issues being touted from a general management standpoint, individual managers will have their own pet peeves and preferences. Some managers may be strong advocates of technology, and thus be willing to consider any proposal for new equipment that's on the cutting edge. Others in the approval cycle may view most new equipment requests as frivolous and excessive. Aside from their substantive preferences on various issues, managers also have differing views as to the format of requests presented. Some may want lots of detail to accompany a written proposal, while others may prefer a quick and to-the-point oral presentation.

What all of this adds up to is that getting the resources you need requires knowing what to ask for and how to ask for it. This is something that you can ignore only at your peril. Your starting point must be to figure out what is likely to gain approval and what isn't. For instance, don't try to add people to your department if the company is trying to reduce the payroll. Conversely, this may be a good time for you to try and get new equipment you want, especially if you can show its labor-saving capabilities.

Timing Isn't Everything—But It Matters

Once you have determined your request for resources has a chance for serious consideration, you can move on to a number of other issues involved in getting your request approved. One important, but often overlooked, consideration is timing. You can't always, of course, control when to make a pitch for additional resources. This is particularly true if it has to go up through the chain of command. At what point in time it will be considered at each step along the way won't be within your control. Nevertheless, there are certain aspects of timing you can control and it's these that you have to use to your advantage.

For example, your boss may be more receptive to listening to suggestions at certain times of the day. If so, try to make your pitch at that time. Conversely, whenever a boss is busy or in an apparent bad mood is the wrong moment to pitch a proposal because someone in a good mood is far more likely to be receptive to what you have to say. These points may seem insignificant, but it's foolish to buck the obvious, and as hard as it is to get additional resources approved, there's no sense in taking any chances.

Incidentally, getting your fair share of resources sometimes hinges on being prepared to take advantage of unpredictable aspects of timing. For instance, you probably wouldn't dream of asking for approval to buy an expensive piece of equipment at the very moment your boss is blasting you for something that went wrong. An automatic rejection of your request would seem to be an obvious given. That's usually true, but if the equipment you want would help cure the problem the boss is unhappy about, you can use this to your advantage. If a boss complains about the need to increase the department's output, then this would be a good opportunity to make your pitch. This will work, of course, only if you can justify that it will alleviate the problem your boss is upset about. You also have to exercise some judgment here about timing. If your boss is angry at the moment, then wait to bring the matter up for a day or so. Doing this will allow the boss to calm down and hopefully be in a more receptive mood toward suggestions for solving the problem he or she was complaining about.

There's a flip side to this coin, however, and you should be prepared to take advantage of it. This opportunity comes about when your boss, instead of complaining about something going wrong, is praising you about some aspect of your department's performance. He or she is obviously pleased and there's no better time to ask for something than when a boss is in a good mood. Take advantage of this opportunity to ask for some resource that's been on your "wish list."

Prepare Your Justification Beforehand

It's always useful to have supporting documentation all prepared and ready to go. This allows you to move quickly when a window of opportunity presents itself. If you don't have the facts and figures ready, you lose the advantage of immediacy in situational opportunities. For instance, a boss who is receptive when you suggest something will likely respond by saying, "Write up your request and let me look it over." If you have already done this, it's a matter of handing it over in short order. However, if no cost estimates or other justification for your request have been prepared, then you are not ready to respond. Depending upon the complexity of the work involved, as well as your ability to fit it in with your other responsibilities, it could be as much as a week before you complete the proposal. By this time, your initial suggestion will probably have been forgotten by your boss, so you will have lost the advantage of getting approval while the boss was favorably disposed.

One of the main problems, however, with a supervisor preparing data beforehand to support a request for additional resources is the time involved. With the pace of work what it is, there's little incentive to try and find time to do anything that's not required at the moment. This is understandable enough, but when it comes to getting resources there are a couple of considerations that you can't overlook.

First and foremost, it's not as easy as it used to be to get approval for additional resources. The new and changing workplace has brought with it a cost consciousness that may not have prevailed back in the days when increases in expenses were often absorbed by raising prices. Global competition no longer permits such a luxury. Therefore, it's difficult to obtain approval for added expenditures unless you have the mandatory justification. So whether you do it sooner or later, the time involved will be the same.

As we have just stated, you should work up this justification before—not after—you make a pitch for resources because you can take advantage of timing opportunities. In addition, there are other reasons that can work in your favor. Suppose it's budget time and your boss calls a meeting of supervisors and states that any requests for resources must be submitted within the next two days if they are to be included in the budget request. Obviously this leaves busy supervisors scrambling to cobble together a request on short notice. Many of the requests will obviously be lacking in attention to detail that can spell the difference between approval or disapproval. If, on the other hand, your request is sitting in a desk drawer ready to go, you don't have to sweat the deadline. You will have a well-prepared package which will cast your request in a better light than some others.

Persist but Don't Insist

Another offshoot of the difficulty in securing additional resources is the need to be persistent without being a pest. Just think of some of the responses a boss may make in denying a request for resources:

- "This year's budget is already submitted. Try again next year."
- "There's not enough detail here to support your request."
- "Top management won't approve any requests for hiring people."

Sometimes these are legitimate reasons, while on other occasions they're excuses used to avoid a direct turndown of your request. Even when the reason given is an excuse, it's generally not a question as to the merits of your request, but rather the fact that it's easier for a boss to say this than to spend considerable time and effort in processing your request.

Keep in mind that requests involving the commitment of substantial sums of money generally have an extensive review procedure which may require several approvals from various management and staff departments. Just as you have to justify the request to your boss, so too does your boss have to plead the case at higher levels. This is reason enough for a busy boss to beg off with an excuse designed to reject your request without having to do so directly.

Because securing initial approval when you're asking for additional resources is difficult, you have to be reconciled to pursuing your case with persistence. Therefore, don't arbitrarily accept an initial statement designed to deny your request. Try to respond as best you can to what was said when your request was rejected. For example, if your boss said something such as, "We can't afford that," or some other statement implying your request is too expensive, look for alternatives.

Perhaps you can revise your request to be less costly. Alternatively, maybe you can come up with a way to spread the costs out over a longer period of time. Another great way to rebut the "We can't afford it" argument is by asserting, "We can't afford not to buy" whatever it is you are looking for. Show with facts and figures how what you want will actually save money. In still other situations, you may be able to get part of what you want if you're unsuccessful in pleading your case for the full amount. For instance, if your request for two people is turned down, try for one or perhaps even some part-time help. The same holds true for equipment: if you are unsuccessful in trying to requisition a new computer for everyone in your department, try to do it a couple at a time. Quite often, you will find that what you can't get in one lump sum you can achieve bit by bit.

Whatever approach you take in responding to an initial rejection, try again at a later date if that's the best you can do. The more convincing you are in your arguments, as well as how persistent you are, will ultimately determine your success or failure. Needless to say, although you want to and should persevere, do not antagonize your boss or anyone else in the approval cycle. Doing that is a golden guarantee that not only won't you get approval for the present request, but there may even be a carryover to future requests.

Enlist Support from Others

With the amount of difficulty involved in obtaining additional resources to do your job, any help you can get is a plus. Try to enlist other people in your cause. How you go about doing this will vary with the nature of your organization, the number of contacts you have who can help, and the type of resources you are seeking. Sometimes you may be able to enlist other supervisors in a joint effort if the resources sought will benefit other departments as well as your own. In other cases, you can enlist various staff personnel as advocates for your cause. For example, the head of computer services, chief information officer, or other technology advocate might be a good ally when you're seeking to update the available equipment.

The relative position of power of those you enlist in your cause will determine how effective they can be in helping out. If you're able to convince one or two high-level managers of the wisdom of your request, then that's the sort of support which greatly increases the odds of approval. Another good way to approach the idea of securing support from others is to incorporate suggestions from others in your request and to make them partners in the idea.

Even better is when you can have senior managers adopt your idea for additional resources as their own. Planting the idea in such a way that they see it as their suggestion will have them carrying the ball for you. This isn't as hard as it sometimes seems. For example, if you're discussing your needs with your own boss and/or some other higher level managers, actively solicit their suggestions. They may come up with something and be so enthused about it that they decide to pursue the approval for you. If you work this right, they may even come to believe it is their own idea. All you have to do is agree that they have come up with something really worthwhile.

In the end, the best approach for getting the resources you need is to use whatever tactic will work. Whatever you do in this regard, don't take "no" for an answer, since without the necessary resources you will end up struggling to keep your department afloat. Getting what you need may not be easy in a cost-conscious environment, but those who can make their case with conviction will ultimately succeed.

THE RIGHT APPROACH TO PROVIDING FEEDBACK TO MANAGEMENT

When you think about securing cooperation from others to make it easier to do your job, you can't overlook the importance of providing feedback to upper level managers. After all, the decisions made by top management will influence your ability to operate your department. Whether it's seeking additional resources, or any number of other matters both large or small, your ability to influence top management will dictate how well you do in protecting your interests.

This goes far beyond the tactics used to obtain resources discussed in the prior section. To succeed on a long-term basis you have to be able to provide appropriate feedback to upper level managers, including your immediate boss. How you do this, and to what extent, will vary somewhat with the circumstances of your job and the desires of your boss. As a minimum, you should provide sufficient feedback to avoid any unpleasant surprises which are just as distasteful to upper level managers as they are to anyone else. But beyond this, the techniques you use can maximize your communication up the chain of command, while expending the minimum amount of time to accomplish.

Know the Details of What People Are Looking For

The starting point in providing feedback on the operations of your department is to learn the desires of those you report to. Of course, the bulk of your feedback will be to your immediate boss, so it's this person's likes and dislikes you should understand. Consider two main factors in providing feedback to your boss.

First is to understand what your boss's expectations are in terms of what sort of information you should be providing. Some bosses want to know all sorts of minor details, while others don't want much more than to be alerted when major problems arise. How much or how little feedback your boss wants shouldn't be ignored. One who wants details will be unhappy about not getting them, and someone who only wants to know about major problems won't appreciate listening to an endless discussion of trivial matters.

The second factor to keep in mind is the format your boss prefers. Some people like written reports, others want computer messages, and still others prefer a face-to-face meeting. Whatever the preference is isn't as important as being careful to observe your boss's wishes.

Watch Out for Quirks

Aside from the basics of what type of information is wanted and how to provide it, there is one nuance in particular that shouldn't be ignored: the peculiarities of the individual you're dealing with.

For example, one boss—let's call him Joe—always wanted lots of information about one department reporting to him. That was perfectly reasonable, but he would also ask questions about seemingly insignificant matters. The subject matter of these trivial details varied from week to week, and it was impossible for Joan, the reporting supervisor, to have all of the answers at hand. Consequently, Joan always offered to get back with the appropriate answers, but Joe, without fail, would say it wasn't necessary. Although Joan spent a great deal of time preparing for every type of conceivable question, more often than not she hadn't covered some obscure topic that the boss would raise.

On the other hand, the boss never got upset about not getting the answers. This left Joan baffled for months. One day she mentioned this to a former employee who had reported to this boss. She laughed long and loud, and then said that this had happened to her too. She went on to say that it was a ploy Joe used to guarantee that supervisors would be prepared to answer any questions they were asked. By always asking about trivial matters that couldn't be immediately answered, Joe was inspiring people to be prepared at briefing sessions.

That's an unusual tactic, to say the least, but many a boss has one or another idiosyncrasy and it behooves you to pay heed. Furthermore, don't let any of these unusual whims get under your skin. In particular, be careful about sending nonverbal messages of dissatisfaction that may contradict what you're saying. For example, although you may be responding favorably to what someone is saying, your nonverbal behavior, such as a frown, or an unpleasant inflection in your tone of voice, may tip your hand and send a different message.

Don't Conceal Problems

One of the most important aspects of feedback when you're dealing with your boss and others is to bring problems to their attention as soon as they arise. There's a natural human tendency to avoid dealing with problems in the hope that they will miraculously vanish or solve themselves. Regrettably, more often than not, they just continue to worsen. Then one of two alternatives is likely to take place. You finally decide the problem is sufficiently serious to bring it to your boss's attention, or your boss finds out about the problem elsewhere.

In either case, it's unpleasant for you. If you're the one to finally tell your boss, the first thing you will likely hear is, "Why didn't I hear about this before?" If the boss is informed of the problem by someone other than you, then you will likely get, "Why didn't you tell me about this? Don't you know what's going on within your own department?" It will be even more unpleasant if your boss first hears about the problem from someone higher in management, since you will have put your boss on the defensive.

Obviously, these aren't situations you want to find yourself in. It's far preferable to face the music early rather than late when it comes to providing this type of feedback. This doesn't mean you have to bring every minor detail to a boss's attention. Nevertheless, once it becomes obvious that a problem can't be handled quickly within the department, or that there will be outside ramifications, let your boss know. Incidentally, when you do this be prepared to make recommendations as to what can be done to solve the problem. You're a lot less likely to hear flak about a problem if you can propose a solution.

HOW TO CO-OPT CRITICS OF THE NEW WORKPLACE

Whenever changes are implemented within a company, whether it's a new policy which impacts everyone or an operational change that affects a single department, critics will find something wrong. On occasion, the criticism may be valid, but for the most part the resistance stems from other factors. It might be the natural resistance to something new, which is to be expected. Or there may be strong personal bias against a change for any number of reasons:

- A reorganization lessens the role of certain managers.
- You have new technology that other managers didn't get.
- Misguided career competitiveness. Other supervisors might oppose anything new that you sponsor with the intent of making you look bad.
- Gut reaction opposition to anything new.
- The "If I didn't think of it, it isn't any good" mentality.
- The idea that it's easier to oppose something rather than learn how to use it.
- A genuine belief that the new technology or procedure won't work.

Whatever the reasons may be, you may on occasion find yourself defending changes to people you deal with. They may be other supervisors, staff personnel, suppliers, or anyone else. Naturally, if the criticism doesn't affect your ability to do your job, you can pretty much ignore the carping. However, if you detect resistance to a change that threatens to hinder job performance, you have to react. How effectively you do this will minimize any problems associated with the change that's taking place. Incidentally, the critics and criticism discussed here relate to people other than those you supervise. The reluctance of subordinates to accept anything new is dealt with elsewhere throughout this book, most notably in Chapter Three.

Educate Critics to Disarm Them

The easiest critic to convert will be someone who is opposing something new merely because of a lack of knowledge about the benefits to be realized. You must spend the time to educate the person about the advantages to be realized by implementing the new procedure or using the new technology. The good news here is that if you have a solid case in terms of facts and figures to support your position, you will probably overcome the objections.

The bad news is that you will probably spend more time doing so than would have been necessary had the person been thoroughly briefed prior to implementation. For this reason alone, it's worthwhile to be certain that anyone even remotely affected by anything new is thoroughly briefed about it before the fact. An even better argument for informing people is that you can convert potential critics beforehand. If the facts supporting the benefits of something new are thoroughly circulated it makes it much harder for potential critics to line up potential opposition. For no other reason than by virtue of having been ignored in discussions beforehand, some people will go out of their way to be critical after the fact. Co-opting this sort of critic is easy to do if you involve people in discussions prior to implementation of anything new.

A Strong Supporter Base Can Silence Criticism

Some critics can be silenced by top management support for new technology and/or procedures. Whenever another manager starts to criticize something new, let him or her know that "X" and "Y" are strong supporters. Most people aren't going to risk their careers bucking top management, so this is a sure-fire way to silence many opponents of anything new. Just be certain that you have the support you claim. Aside from top management support, you can also silence a faultfinder if someone with influence over the critic favors whatever is new over the old. Most typically this will be someone's boss. Consequently, if you know that someone opposes something, see if you can win his or her boss over to your side. If you are successful, it becomes extremely difficult for someone to be critical vocally in opposition to the boss.

Don't Let Critics Put You on the Defensive

Critics of anything new will use a two-pronged approach in their attacks. They will offer reasons why something won't work, and also bombard you with questions that you may not be able to answer. Be prepared to respond with facts and figures to show why doing something differently will work better. Don't be put on the defensive, however, since critics find it a lot easier to attack than to defend their own position. Ask questions that force critics to prove what they are saying. This can be very effective, since critics sometimes tend to use very shallow arguments to support a position that isn't very sound. You thus put critics on the defensive and the longer they have to spend defending what they say, the greater the chance of them looking foolish.

Incidentally, don't fake it if you can't answer a critic's question. You can make yourself look bad if your answer is ultimately proven wrong. It will also validate the critics' opposition. Instead, just say you don't have the answer. If it's something you can research, offer to look into the matter and get back with an answer. Whenever possible, take advantage of your "I don't know" answer to expand upon the virtues of whatever you are defending. For instance, say something such as, "I don't know about that, but there are over a dozen advantages to using the new technology. These include..." This gives you an opportunity to elaborate upon the benefits of whatever it is that's being challenged.

Last of all, demonstrate your enthusiasm for whatever it is you're defending. Communicate your thoughts positively and take advantage of every opportunity to elaborate upon the benefits of anything new introduced into your department. Being convinced about something doesn't do you any good with critics if your enthusiasm isn't apparent to them. You can't hope to convince anyone of the virtues of anything if you don't demonstrate your convictions.

BREAKING DOWN INTERNAL BARRIERS
THAT HAMPER TOP PERFORMANCE

Although it's not supposed to be that way, and even though top management might deny it, there are frequently a number of internal barriers that can serve as obstacles in getting your work done. These can range from internal competition for promotions, which can cause people to place their own interests ahead of the job, to individual bottlenecks such as procrastinators and indecisive people.

The modern workplace with its emphasis on teamwork and cooperation was supposed to eliminate practices such as empire-building and buck-passing which deter the kind of cooperation needed for maximum efficiency in the workplace. And although these practices may not be as prevalent today as they were in the past, there is still a long way to go before all of the non-cooperative obstacles are overcome. In fact, human nature being what it is, there will always be some barriers in existence which you have to learn to circumvent. Otherwise individuals, either through incompetence or in pursuit of personal agendas, will hold up progress on your most important projects.

Avoid Departmental Bickering

The first step in overcoming internal bottlenecks is to be aware of their existence. Sometimes you can fail to see that a less than cooperative atmosphere exists. For example, line managers may readily place the blame on the Human Resources department when less than satisfactory job candidates are brought in for interviews. On the other hand, the Human Resources people may grumble among themselves about the failure of line departments to properly identify the skills they are seeking to fill positions.

The same sort of cross-departmental conflict and misunderstanding can exist in any number of settings. Production and quality assurance is another area ripe for conflict as the former strives for quantity while the latter emphasizes quality. Sales and credit departments are yet another possibility, with sales people concentrating on selling, while the credit department wants to be sure people can pay for what they buy. This interdepartmental bickering is generally subdued and on the surface, at least, cooperation is satisfactory. But true cooperation may not exist, and when the opportunity arises, someone may impede the orderly flow of work for another department rather than look for a way to simplify getting the work out.

Despite such interdepartmental feuding, you can stay above the fray by concentrating on establishing good individual relationships with those people you work with in other departments. Once you get beyond the organizational bickering to the personal level, you separate yourself from the quarrel. This will help you get your work expedited while other supervisors may find themselves caught up in organizational politics.

To some degree you have probably experienced these problems in the past. If you have always tried to deal with people fairly, you may have noticed how much more successful you are than others in working with other departments. People who work at getting along with others are recognized as such and dealt with accordingly.

When departmental rivalries are strong, cooperative people tend to be singled out from their department. They tend to elicit comments such as, "Frank's the only one in Accounting that knows what he is doing," or "If everyone else in Sales was like Martha we wouldn't have all these credit problems to deal with." Basically, it boils down to being liked so you get your work done without the hassles other people face. How do you go about achieving this? All it really takes is a willingness to understand the problems that may exist from the viewpoint of the departments you deal with. Every group has its own set of particular difficulties in terms of its workload. Understanding these problems can keep you from making requests or unreasonable demands that make life difficult for another department. In addition, be willing to listen to the advice of people from other groups. They may not know much about your particular field of expertise, but they are well versed in their own area. So using their knowledge is not only directly beneficial, but it also gives you the indirect benefit of being viewed positively. And over the long haul, that gets your work done, while others fuss and fume about the lack of cooperation.

Use Finesse with Individual Bottlenecks

Various individual roadblocks can slow you down in accomplishing your work in a timely fashion. Some people are unintentional bottlenecks, while a few may be deliberate about what they are doing. Whatever the case, gaining their cooperation, or at least working around them, is essential to a timely completion of your tasks.

One of the most common barriers you can run into is an indecisive individual. These people aren't deliberately trying to hold up your work, but are trapped by their own inability to make a decision. What you have to do here is make it easy for them to make the necessary decision. For all intents and purposes you will be making the decision, but at the same time making it appear as if the bottleneck made the move.

How you do this requires discretion, since you don't want to appear to be forcing the decision upon the individual you're dealing with. For example, say something such as, "Of the four choices available, (a) is the only one that doesn't have any negatives attached. From my viewpoint that's the only choice that can avoid future problems. Does that make sense to you, Franklin?" The phrasing pretty much leaves the other individual little choice but to agree with you. That, in fact, is what you always want to try to do. If you can phrase the decision-making choice in such a way that it virtually requires a "yes" answer, you have pretty much guaranteed yourself a favorable response.

Another good tactic to encourage agreement by indecisive people is to imply that top management is in favor of what you're proposing. Of course, don't be foolish enough to try and wing it here if that isn't true. Otherwise, you may find yourself with more problems than you bargained for.

Deadlines provide another way to deal with indecision. Beware, however, that this approach can backfire since, if you're looking for approval of something, the indecisive individual may find it easier to reject what you're proposing. The situation can be complicated even further when a rejection is based on a lack of enough information to allow any decision-making. This can leave you with even more work to do, so don't try to paint someone into a deadline corner unless you can make it stick.

How best to deal with individual bottlenecks? Avoid them at all costs. This is especially true if otherwise you would have to deal with them on a regular basis. Try to find some other person who can substitute for direct contact with the bottleneck. Usually this will be someone else within the individual's department. If this tactic isn't feasible, then look for a way to accomplish what you want by eliminating the need to go to this person in the first place. Of course you will occasionally encounter one form of bottleneck or another. Use whatever means possible to keep it from slowing down the progress of your work, but even if you don't succeed, keep your cool. Losing your temper won't accomplish much other than making you look foolish. With some sadistic bottlenecks that may spell success, since that may have been their objective in the first place.

SEVERAL WAYS TO GET CLOSER TO YOUR CUSTOMERS

One of the attributes of the new workplace is a focus on customer service which, in part, means more cooperative behavior rather than age-old attitudes which sometimes amounted to a "take-it-or-leave-it" philosophy. Furthermore, the definition of a customer has been greatly broadened. You may have a supervisory position where your unit or department has a great deal of customer contact in the traditional sense; on the other hand, your job functions may require no customer contact in an external way.

No matter what your role is, however, if you broaden the definition of "customer" to mean the group or groups your department services, then most everyone has some form of constituency to call a "customer." It may be the next step in the production process, or even all of the company's employees if you supervise a department such as Human Resources. Whatever your particular situation, it's imperative that customers be serviced well. Although there are innumerable ways to work more closely with customers, which will vary to some extent with the nature of your work, several common measures work well in any situation. Let's look some of these and how you can apply them to improve customer relations.

Communicate with Your Customers

First of all, recognize that pleasing your customers isn't an easy task. They can be demanding and sometimes unreasonable. Accepting this as a fact makes it much easier to cope with the inevitable hassles that you may eventually confront. Perhaps the starting point in establishing a more cooperative relationship with customers is to learn to be a good listener. You have to know what the expectations of your customers are and you can't do this without listening to what they have to say. But at times you have to go beyond listening and actually ask your customers what you can do to better meet their needs. This is something that isn't often attempted, since it opens up the door for plenty of criticism, and most folks don't go looking for that.

Get Your Employees Involved in Customer Service Efforts

It's also crucial to get your employees involved in customer service. Unless your subordinates see its importance, they may well neglect it from unawareness more than anything else. This is particularly true if you supervise a unit which doesn't have customers in the traditional sense of the word. For example, if the output of your department is of a strictly internal nature, your employees may not recognize that they have customers. It's up to you to educate them continually to the fact that everyone they serve and deal with in the company is a customer. This is critical especially where the notion of serving customers is neither obvious nor ingrained in the corporate culture.

New Technology Can Cause Customer Complaints

Whenever new technology or equipment is introduced into the workplace, the inevitable glitches have to be ironed out before the benefits of its adoption can be realized. Sometimes this is a relatively quick and painless process, while on other occasions the problems may appear to be never-ending. Naturally, in these situations, every effort should be made to avoid any negative impact on customers.

Unfortunately, that goal can't always be met and sometimes mishaps of one kind or another have customers very unhappy. When this happens you have to make the effort to explain that new equipment is causing temporary problems. Apologize for any inconvenience and solicit their suggestions as to any errors resulting from the new equipment. Close cooperation with customers can provide valuable feedback.

By the way, you can minimize many customer problems of this nature by letting customers know beforehand that you will be updating technology or equipment in order to provide better service.

Furthermore, solicit any suggestions they might have on how changes can be made that they would like to see. Discussions of this nature can give customers a sense of being business partners and can do much to improve customer relationships. Incidentally, it's not just a major introduction of new technology that can cause these problems; it can be something as simple as shuffling responsibilities in an internal personnel realignment. Therefore, even minor aspects of doing something new should be viewed with the customer's viewpoint in mind.

Dealing with Problem Customers

One of the trickiest aspects of customer service you have to deal with is keeping unreasonable customers relatively happy even though you don't give in to their every whim. Some customers will push you to the limit and, although you might want to let them go, it's a lot easier to retain an old customer than to get a new one. Actually, in some situations where your customer is within the company—such as another department—you're stuck whether you like it or not. Therefore, for one reason or another it pays to try and work out the differences when you have problem customers.

How do you handle problem customers as opposed to customer problems? It depends upon the circumstances, but some practical steps include:

- Insist on fair treatment for both you and the customer. Let the customer know that you will be reasonable in trying to work out problems, but that you expect the customer to do the same for you.

- Be specific about what you will do for a customer in the future. By agreeing on what sort of performance the customer can expect from you beforehand, you avoid the hassle of later disagreements.

- Keep discussions on an unemotional level. It's very easy to get ticked-off when a customer makes excessive demands, but don't take it personally. A few will push you to the outer limits to see how many concessions you will make. If you have to say "no" to an unreasonable demand, do it without hostility. State why you can't meet the customer's demand, what you are willing to do, and do it in a firm but pleasant manner. That may, on occasion, seem to be the hardest part of dealing with problem customers.

USEFUL TACTICS TO GAIN COOPERATION FROM SUPPLIERS

Just as with customers, your job may not require you to deal directly with suppliers in the traditional sense. However, with the closer coordination and cooperation that's essential today for efficient operations, more corporate departments are working closely with outside suppliers. This is particularly true as companies outsource functions that were formerly performed in-house. So even though your present job doesn't require this type of contact, that situation could change in the future.

Insiders Are Also Your Suppliers

Internal departments and individuals that supply your group with necessary input on a continuing basis should be considered suppliers in every sense of the word. Look at it this way. Suppose another department furnishes parts to your group, but a decision is made to outsource that function to another company. Let's also assume that the new supplier hires the same people who formerly worked for your company to do the work. In other words, you're still having the same people supply the same parts; the major differences are that they have a different employer and your company now has a contractual relationship with a supplier for the parts.

Many people wouldn't think of the internal arrangement as that of a supplier/customer, while the outsourcing arrangement would fit their traditional definition. Yet apart from geographic location and contractual documentation, outside suppliers and internal suppliers both work to meet your needs. Therefore, it's of value to understand the measures necessary to maximize cooperation and understanding with supply sources whether they be external or internal. Let's look at how this can be achieved.

If there's one overriding reason for improving cooperation with suppliers, it's that they can screw things up royally if they don't perform the way you expect them to. For example, not supplying your needs on time can prevent your department from doing its job. To prevent such a disaster, as well as to foster a sound, on-going relationship, requires honesty, trust, and constant communication.

Communication Is the Key to Cooperation

The entire process starts with on-going communication, whether your suppliers are in-house or external, since without that you won't be able to develop attitudes of honesty and trust. Don't confine discussions to when problems arise, but instead establish an environment where you work closely together for continuous improvement of the relationship.

Incidentally, don't just look at things from your viewpoint, but also be willing to work toward resolving difficulties your supplier may be having. Be fair in your demands. It's all too easy to impose unreasonable demands on suppliers. Sometimes there's even an unintentional attempt to make a supplier the scapegoat when something goes wrong, for instance, when you blame the failure to meet a deadline on an inability of a supplier to meet requirements. Sometimes, of course, this is a valid excuse, but in other situations it's not always the supplier's fault, for instance, when you change requirements mid-stream.

In addition to being fair with suppliers, try to work with them in resolving their problems. Suppliers complain most about unreasonable demands which can take many forms, but no matter what the specifics are, discuss how to come up with a satisfactory solution that meets both of your needs. Frequently, this requires some sort of compromise and you should be willing to do your part to reach an agreement. Even on matters where a supplier is having a problem you can't help with, at least be willing to listen and be empathetic. It's the personal side of a business relationship that often spells the difference between success or failure.

The better you become at communicating with your suppliers, the easier it will be to build a relationship of honesty and trust. Unless both you and your suppliers are willing to level with one another, it becomes impossible to forge the kind of link that will allow for continuous improvement to consistently yield productive benefits for both parties. Do your utmost to not conceal matters from your suppliers and expect them to do the same with you.

Incidentally, it's easy to neglect the need for honesty, trust, and communication when you don't deal with outside suppliers. If your sources are internal, you can often assume they don't need the care and feeding that outside sources do. There's also the potential for internal competition in terms of promotions and allocation of resources. This can lead to corporate in-fighting which is both destructive and debilitating. Therefore, even if this is commonplace within your company, do your part to overcome these attitudes by working closely with the departments who serve your needs. All in all, whether your supplier is down the hall, down the road, or across an ocean, cooperation is essential.

HOW TO BUILD VENDOR RELATIONS THAT GUARANTEE RAPID RESPONSE

With companies continually searching for ways to gain an edge on the competition, the ability to get new products into the marketplace on a timely basis is imperative for corporate success. This means maximizing cooperation with suppliers as discussed in the previous section. But even beyond this, it requires a total change in philosophy to build long-term vendor relations that can guarantee rapid vendor response when you need it most.

Plan your needs and work closely with suppliers to achieve your goals. Incidentally, don't ignore doing this if you happen to supervise a unit where your suppliers provide services rather than products. It's easy to overlook vendor performance if you don't work in a manufacturing environment.

Wherever possible, simplify your requirements to make it easier for your suppliers to serve you. Sometimes you can devise your own ways of doing this; other times your suppliers may make suggestions that will make it easier for them to comply with your requirements. By the way, something that is relatively meaningless to you may be extremely burdensome to a supplier. For instance, perhaps you require some form of documentation, which actually serves little purpose for you, but is time-consuming for your vendor to prepare. Eliminating things of this nature can benefit both you and the vendor with no cost in terms of efficiency.

Incidentally, e-mail and electronic data interchange systems have eliminated much of the paperwork burden involved in dealing with vendors. Nevertheless, as technology continues to simplify things, it also requires equipment and training. You may find that some of your vendors lack the latest in equipment, and/or their employees aren't trained to use it. Whenever possible, encourage them to modernize and, if it's feasible, assist in training their employees. This isn't always as difficult as it might seem. For example, if your people are to be trained in a new software program for interacting with vendors, why not offer training to vendors you deal with on a regular basis?

Learn to Live with Just-in-Time Inventory Techniques

One of the hardest changes you may find yourself adapting to is operating with just-in-time (JIT) inventory techniques. JIT, as you know, is fundamentally the process used to provide exactly what you need when you need it. It essentially requires vendors to maintain inventories to meet your needs, and it further requires the vendor to assume the quality control function. The good old days when inventory levels were such that there were never worries about running out of components or materials is a thing of the past. Now it's necessary to plan requirements so that needed materials arrive in time to go into the production process. This, of course, isn't always easy to do. However, rather than resisting the process, the better approach is to learn how to adapt to JIT practices and make them work to your advantage. The assumption of these new roles by vendors requires a close working relationship. However, whether or not you work where JIT is used, good vendor relations will guarantee a rapid vendor response to your requests.

9 Dealing with the New Workplace From a Supervisory Perspective

The new and changing workplace that continues to evolve requires an adjustment in supervisory practices. From a broad perspective, the shift toward less bureaucracy and greater worker participation necessitates a different approach to getting the job done. However, as you know, if you have been doing things a certain way for a number of years, it's not easy to adopt new supervisory techniques. The following pages cover the many aspects of how to do this.

The first step toward supervising in a more democratic fashion is to spend some time thinking about your present methods of supervision and deciding what aspects might need a change in focus. Included are tips and tactics on how to be both a leader and mentor within the context of participative management. Not to be neglected in this regard is the need to encourage workers to become active participants in workplace decision-making.

There are, of course, a number of troublesome issues you have to contend with in the modern workplace. One of the most difficult is attempting to operate with limited resources. This requires you to work hard at keeping up morale, while also learning how to tactfully avoid being overloaded with work. Beyond this you also have to convince employees of the wisdom of new policies and procedures used to implement changes in the workplace. This is not an easy task, particularly when some of the changes may be unpopular with your workers. The topics in this chapter offer plenty of solid tips and techniques for accomplishing these tasks.

RETHINKING YOUR TRADITIONAL ROLE AS A BOSS

If you have been a supervisor for any length of time, you may be conditioned to supervise in an environment where you were little more than a conduit for directives issued by upper level managers. You received the directions and then implemented them within your department. There were no prior discussions of the pros and cons of how things would be done. Employees were essentially expected to do what they were told. This, of course, is the way management traditionally functioned.

Of course, there were exceptions to this rule and perhaps you worked in a more cooperative atmosphere. Despite common perceptions, not every workplace was modeled on a military structure of issuing orders and expecting them to be carried out; some were more democratic by virtue of the personalities of top management. Smaller companies also tended to be friendlier than their larger competitors. Nevertheless, whatever management style you used in the past, the accepted method today is to treat workers as team members engaged in a common undertaking. There's been a realization that no one knows better how to get work done than the people doing it.

Naturally, there's always a gap between what you read in the latest management treatises, advocating new methods of management, and the realities of the workplace. What this means is that, although some articles and books you read would have you believe that certain practices are the standard of the future, in actuality they are at best a passing fad. The truth is that even though the workplace may change, these changes will be gradual and nowhere near as revolutionary as some of the more radical recommendations of the crystal ball crowd. All of which is to say that the management changes that take place will be more a matter of style rather than structure.

Do Some Self-Evaluation

Dealing with a more participatory workplace where employees are encouraged to contribute their ideas is a fundamental reason why you should take some time to rethink your traditional role as a boss. This doesn't mean that you are doing it wrong, but only that you probably haven't taken the time to evaluate your supervisory practices. Therefore, it's worthwhile to make the effort to sit down and think through your role as a supervisor.

In doing this, it's helpful to ask yourself some questions about how you handle supervisory relationships with employees. For example:

Do you fly off the handle at employees if they question anything you say? Losing control of your emotions isn't good under any circumstances, but it's particularly devastating when you are trying to establish a working environment where employees are encouraged to communicate openly. If they are treated rudely when they ask questions, they will soon learn not to do so, and any attempt to establish good two-way communication will be defeated from the start.

Do you continually cut workers short when they are trying to tell you something? If you aren't willing to listen, workers will quickly assume that it's because you believe nothing they say is important. So you won't hear about problems in their early stages when it's possible to straighten them out without too much difficulty.

Do you actively solicit suggestions from employees? Workers aren't likely to make suggestions on how operations can be improved until they are secure in the knowledge that you believe in the soundness of their advice. Therefore, at the beginning you will have to take the initiative by openly soliciting suggestions. This requires a great deal of patience, since some of the suggestions you will receive won't be workable. Nonetheless, it doesn't pay to cut workers short when you are trying to open the lines of communication. Hear people out, and always take the time to explain why a suggestion can't be implemented. After all, the same person who is touting something foolish today may have a very useful suggestion to make sometime in the future. For this reason, you don't want to discourage people from offering their ideas to improve the workplace.

Do you encourage employees to make decisions on how they do their jobs? If employees are required to clear every detail with their boss, they won't take any independent action for fear of being criticized. Such a policy also conveys an attitude that employees aren't capable of making decisions on their own. Workers find this to be insulting. Furthermore, supervising in this fashion consumes a great deal of time spent on details which could have been delegated.

These are just a few of the questions you might want to think about in terms of your current supervisory techniques. It's admittedly not an easy task to be honest with yourself in this regard. Nevertheless, it's a necessary first step in deciding what adjustments you want to make better attuned to the supervisory techniques of the new workplace.

HOW TO ALTER YOUR "OLD SCHOOL" MANAGEMENT TECHNIQUES

Once you complete a self-assessment of your supervisory practices, you may discover that you tend to operate by the "old school" rules of issuing orders and neither wanting nor expecting employee feedback. Even short of pegging yourself as a full-blown advocate of drill sergeant tactics, you may feel there are a few things you can do better in the future. These adjustments may not be as easy to make as simply renouncing your past practices. After all, they are ingrained habits and habits are hard to break.

From another perspective, employees are used to reacting to your tried and true management style, so changing your supervisory techniques also has to take this into account. So you may find it better to implement gradually any changes in your style of supervision. In the same vein, you shouldn't get discouraged if you occasionally lapse into the old way of doing things.

Although they may not apply to you, it's useful to look at a few outmoded supervisory practices that may need to be adjusted.

The boss-subordinate affliction. Some bosses have an almost reflex action in dealing with direct reports. It conveys an attitude of superiority and aloofness which discourages employees from directly communicating with a boss unless it's unavoidable. Even then, employees are likely to contribute little to the discussion.

The "just do it" attitude. This old-style military approach leaves no room for questioning anything. Anyone who challenges such a supervisor will likely be subjected to an angry outburst.

The finger-pointing boss. This is a person who, when something goes wrong, immediately looks for someone to blame.

The benevolent benefactor. This is a boss, usually well liked, who treats his or her employees more like grandchildren than peers. But the failure to deal with employees on an equal footing can create resentment and behind-the-back comments such as, "What does he think I am, a dummy?"

None of these methods of supervision are conducive to encouraging the level of teamwork and cooperation from employees that the new and changing workplace demands. They all represent an attitude of superiority and a lack of real two-way communication. Your supervisory techniques are probably a lot more moderate than any of those listed, but your self-evaluation may lead you to make a number of minor adjustments.

In general terms, the foundation for becoming a better supervisor is to establish solid back-and-forth communication with your direct reports. Let them know you are open to their ideas, and show a genuine interest in them as people—as opposed to resources required to do the job. Getting employees to level with you about all aspects of their work will be a gradual process as employees learn over time that you genuinely mean what you say. Some specific tactics to encourage a better working relationship will help immeasurably.

1. Show a genuine interest in your direct reports. Take the time to engage in casual conversation unrelated to work. This isn't always easy to do in a busy workplace, but whenever possible take a few minutes to chat with workers on an individual basis. It helps to build a level of familiarity which makes it easier to establish a high degree of trust and lays the groundwork for teamwork and cooperation.

2. Be careful about correcting mistakes. You want to encourage people to accept greater responsibility, which means mistakes will be made as workers learn new tasks. If you are sharply critical when people make errors, they will become reluctant to take on additional duties. Always concentrate on the learning aspect when a mistake

is made. Focus on ways to prevent a repetition of the error, rather than on criticism of an employee.

3. Encourage workers to make decisions without consulting you on every minor matter. Learn to toss the decision back to the employee who comes to you asking for advice. Say something such as "What do you think?" or "What are your suggestions?" rather than routinely answering the question. Naturally you have to be selective in doing this, since employees will from time to time encounter situations which require a decision from you. For the most part, however, if it concerns some aspect of the employee's job, rather than an administrative matter, try to encourage some independent thinking.

4. Consistently discuss and encourage teamwork with your group. A good way to show your belief in teamwork is to solicit the group's thoughts on matters you are trying to resolve. If they see you have enough confidence in them to ask for their advice on something you are doing, then they will know you are sincere about working together as a team.

5. Express appreciation when you see employees working effectively as team members, or helping each other out with work-related problems. This helps to reinforce that the concepts of teamwork and cooperation are important to you. It also demonstrates to those you supervise that you recognize their efforts as team members.

ADJUSTING TO YOUR NEW ROLE IN A LESS BUREAUCRATIC ORGANIZATION

As companies continually look for ways to cut costs, the workplace will become less bureaucratic. There just isn't the luxury today of maintaining many former staff functions, and the layers of management will be trimmed. In many instances you may already have contended with these changes, but if not, it's a likely prospect your employer will thin out the ranks in the future.

A more flexible management structure will affect you in a number of ways. For one thing, you will likely have to assume additional duties. Chores formerly performed by middle managers will be thrust upon first-line supervisors. In fact, you may have already experienced this misfortune. In addition, employees will be more active participants in workplace decisions, which will be a bit unsettling if you are a person who likes to make your own. There are definitely a number of adjustments you will have to make in order to be more attuned to the role of a supervisor in a more flexible organization.

The first imperative as a supervisor in adapting to a workplace where teamwork and cooperation are emphasized is to put your role as a boss in perspective. Recognize that there will always be a role for supervisors even in the modern workplace. You can have all of the teams, committees, project groups, or whatever else you want to call them, but they won't replace the need for an ultimate decision-maker. Some people don't like to make decisions, others don't want the responsibility, and still others may not have the competence. Just envision the prospect of teams deciding who will lose their jobs if cutbacks are necessary. This and a lot of other distasteful functions you have to perform as a supervisor will still have to be done. Therefore, there will always be the need for supervisors to fill this void.

The most important key to adjusting to the new workplace with its emphasis on cooperation and employee participation is to be willing to exercise a great deal of patience. Learning to work closely with your employees to solve problems can be difficult. However, if you show even the slightest signs of impatience, the process can be even harder. This is so, since employees also have to adjust to the new flexibility of the organization, and without saying so directly they will be looking to you for clues.

The modern workplace requires that you be flexible in accepting new technology and procedures. Always try to stay on the front end of the learning curve whenever anything new is introduced. This not only will give you the skills you need from a career standpoint, but it also will provide you with the tools to teach the people who work within your group. Treat your training needs as continual rather than as a sporadic or occasional endeavor. In other words, you always want to be engaged in learning something. By doing this you will broaden your perspective and encourage your employees to do likewise.

Learn How to Let Go

Always be looking for new ideas and better ways to do every aspect of your job. As part of your efforts to promote teamwork and employee involvement in all aspects of the department's operations, train your people so everything functions smoothly when you're not there.

This is one adjustment that is harder for some supervisors to make than for others. A manager who has always freely delegated duties won't have much trouble in this area. On the other hand, a boss who has been reluctant to parcel out any responsibility to subordinates will have to work hard at learning to let go. With plenty of work to go around and fewer people to do it, it becomes almost imperative to share the work. Therefore, show some confidence in the abilities of those who work for you by assigning them greater responsibility. In the past supervisors used to complain to their bosses about a personal overload of work and receive some sympathy. Today the response is likely to be, "You shouldn't be doing that work anyway. Give it to your people to do."

Aside from practicing the virtues of delegating, learn how to plan your work to accomplish your duties without having everything back up on you. Prioritize everything in whatever way works best for you. It's also beneficial to encourage everyone within your group to do likewise. In this fashion, the important things will always be done by everyone within your group. It may turn out that the nonessential things never get done. That in itself is one of the windfalls of a less bureaucratic organization.

HOW TO MAKE WORKERS PARTNERS IN PARTICIPATIVE MANAGEMENT

A more difficult assignment that the new workplace thrusts upon you is the need to make workers partners in participative management. There is often a good deal of confusion here, with some people scoffing at the notion as one of "touchy-feely" management. This isn't the case, and it shouldn't be construed as such. What we are really talking about is instilling in workers the sense of being partners and associates in the work process. This sounds great and it wouldn't at first blush seem to present too much difficulty.

Unfortunately, like so many others things that aren't as easy to do as they appear to be, worker participation in decision-making also has its share of difficulties. Unless and until you overcome these problems, your department will never function as a closely-knit group working toward common goals.

First of all, let's define participative management in a way that you can relate to. It's getting the people who report to you to become participants in making decisions on how the work is done within your group. What you want is to encourage workers to suggest ways for improving how the work is done, ways to make tasks easier, and duties that can be eliminated. You want people to cooperate in a joint endeavor to make the department function smoothly. You also want workers to be willing to make work-related decisions without coming to you on every minor detail.

There are, of course, a few academics and consultants (one and the same in many instances) who preach that participative management goes beyond this to the point where worker teams run groups. They supposedly do this without a supervisor; where the impracticality of managing by committee is recognized, they use terms such as "team facilitator" or "team leader" to disguise the fact that there will always be a boss. These views tend to be unrealistic and ignore the realities of the workplace.

There is, and always has been, a place for the limited use of cross-functional and other forms of teams, but they are by no means as prevalent or efficient as their proponents would have you believe. From a practical standpoint, participative management is merely an extension of what some managers have always done, which is to encourage and promote teamwork within their groups. For this reason, it is more evolutionary than revolutionary, with the main contribution of the concept to be a wider recognition that teamwork works better than coercion.

What are some of the hassles you face and what can you do about them? One of the first problems you have to recognize is how diverse your group is in terms of welcoming participative management. Some employees will eagerly embrace the opportunity to accept more responsibility. Others won't want to budge from the old way of doing things. As surprising as it might seem, there are people who want to be told what to do, then do what they are told, and collect their paychecks at the end of the pay period. However, even before you attempt to cope with the reluctance of individuals within your group, you first have to lay the groundwork with your group as a whole. Essentially what you have to do is convince the group that soliciting their ideas on how things should be done isn't the latest in a long list of management fads.

Sincerity Sells

If you happen to work in an organization where top management has a history of jumping on and off the management fad bandwagon, then you may find your subordinates to be skeptical of participative management. This will even be true to a lesser degree in companies where teamwork and employee suggestions have traditionally been welcomed. The common arguments you may hear from employees will have the following themes:

"I'm not being paid to make decisions."
"This is another gimmick to cut jobs."
"I'm already overworked. I don't need additional burdens."
"Am I going to get more money for taking on greater responsibility?"
"Why waste my time? My suggestions never get acted upon."

What you have to do to overcome these arguments, along with other more general suspicions, is to prove your sincerity to the group. If you have traditionally been a straight-shooter in communicating with subordinates, then it won't be as difficult to convince them that their input is welcomed.

It will, of course, take longer to overcome the resistance of some members of your group, but don't let this discourage you. Listen to and implement ideas suggested by those people who are more willing to practice teamwork and joint problem-solving. Give these people greater responsibilities and encourage them to make decisions about their work without consulting you. Equally important, when mistakes are made, don't place blame. Instead, in a low-key way go about discussing what caused the error and what can be done to prevent repetition.

When employees see you are sincere about letting them assume greater responsibilities in doing their jobs, some of them will start to exercise greater independence. The more experience that people gain in taking on a greater role in determining how their work is done, the fewer the details you will have to get involved in on a day-to-day basis. Ultimately that should free up some of your time to concentrate on some of the other aspects of your job that have never gotten the attention they deserved.

Recognize Differences in Temperament

Once some members of your department start to work more independently, you will have more time to concentrate on those who don't show a great deal of interest in participative management. These people will be reluctant to either make decisions on their own, or offer suggestions on how their work can be simplified. What you are dealing with to a large degree are differences in personalities. Another aspect of the problem is that some of your more experienced people are conditioned to being told what to do about every aspect of their jobs. They are likely to be more hesitant to change their practices than newer employees who aren't as set in their ways.

Be alert to recognize these individual differences and don't try to force feed your ideas upon them. If a supervisor demands that an employee become an active supporter of participative management, that approach becomes self-defeating. In fact, this authoritarian approach is precisely what participative management is supposed to overcome. Rather than pressuring people, you have to slowly and subtly convince them to adopt a new way of doing things. With some it will take longer than with others, and some workers will carry the concept further than others. The important issue is to recognize the differences in both personalities and desires and operate on that basis.

Play to Individual Strengths

One good way to get some of your reluctant workers to become more active participants is to appeal to their strong points. For example, if a worker is particularly good at a certain skill, ask that person to train others. An employee who learns to relate to group endeavors by utilizing a skill he or she excels in may gain the confidence to become less of a loner.

By the same token, some workers may feel quite comfortable in discussing changes with you, but be quite unwilling to participate in group discussions. Whatever the particular trait may be, it isn't as significant as identifying individual strengths that can be used to encourage workers to participate more in determining the operations of the group. In the end, you will find that your efforts will succeed with most workers.

Despite this overall level of participation, however, the degree to which different workers approach the concept will vary greatly. If you think about it, that's quite appropriate when you're talking about a concept such as participative management, which is designed to give workers a greater voice in how their work is done. By definition it should also give them the freedom to decide how much of a voice they want. All of which is to say that you may still have a worker or two who wants you to decide everything they do right down to the last detail.

PRACTICAL WAYS TO OPERATE IN A "LEAN AND MEAN" ENVIRONMENT

If you're like most supervisors, you are probably in a position where it's a constant struggle to accomplish the workload with the resources available to you. You may be operating your department shorthanded, with no hope of additional help in the foreseeable future. You may also be constantly trying to upgrade outdated equipment and repeatedly hearing responses such as, "We can't afford it in this year's budget. Do the best you can with what you've got." When you hear comments such as these from senior management levels, it may be tough to keep from replying that you are being asked to do the near impossible.

There's little question that operating a department with scant resources and increasing workload is a real headache. Nevertheless, you must do it, so the important aspect to emphasize is getting the job done with what you have. This requires all of your energy, so there's little point in wasting time worrying about the difficulties that confront you.

Look for Easier Ways to Do the Work

There are several approaches you can take to stretch your department's resources to their limit. What you have to consider first is what is doable and what isn't. Examining the work processes within your department may reveal areas where you can take short cuts, eliminate unnecessary steps, and combine job elements. None of the measures you come up with may save a lot of time individually. But cumulatively the time-saving benefits can be substantial. The trick to squeezing the most out of what you have to work with is constantly searching for little ways to become more efficient. Some supervisors fail to recognize this, and as a result become extremely frustrated at not being able to manage a department that's stretched thin.

Avoid Gratuitous Work

One often overlooked way to trim your department's workload is to avoid unnecessary work. For example, if your boss is looking for a volunteer for a pet project, don't jump at the opportunity. If you're asked, give some type of reply such as, "That's a great idea, but I'm probably not the best choice for the project right now since I'm working on that rush order that top management is so interested in." In this manner, you display your enthusiasm for the idea, but indicate your other responsibilities make you ineligible for the assignment at the moment. Note that you must take yourself out of contention for the assignment, but you must still demonstrate your enthusiasm. Let's look at how this can be done:

Background Maureen, the section manager, approaches Shirley, a unit supervisor, with a pet project that Maureen has been mulling over for a couple of weeks.

The discussion

Maureen: "Shirley, did I mention the idea I had on reviewing our customer database to pinpoint customers who reorder at a certain dollar value? As you know, we keep track of repeat customers, but we don't distinguish between those who reorder $200 worth of merchandise and those who order $20,000 or more. If we had this information, we would know who our most profitable customers are. I know we have a rough feel for this now, but I don't think we actually have a list of the names and numbers. It's certainly something that's easy enough to do. It just requires a little bit of time massaging our database. I was wondering if you would be able to take this project on?"

Shirley: "It certainly sounds like that would be a really worthwhile project. I really appreciate you asking me since I'm always interested in doing something different. Unfortunately, I've got those two priority jobs to finish that I talked to you about last week. Therefore, if this is something you want done within the next four weeks, you would probably be better off giving it to someone else. Jean is very detailed and good with numbers so she might be a good candidate if you don't have someone else in mind."

Maureen: "Oh, that's right, Shirley. I forgot about those priority projects. How are they coming along?"

Shirley: "They're right on schedule, but I don't have any slack to spare, so I'm staying right on top of them."

Maureen: "Good for you. In the meantime, I'll talk to Jean about doing this job for me."

Comments

Notice how Shirley let it be known that she liked the boss's idea but didn't think it wise to take it on in conflict with her other work. She then went on to suggest someone for the assignment and also gave reasons for her choice. This made it easy for Maureen to agree. At the same time, Shirley reassured Maureen about being a team player and not someone who only thinks about her own self-interest. The trick to avoiding assignments is to do so in such a manner that it doesn't have a negative impact.

Eliminate Excess Requirements

Another form of unnecessary work is that which may be purely routine. A lot of unnecessary paperwork falls into this category. When you next receive a periodic report or similar document, take a moment to think if it has any real value in the operations of your department. If not, get yourself taken off the list to receive such documents. If it's a report your department generates, then eliminate it from your workload. Frequently, when companies had plenty of resources before they downsized, they generated all sorts of "nice to have" reports and documents. However, when companies slimmed down and reduced their work force, efforts weren't always made to trim nonessential work requirements. You may find now a few relics of the past to eliminate and make your job a little easier.

Farm It Out to Others

When companies slim down and reorganize there's often some confusion as to who does what. This is particularly true where jobs have been eliminated. After all, if the person doing the job is no longer there, who is to take on the workload of the departed employee? It pays to be aggressive in finding a home for this workload in someone else's department. Your ability to be creative in suggesting realignments of workload to your boss will benefit your own interests. Rest assured other supervisors will be equally interested in dumping work into your department.

Obviously, you can't be blatant about trying to dump work someplace else. Take the time to show how efficiency will result from any realignments you recommend. This can work in your favor with upper management, since some department heads will merely try to point the finger and show they have more work than someone else. For this reason, if your arguments are made in the interests of the overall welfare of the organization, you are the one who will be heard.

To be successful at this you may even want to suggest taking over some work currently being done by another group. This shows you're not solely interested in dumping work. Of course, be careful how you do this, since the net effect is to make certain your own department isn't swamped with work. In offering to assume any work currently done by other groups, look for what holds promise over the long-term (for example, new technology, new products the company has introduced, and so forth). The trick here is to position your department for both growth and survival down the road. In the scramble to position your department after one reorganization, it's smart to look toward the future in the event history should repeat itself. In this way, you will be able to maneuver your department into position for both the present and the future.

HOW TO BE A SUCCESSFUL MENTOR IN THE NEW MANAGEMENT ENVIRONMENT

With constantly evolving technology and frequent reorganizations affecting the workplace, employees can be expected to be confused and concerned about all of the changes taking place around them. Naturally enough, these changes present their own set of hassles for you as a supervisor. One of these is the need to concentrate on being a mentor for employees who are experiencing difficulty in making adjustments as change takes place within your department.

This can be a time-consuming task, but fortunately not every employee will need the same extent of guidance and counseling needed to keep them focused and productive. Some will readily accept changes while others, although not welcoming it, will muddle along doing their jobs without any negative impact on their performance. It's the one or two members of your group who always experience problems with anything new that will require your hands-on guidance.

Be Reassuring When Changes Take Place

One of the things that some workers miss most when rapid changes are taking place is a sense of stability. This is particularly true for workers who may have been doing the same job for a number of years. They have developed a routine in their work life which is almost second nature to them. It comes as a shock when they see this constancy disrupted by a reorganization, or when they are told they will have to learn to use some new form of technology. What you can do to help here is offer some form of reassurance that things will settle down in short order.

Sometimes your willingness to listen and spend some time with these people will help immeasurably. For them, you are one of the things that hasn't changed, which makes you their link to the past. Naturally, you can't spend large blocks of time trying to bolster the spirits of individual workers, and actually that isn't really necessary. Just taking a few minutes now and then to discuss how a worker is adjusting to the latest change should be sufficient. Furthermore, the initial shock of a substantial change wears off quickly with the passage of time.

Be a Technology Realist

With some employees one of the difficulties you will encounter is their technophobia. Many workers may initially experience reservations and hesitancy about new equipment and technology. Most of them, however, with the proper training will soon adjust. A few others may take an extended period of time to become proficient in using the new equipment, and one or two may seem to be beyond help. What you have to watch for here is not to have inflated expectations of how easy it should be for someone to learn the new technology.

This is particularly true if you happen to be technically proficient. You have to always keep in mind that some folks have trouble using a screwdriver, and one or two of them may be working for you. The point is that you shouldn't be impatient with those who don't learn as quickly as others. Given time and adequate training they will eventually acquire the knowledge necessary. In the interim, try to be as helpful as you can, which as a minimum means giving them a little reassurance that they will succeed in learning as long as they don't give up.

Although rare, you may sooner or later have a situation where an employee just can't seem to learn how to work with new technology or equipment that has been introduced within your department. This is most likely to happen where the technology is complex and math or other skills are necessary to use it properly. Several forms of training may have been tried to no avail. In these instances, you are left ultimately with little choice but to find another position for the individual, either within the department or somewhere else in the company. With rapid technological advances taking place throughout many industries, it becomes necessary for individuals to keep updating their skills. For your part, you should continually emphasize this point with your employees.

Be a Mentor of Change

To ease your workers through periods of change, one of the more meaningful factors is your own attitude. You are the boss and how receptive you are to a given change will be closely observed by your direct reports. If you openly oppose it, they can't be expected to happily embrace it. Even if you are more subtle, if they perceive you to be less than enthusiastic about something, then they will have their own reservations.

All of this doesn't mean you have to perfect the skills of a cheerleader. Nevertheless, the more enthusiasm you display, the more likely workers are to accept any given change. Don't fake it, though, since employees will see you as being insincere. When that happens their trust in you will quickly evaporate. If a change is initiated that you aren't enthusiastic about, accept it with a matter-of-fact attitude in the hope that it will work out as planned.

Talk to your people about their concerns and try to answer their questions. If you don't have the answers immediately available, try to find them. Most of the harder questions you can expect will involve issues such as job security. Whenever changes such as reorganizations or mergers are announced, employees start to worry about losing their jobs. From a historical viewpoint that isn't necessarily an unreasonable attitude, since these actions are often accompanied by layoffs. But on the other hand, there are mergers where expansion occurs and additional jobs are created. These, however, don't get the media play of the layoff situations, so workers are necessarily conditioned to associate certain management actions with layoffs. In any event, try to be as realistic as possible in answering employee concerns. Often you may not know much more than they do, but as long as you level with people you will have their respect.

TIMELY TACTICS TO KEEP MORALE UP

You may experience occasions when management actions—or even rumors—tend to lower the morale of your employees. Causes can be varied, with the most common arising from cutbacks in the work force that result in layoffs. In times like these it's necessary for you to keep morale as high as possible. Otherwise, not much work will get done as employees spend their time discussing the latest rumors. Of course, if layoffs directly affect your group, you have to deal with notifying individuals who will be let go. But beyond this, you will have a continuing problem in boosting the morale of the survivors.

Sometimes companies make it difficult for supervisors to do this by having round after round of layoffs. When this happens, employees are constantly on edge wondering when the ax will descend upon them. This could be avoided if companies had one-time cuts and were done with it. Unfortunately, this isn't always the case and you as the supervisor are stuck with a mammoth morale problem not of your making.

Beyond the really traumatic events such as layoffs which certainly affect morale, the general operating environment may also be a contributing factor. Poor working conditions, inadequate pay raises, a lack of communication between managers and employees, are just a few of the day-to-day difficulties that can do damage.

So even though you may be fortunate enough to work for a growing company where personnel cutbacks haven't been an issue, you can still have a morale problem to deal with. In fact, the growing pains associated with rapid expansion can cause a level of stress and confusion that in itself can affect morale. The fact is that employee morale is something you have to stay attuned to, and if it starts to deteriorate you have to take measures to counter it.

Alert Top Management to the Problem

One of the first actions to take when you become aware of a serious morale problem is to bring it to the attention of your boss. This isn't easy, since it's always difficult to bring any form of bad news to your boss, and particularly tough if the issue is employee morale. For one thing it's something that can't be quantified. Beyond that, in many instances actions taken by top management have brought about the problem.

Needless to say, it requires some degree of diplomacy to suggest to upper level managers that their policies are causing serious problems. But if morale sinks so low that it impacts the productivity of your department, you better let your boss know what's causing the problem. Otherwise you may find yourself on the spot when the boss wants to know why your output is declining. If at that point you bring up the morale issue, then a boss is likely to say, "Why didn't you tell me about this before?" In some instances, a boss may also decide that you are just using poor morale to cover up some failure on your own part.

On the other hand, if you go to the boss with this problem, you have to be prepared to state why you think morale is bad. This isn't always so easy to do, since employees aren't always willing to level about such issues. However, if you have good communication with your direct reports, then this shouldn't be a difficulty. Frequently, of course, the cause of a morale problem is obvious, such as when layoffs or other adverse actions that directly affect employees take place.

When you confront your boss over a morale problem, there are two fundamentals to consider. One is how you approach the subject matter, and the other is what, if any, recommendations you have for curing the problem. Never forget the cardinal rule that when you bring any problem to your boss, you had better bring along a solution. This is especially true in situations where a boss will have to go to higher levels of management with the problem. Top managers will look to your boss for a recommendation, which means that if you don't provide one, he or she will have to be creative and come up with one. This naturally isn't a course of conduct designed to make any boss very happy. Suffice it to say that when you bring an issue to your boss, have a solution ready or else a darn good explanation as to why you don't.

The approach you use in alerting your boss to low morale within your department will vary somewhat according to its cause. If there have been layoffs, or other actions such as a pay freeze, which are virtually guaranteed to impact upon morale, the obvious speaks for itself. All you have to do here is avoid being critical of any top management action that created the morale problem.

When you're asked what can be done about the morale problem, you usually won't have many alternatives to offer. For instance, if low morale follows a layoff, you certainly can't recommend that people be rehired. About all you can do is suggest tactfully that perhaps top management could issue some reassurance to surviving employees that their jobs are secure.

On many occasions, your boss may tell you not to worry, since with the passage of time morale will improve. This is a fairly common response to expect, since with layoffs and large scale reorganizations it's natural to expect morale to suffer. Your boss knows this and recognizes that there really isn't much to be done, especially if top management isn't likely to issue any forms of reassurance about the future. As a consequence, your boss doesn't want to take the problem up the ladder. Whatever the result, the crucial issue is that you let your superiors know about the problem. The main point of doing that is to protect yourself from being the scapegoat if the productivity of your department hits the skids.

Don't Ignore the Little Things

In addition to the major factors we have just discussed, sometimes less consequential events cause morale to fall. It may even be something that bothers one or two employees rather than the entire department. Fortunately, unlike morale problems resulting from layoffs and reorganizations, there are many aspects of morale you can do something positive about.

The most effective way for you to prevent these problems within the department is to respond promptly to employee complaints. You may not agree with every employee complaint, or even be able to resolve it, but you can listen, learn, and react. If you give workers a fair hearing and explain what you will or won't do, they will respond favorably. If your decision departs from what the employee is seeking, you should also give your reasons for taking such an approach.

Heavier Workloads Can Be a Source of Morale Problems

With the new and changing workplace, one where people are often assuming heavier workloads, there are other sources of morale problems: the overloading of people with work and the making of unreasonable demands. Admittedly it can become difficult to handle increased workloads with a stable or declining number of people under your direct supervision. This brings with it a burden not to place too much pressure on subordinates by assigning them more work than they can handle.

Avoid the trap of expecting everyone to be able to work at the same pace. Experience, skill levels, physical factors, and personality all come into play in determining individual capabilities. Your departmental hotshots may have output which far exceeds their laggard co-workers. Nevertheless, you shouldn't set performance standards based on a peak performer's output. Everyone can't work to that standard and it's foolhardy to expect it. It can also create a morale problem if you ask your best workers to pick up too much of the department's work overload. They also have their limits and, if pushed beyond them, are likely to take their talents elsewhere, which will only make a bad problem worse. It's not an easy issue to deal with when you have limited resources, but overloading your workers isn't the answer. If it causes morale to suffer, then productivity might actually drop, which is the opposite of your original intent in giving people additional work to do.

To keep morale as high as possible, you can't overlook the need to keep track of the rumor mill. Whenever you hear rumors that could contribute to lowering morale, get the facts out to your people. Otherwise rumors can get out of control and cause considerable worker concern. Beyond that they can waste a lot of time as employees gather around the water cooler for the latest rumor update. If this happens too frequently, the lost productivity may even cause your own morale to suffer a dip.

WHY YOU SHOULD SEEK OUT BAD NEWS FROM WORKERS

No one likes to hear bad news, and enough of it comes your way without your seeking it out. But if you aren't in the habit of looking for problems by actively soliciting bad news from your employees, then you are limiting your effectiveness. Furthermore, by ignoring bad news you may inadvertently contribute to even bigger problems in the future. On the other hand, if you continually seek out the minor problems that arise within your department, you may be able to prevent bigger debacles from developing.

Aside from preventing the escalation of minor mishaps into a major crisis, insisting on knowing about workplace difficulties cements open communications with those people who work in your unit. When employees realize that you want to know about bad news, their concerns are alleviated. After all, there's a great deal of reticence about being the bearer of bad news. So until workers recognize that you welcome knowing about the daily minor mishaps, they aren't likely to seek you out with this information.

Handle Problems Diplomatically or You'll Be Left in the Dark

Naturally, how you go about dealing with problems when you learn of them will largely influence how successful you are in gaining worker confidence in leveling with you. More than one boss has sat in meetings and said, "I want to know about it right away if you have any problems." What unfortunately happens in some instances is that these same bosses counter this advice by blowing their top at the first person who brings a problem to their office door. Obviously avoiding anger and criticism is a necessity if you really want to know what's going on within your group.

When problems are brought to you, deal with them to seek a solution, not to pin the blame. If a worker makes a mistake, keep in mind that occasional mistakes are inevitable. If they tend to be repetitive, then perhaps the worker needs some training. Alternatively, perhaps the worker isn't suited to the type of job he or she is performing. If that's the case, perhaps the job can be altered to make it doable, or maybe the worker can be reassigned. The important point is not to lose your temper. After all, it's highly unlikely someone will continually make mistakes on purpose. Concentrate on curing rather than complaining about the errors.

Make Employees Participants in Curing Problems

When an employee brings you bad news, always try to involve that employee in resolving the dilemma. After you listen to what he or she has to say, ask for suggestions on ways to cure the problem or prevent a repetition in the future. By making the employee a partner in coming up with a solution, you promote the sort of teamwork and cooperation you want to cultivate within your group.

When employees come to you with problems, let them know that it's a positive, not a negative action. For example, in some situations you may be able to reassure a worker that the problem isn't as bad as originally thought. Your reassurance serves dual purposes: it provides relief to the worker who may have thought the problem was of a much more serious nature, and it gives the worker greater confidence in being able to bring you bad news in the future.

Incidentally, the thought of employees bringing bad news to your office door may not have much appeal on the surface, but there are a number of practical benefits:

- prevents minor problems from becoming big ones
- allows remedial action such as providing additional training
- encourages employees to take risks without fear of criticism
- promotes cooperation with subordinates
- prevents unpleasant surprises because you weren't informed
- minimizes damage by allowing prompt action to prevent repetition

Always try to soften the blow for employees when they bring you problems. After all, it's not an easy thing to do, and no one likes being in the position of being the bearer of bad news. So it's not a bad idea to spend some time chatting about incidental matters once the worker has told you what the problem is, unless, of course, there's some basis for taking immediate action. Above all, avoid anger at all costs even if it's not directed at the person who brings you the bad news. An angry person makes anyone feel uneasy even if the anger is directed elsewhere. So keep your cool if you want the comments to keep coming.

FERTILE WAYS TO BE A LEADER IN THE NEW WORKPLACE

With teamwork and cooperation established as the standard in the new workplace, strong leadership skills are essential for effective supervision. This wasn't always so, since in the past workers were expected to follow orders with little or no discussion of their thoughts on the matter at hand. Now, as workers are recognized as valuable contributors to fundamental decisions about how the job is done, it's far more important to achieve some form of consensus within the group you supervise. Admittedly this isn't always possible, but that isn't the essential point. What matters most is that there are open discussions which allow employees to be heard, even though ultimately every employee suggestion can't and won't be implemented. After all, no matter how much teamwork and cooperation there is, the buck always has to stop somewhere. By the way, there is no requirement for overall agreement in every workplace decision.

The Buck Stops with You

You, as the supervisor, are ultimately responsible for the final decision, so you shouldn't sweat the teamwork angle so long as you genuinely encourage employee contributions to how the work is done. In fact, employees themselves don't necessarily want to be decision-makers. What they do want is to be part and parcel of any discussions involving changes in their jobs, and how their work is performed. Who makes the final decision is something most workers expect to be done by their boss. Furthermore, as long as workers are consulted, they will accept changes they may not agree with as long as they know they contributed their input to the decision-making process.

Of course, leadership in the modern work environment is essential to gain the respect and cooperation of the employees you supervise. In the past, leadership skills weren't as essential since in the extreme the policy was "Do as you're told, and don't ask any questions." This made life a lot simpler for supervisors, at least as far as communication with workers was involved. Of course, that didn't ensure the work was done right, and it certainly didn't encourage workers to be productive.

Establish Credibility with Your Employees

To be an effective leader of those you supervise in the new and ever-changing workplace, it's essential to earn those spurs by your daily actions in communicating with the members of your department. First you must establish credibility with employees. You can do this in varied ways, but basically you have to start by demonstrating that you genuinely seek the contributions of workers in how the work is performed. It's of no value to simply make pronouncements of how you want people to contribute their ideas if you habitually ignore what they tell you. It won't take long for workers to recognize that you're just giving the employee participation concept lip service.

Once that idea sets in, employees will quickly stop offering any advice and assistance on how the work should be done.

Of course, not every employee idea will be workable for any number of reasons. But at the very least you should hear out every suggestion in detail. Discuss the pros and cons with workers. If an idea isn't able to be implemented, explain why. When this is done properly, then workers are more willing to accept the ultimate choice than they would have been if no discussion was involved.

Keep Employees Informed

Everyone wants to be knowledgeable about matters that affect them directly, whether it's at work or in their personal lives. Yet traditionally there have been only nominal attempts to keep employees advised as to corporate actions that may inevitably impact how they do their jobs. Even where there are sound policies on paper in terms of employee communication, in practice employees are ignored when it comes to decision-making.

Whether it's the procurement of new equipment, the realignment of an assembly line, or the reorganization of workload, the decisions are often made at middle and upper management levels with little or no consultation with the people who actually do the work. On the other hand, employees are expected to contribute their ideas on how to do their jobs better. What this boils down to is that the individuals who best know the details of doing the work are kept out of the loop when decisions are being made to make changes that will impact how the work is done.

What does this have to do with leadership? If employees don't respect you they certainly won't trust you. Obviously employees aren't likely to respect a boss who keeps them in the dark about matters that affect their jobs. So without respect, there won't be trust, and without trust it's impossible to be an effective leader. Therefore, whatever the overall corporate policy is concerning effective employee communications, do your best to level with the people you supervise. As long as employees see that you are sincere in your efforts to keep them informed, you will have built a base for the respect and trust that form the foundation of effective leadership.

Know When to Step In—And When to Step Aside

Leadership in the modern workplace requires a balancing act between knowing when to assert yourself and when to step aside and let employees solve the problem without your guidance. Cooperation and teamwork succeed best when employees are empowered to take responsibility for their work and to participate in the decision-making process. However, you still need to maintain oversight and guidance to keep everything in focus. The trick is to do so in such a way that you won't seem to be still making all the decisions. Frankly, even when you still are, it may be beneficial to give it the appearance of a group decision. Naturally, that's not always possible, and if it's obviously your decision don't try to hide that fact.

The important detail is to involve your employees in the decision-making process concerning their jobs without relinquishing your management responsibilities. This requires you to balance management control against employee empowerment. It isn't as hard to accomplish as it sounds if you have good communication with your subordinates. Under those circumstances the general practice will be for employees to make basic decisions on doing their work. At the same time, if they hit a snag or aren't quite sure of what to do, they will consult you. In other words, leadership in the modern workplace doesn't mean "management by committee," nor does it mean the arbitrary direction by a boss that sometimes existed in the past. It really represents a balance somewhere between the two.

HOW TO MAINTAIN A POSITIVE ATTITUDE

Although you are all too well aware of the problems you face as a supervisor, let's just look at a few of the more common headaches most supervisors have to confront:

- A department that's understaffed
- Excessive workloads
- Tight budgets that don't provide any operating flexibility
- Outdated equipment that is always breaking down
- Low employee morale

- Inadequate provisions for employee training
- Upper level managers indifferent to your concerns
- Lack of cooperation from other departments and staff personnel
- Difficulty in getting satisfactory answers from your own boss

These are just a few of the general burdens most supervisors have to contend with, along with dozens of others that are specific to each particular situation. It's easy to understand how the broad scope of these problems can easily lead to a less than stellar attitude toward your job. However, adopting a sense of futility only serves to make matters worse. On the other hand, maintaining a positive attitude helps you place things in perspective and can make coping with problems a lot easier to do.

Have Open Discussions with Other Supervisors

A place to start in developing a positive attitude is to discuss problems with your peers. Most likely, other supervisors encounter the same difficulties. So, regular discussions over coffee could help you realize you're not alone in facing seemingly impossible workload demands. Don't be shy about asking other supervisors how to deal with specific situations. They may well have handled such a difficulty in the past and would be more than willing to discuss how they dealt with it. This is particularly useful in problems you may be having with employee discipline. It's sometimes easy to conclude that you have the world's worst employee working for you; but in conversation with other bosses you may learn they have had the same problem to contend with in the past.

NOTE: Although you want to be able to discuss problems openly, there are certain areas where you should observe extreme caution. One is not to be openly critical of your boss or other upper level managers. This sort of discourse can come back to haunt you if other supervisors have a close relationship with the people you are criticizing. The same also holds true if another supervisor knows one of your employees who is giving you difficulty. How much you can and should discuss will evolve around how well you know your peers. If it's not a close relationship where you know you can trust the other person, then confine your discussions to technical aspects of the work, and leave personalities out of it.

Get Control of Your Work Environment

Even though you may be overwhelmed with work, you don't have to appear that way. Just getting control of your work in terms of organizing it will give you a feeling of control. Straightening out your physical environment such as your desk and office will also help the situation. A few people are neatness freaks, but many others will tend to do the minimum to keep their lives in order. However, as workload starts to mount, there's less and less time spent in organizing and prioritizing. The end result is that people become even more pressured because paperwork gets misplaced, e-mail is ignored, schedules aren't kept, and nothing seems to get done. Taking the time to bring order out of chaos will accomplish a couple of things. First and foremost, it will allow you to prioritize your work so you can concentrate on what's essential. Even more importantly, it will give you a feeling of control over your workload which makes it seem far less threatening.

Balance Your Interests

Putting your work in the proper perspective can go a long way toward helping you maintain a positive attitude no matter how busy you may be. One of the pitfalls of many supervisors is working longer and longer hours to meet an increasing workload. This leads nowhere but to defeat, since your work can keep expanding; but the number of available hours is finite. It also causes other difficulties. It's much harder to seek relief from an overwhelming workload if you are managing to get the work done. After all, your boss may sympathize, but as long as you get the job done why should he or she worry about how many hours you work? He or she will far prefer not having the work back up. On the other hand, if you can't finish everything you have to do, sooner or later your pleas for help will have to be addressed.

You're far better off making sure you give yourself the personal time necessary to conduct some form of social life. If golf is your game, go for it. Whatever your interests may be, leave time to enjoy them. Over the long haul you will find that doing this helps you keep a positive outlook on life in general and work in particular.

As much as possible, avoid bringing your work home. This is increasingly difficult since, with computer and telecommunication networks, where you are doesn't always matter. Nevertheless, just because you have access to work doesn't mean you have to do it every moment of the day. Incidentally, even while you're at the office, don't neglect to take even short breaks to get away from the routine. If it's impossible to get any free time while you're in your office, take a walk even if it's to visit someone else on business in another part of the building. Any way you can, find a few free moments to enjoy thoughts of something other than the next problem you have to deal with.

STRATEGIES TO PROTECT YOUR OWN JOB IN A REORGANIZATION

As discussed elsewhere in this book, reorganizations within the business world are something that every supervisor is involved in at one time or another. Managing various internal aspects of a reorganization were covered in the Chapter One topic on overhauling an organization. Also, the opening topic in Chapter Eight discussed reorganizations in the context of customers and suppliers, as well as locating jobs for displaced workers. Here the focal point is on tactics to protect your own job if and when a reorganization takes place.

The practice of combining two groups under one supervisor is common enough, especially where the number of employees has been thinned out over time by attrition, or in extreme cases by layoffs. However, reorganizations can occur for any number of reasons, some of which don't seem to make sense, except perhaps for the person who redrew the blocks on an organization chart. They can range in scope from the realignment of a major business division to the sort of inconsequential juggling that ultimately turns out to be little more than a nuisance for anyone who has to deal with it.

Plan Now to Survive Later

Whatever the situation may be, you have to know how to survive reorganizations with your position intact. Being successful at this is an on-going process, since it's the groundwork you do ahead of time that is most likely to protect you if and when a reorganization takes place. One of the best ways to plan ahead is to take some time and think about the reorganization possibilities that might exist. Of course, you will never be able to conceive of all the novel notions that some managers charged with reorganization can dream up. For the most part, however, you should be able to identify any obvious changes that could be made. There are a number of questions to ask yourself to assist in doing this.

From a work standpoint what groups could be combined? Technology and streamlined procedures can combine to increase productivity in many areas. As a result, greater output is possible with fewer people. Perhaps this has happened within your company, but even though the number of people in your department has decreased, there's been no action taken to combine similar groups. The reasoning for this may well be that top management just hasn't taken that step yet. Perhaps they are waiting to get the kinks ironed out from the transition to new technology, or waiting to see how new working procedures will pan out. If it is apparent that two or more groups could be combined under one supervisor, then you ought to take whatever steps you can to make sure that person is you.

Are some departments currently understaffed? In the competitive environment that exists in the business world today, a quick answer here would be that every department is understaffed. However, what you're looking for here isn't the obvious. What you want to watch for are departments where essential positions aren't being filled. Under these conditions, jobs are left vacant until the point where a department can no longer function as a separate entity. At that point, it gets absorbed into another group.

This situation can occur when a company decides that, rather than lay people off, it will cut the payroll through attrition. Needless to say, when this happens there's inevitably an excess supervisor. You might think that since it's not your group where this is taking place, there isn't any need for worry. But who's to say that the supervisor of the group that's ultimately abolished won't be placed in charge of a combined department which includes your group? Perhaps not, but it's certainly something to keep in the back of your mind.

Have you noticed that one or more groups seem to be receiving second-class treatment? This can be very revealing, since a management that is planning a future organizational change may subtly signal this in a variety of ways. If a supervisor's requests for resources are regularly turned down by a boss, while a peer's requests are frequently honored, it might be because the group is going to be realigned in the near future. Needless to say, if your own department is the victim of this sort of treatment, you may be in real trouble.

On the other hand, don't become paranoid about your own group when you do this kind of an assessment. Isolated management actions can be easily misinterpreted as preferential treatment for certain groups at the expense of others. It may even be true, but it doesn't necessarily follow that because of this your group is going to be abolished. For example, your immediate boss may favor another supervisor who plays golf with him on the weekends. That fact, in isolation, doesn't mean your group will soon be combined with the favorite's group.

It doesn't even necessarily mean the favorite will survive while you're out of a job if a forthcoming reorganization combines the groups. Why not? Perhaps your boss has little or no political power within the company. It could well be that this manager isn't either liked or respected by top management. This could mean that perhaps both he and his golfing partner are prime candidates for dismissal if and when a reorganization takes place. With this scenario, contrary to the assumption that being this manager's friend and golfing partner will give someone's career a boost, it could actually be a liability.

Is there unusual management interest in your department? One factor that should arouse your suspicions about the potential for being reorganized out of a job is if an otherwise hands-off boss and others start to display an unusual interest in the details of how your department functions. This is especially true if this goes hand-in-hand with rumblings in the rumor mill about reorganizations and layoffs. The more facts that dovetail to confirm your suspicions, the greater the possibility that something is afoot.

Are you being left out of the information loop? It's easy to take comfort in the hope that whatever changes take place perhaps your own job won't be affected. That's an assumption at best and outward indications can detect signals that may indicate the opposite is true. For example, if you notice a difference in the way your boss treats you, this could mean you're on the firing line. Perhaps you notice a certain hesitancy about getting involved in talking about a reorganization that's the subject of scuttlebutt throughout the company. It may even be that you suddenly notice other managers avoiding you. These actions don't have to be blatant, but could be rather subtle.

Don't overdo it in drawing conclusions from these actions or any others. The key point is that you want to think about the possibilities that could develop in the future that may affect your job. Only by doing that will you be able to position yourself to survive a reorganization. Awareness of the potential for being reorganized is only one aspect of protecting your job in a reorganization. In fact, the groundwork to protect your job should be done long before any reorganization takes place.

The blocks on the organization chart and who will fill them are completed early on, and making sure your name is in one of them requires much preparatory work. Obviously, your skills and experience will weigh most heavily. However, rather than rely on those alone, there are other measures you can take to position yourself for survival.

Play Politics

Don't overlook the political angle. Do your best to be thought of favorably by those in a position to help you, should a reorganization take place. This goes beyond your immediate boss to senior managers who will hold the key to the final decisions when a reorganization takes place. Always go out of your way to satisfy work requests made by senior managers. This seems to be obvious, but there are times when it's busy and a senior manager may make an unreasonable request. It's easy to give it short shrift just to get the person out of the way. You may have little interest in wasting valuable time on some inconsequential work for a senior staffer who has no line responsibility. Ultimately, this person may wield significant power over personnel decisions for a pending reorganization. Give every request from anyone with potential power over your destiny the greatest respect. Although you may have little day-to-day interaction, if you have responded well in work situations, upper management will know who you are when it counts.

Be a Technology Booster

Technology will continue to play an increasing role in the operations of almost any business endeavor. Some people tend to resist it while others welcome it with open arms. Still others adopt a wait-and-see attitude as to whether something will be helpful or just a lot of hoopla. If you are technology resistant, then you better change your ways. When decisions are made about whom to keep and whom to jettison the next time the business is realigned, anyone who is a technology dinosaur is destined to be dumped. What a business will increasingly want are supervisors who are advocates of technology and can convey this attitude to those they supervise. Those who don't keep up with the latest in technology will be seen as liabilities in the race to outpace the competition.

Show Flexibility

You have a better chance of surviving a reorganization if you display a great deal of flexibility both in working with technology as well as with different groups of people. Some supervisors concentrate exclusively on their own department and the functions it performs. Yet the workplace is increasingly one where cross-functional teams operate and other cooperative endeavors take place. In a reorganization, a company will look to retain those supervisors who can best operate within the modern mold. You should try to demonstrate your flexibility on a day-to-day basis by willingly accepting new responsibilities and cooperating closely with everyone you interact with.

TACTFUL WAYS TO SAY "NO" WHEN YOUR BOSS TRIES TO OVERLOAD YOU

There's one change that the modern workplace practically guarantees you will have to cope with, and that is a heavier workload. That's probably no surprise to you as you struggle to keep pace with the daily demands of the job. To some extent at least, there are measures you can take as your workload increases to help relieve the pressure. But beyond a certain point, you will inevitably find that there are no more short cuts or efficiency moves to help you manage the burden.

Naturally, in theory at least, your boss should recognize the outer limits of how much work you can handle and should ease up on passing the chores along. Unfortunately, that isn't necessarily so, and your only salvation is to let the boss know you have more work than you can handle. This is always a tricky proposition, and with some bosses is a task that requires a great deal of valor. Nevertheless, at some point you will have to communicate that you can't handle any more work. It may seem difficult, and it's easy to worry about the ramifications of such an action. But keep in the back of your mind that human nature tends to follow the path of least resistance. If you accept additional work without protest, it's only natural for your boss to think you're capable of handling it.

You also have to remember that if other supervisors have already protested that they have too much work, you are then stuck with absorbing an unfair share of the additional workload. Therefore, despite all the misgivings you may have, there can come a time when you have to send a signal that you're overloaded. The trick is in doing it in ways that don't alienate or anger your boss. Let's look at a few possibilities:

Suggest that you're nearing your limit. Say something such as, "I'll squeeze this into the production schedule, but I don't think we'll be able to add anything more this month." Since you are accepting the additional work, your boss isn't likely to be critical of this statement. At most, he or she may ask what you mean by your comment. If so, this will give you an opportunity to explain how much work you already have, and why additional assignments will overburden the unit.

Document your dilemma. It's one thing to state you are overworked, but it's far more effective to be able to prove it. A boss may not place too much credence in your conversational claims of having a department that's overloaded with work. Sometimes it's assumed to be a little puffery and self-promotion by a supervisor. On other occasions, it may just be that your boss isn't a good listener, which isn't unusual when the subject is a complaint about overwork. To be far more convincing, you should document the excessive level of the workload. If it's feasible, show comparative figures for past periods and how the workload has increased without a corresponding increase in employees.

What is really impressive is to have figures showing comparable workload for units performing similar duties within the company. However, comparing with other groups should be done subtly without making overt statements. Furthermore, it's preferable if figures used to support these claims have been calculated by a department other than your own, such as accounting or production control. That way, there's no inference of built-in bias and the figures have a lot more credibility.

Give your boss alternatives. You may be able to offer your boss a creative alternative to assigning additional work to your group. What this might be will vary with the specifics of the work. It could be something such as combining the assignment with a similar one which would make it easier to do. Naturally, the similar job you're thinking about is being done by another department. Another approach may be creative rescheduling of delivery dates on the new assignment or other work. Whatever the alternatives may be, the important point is to explore all the possibilities before you resignedly add to your workload.

NOTE: Refer to the additional discussion on fending off work when your department is overloaded in the section in Chapter Five on preventing worker burnout.

Make your boss the decision-maker on additional work. Of course, no matter how much work your department has, there's nothing to prevent your boss from giving you an additional assignment. You can and should argue your case as persuasively as possible. You can't, however, simply refuse to take it. There will be times when, no matter how good a job you do at convincing your boss that your department is overburdened, you will still get the additional work. When this happens a boss will typically make some explanatory statement such as:

Everyone is overworked. "I understand your situation, but everyone else is overloaded too. You'll just have to do the best you can." (Interpretation: I have to give this to someone, and I'm here so you're it.)

Offering future hope. "Work on this assignment, and I'll give the next few that come along to someone else." (Interpretation: If you mention this in the future, I'll just deny it.)

Help is on the way. "I know you're overloaded with work, but I've put in a requisition for two more people for your group. We should get approval shortly." (Interpretation: Don't hold your breath while you're waiting for additional help.)

Even though a boss may be sympathetic to your predicament there may be little or nothing in the way of alternatives. So you may be stuck with more work than your group can handle. When this happens, make certain this is documented, since inevitably in these situations delivery dates and other deadlines are missed. As a result, everyone starts looking for a scapegoat and unless you have a stalwart boss who supports his or her supervisors, he or she may be quite willing to let you take the rap. However, if you can prove that you did everything you could to communicate about your overload of work, then you're off the hook.

SELLING NEW POLICIES AND PROCEDURES DICTATED BY TOP MANAGEMENT

As companies strive continually to improve their competitive position, new policies and procedures will be introduced to the workplace on a regular basis. Many of these will be designed to make it somehow more productive. However, since changes are not always welcomed with open arms, employee resistance to and resentment of some of these policies are inevitable. Even when workers don't openly object to a new procedure they don't agree with, they may silently resent the change and subtly work to undermine its effectiveness.

Unfortunately you, as the supervisor, are caught in the middle of these situations. It's your job to implement new policies and procedures at the working level. On the other hand, this presents problems when employees don't like the changes. Furthermore, you may not even like them yourself, but implement them you must—unless of course you can present highly compelling reasons why the procedures shouldn't be put in place. This isn't likely, so for the most part you may find yourself with a selling job trying to convince workers of the value of these changes.

There are a number of approaches you can take to convince otherwise reluctant workers of the value of a new policy or procedure. Sometimes you can make your case by simply taking the time to communicate the reason for the change. This is especially true where changes are sent down through the management pipeline with little or no prior knowledge on the part of lower level managers. In fact, in many instances you may find it necessary to talk with higher level managers to learn the whys and wherefores of a new procedure before you can go about explaining it to your employees.

With a bit of communication many workers will gradually accept most changes in the form of new policies and procedures. You may have a few diehards that seemingly find any and every change to be objectionable; that is to be expected. Even most of these people, with the passage of time, will fall into line. On occasion, however, you may have a new policy or procedure that causes some form of difficulty or inconvenience for one or more of your employees. These constitute the tough sell and to be successful you have to find an angle that is convincing. What that is will depend primarily on the change and the individual circumstances of your situation. Let's look at one such difficult situation that a supervisor had to face:

Background Jane was the supervisor of fifteen people in the Customer Service department of a telecommunications firm. The company had recently issued a new procedure whereby the department would work expanded hours. This meant that the employees within the department would have staggered work schedules, with different starting and ending times. Five employees would work from 7:00 A.M. to 3:00 P.M., five others would work from 9:00 A.M. to 5:00 P.M., and the last five would cover the 11:00 A.M. to 7:00 P.M. shift.

Jane held a meeting with her people to discuss the new scheduling which would take effect in two weeks. There was a considerable amount of grumbling when Jane announced what was going to happen. She explained that one of the measures being adopted was to improve customer service and asked for suggestions on the best way to handle the scheduling.

After considerable discussion, it boiled down to two choices. One was to have everyone alternate week by week, while the other was to permanently assign people to specific times. Most of the employees didn't like changing their working hours every week. Many had personal commitments such as child care arrangements which would cause problems. Therefore, the consensus was that everyone should work a set schedule, although from the discussion it was obvious that at least a couple of people were unhappy with working anything other than their present 9:00 A.M. to 5:00 P.M. schedule.

Employees were allowed to select their preferred shift in order of seniority. They each wrote down their three choices in descending order of preference. Jane collected these and the next day went over them to start setting up a schedule. As it turned out, more people than Jane had expected listed the earliest and latest shift as their top priority. After making assignments according to the preference sheets, Jane held another meeting with her department and handed out the assignments. She suggested that anyone who had a major problem should see her privately. Shortly thereafter, Erika asked to talk with Jane about the schedule.

One-on-one encounter

Jane: "What seems to be the problem, Erica?"

Erica: "It's the new working hours. I'm assigned to work 11:00 A.M. to 7:00 P.M. and there's no way I can do that. I take my two kids to school every morning and pick them up at the after-school day care center. They are eight and nine years old so there's no way they can get to school or home by themselves."

Jane: Don't mind me, Erica, if I say something that's foolish. I'm just thinking out loud to see what we can come up with. For instance, can they take the school bus one or both ways, or do you have a neighbor or friend who could transport them?"

Erica: "They attend a private school so there's no bus. Even if there was, I couldn't let them stay at home by themselves. I know there's no one else in my neighborhood that sends their kids to the same school as mine. I just don't have any alternative. If I have to work 11:00 A.M. to 7:00 P.M. I'll have to resign."

Jane: "I really don't want to lose you, Erica, but it would be unfair of me to ask someone else to change shift since it was based upon seniority. Give me a day or two to see if I can come up with something. I'll get back to you no later than Monday, alright?"

Erica: "OK."

Resolution

Jane meets with her boss, explains that the new work schedules have been assigned, and states that despite some grumbling, with one exception, everything has been worked out. She then states that she would like to have some flexibility in terms of scheduling for a couple of reasons. First of all, depending upon the amount of customer demand during the various time periods, she would like to be able to adjust the number of people working any particular shift. This would maximize customer service which is the purpose of having the additional hours of coverage in the first place. Second, it would also give her some flexibility in juggling assignments to accommodate the needs of her people. Her boss readily agrees and, with this change in procedures authorized, Jane calls Erica into her office.

Jane: "For the near term, Erica, I'm going to keep you on the 9:00 A.M. to 5:00 P.M. shift. It's not definite at this time how many people we will need in that time slot, but at least for the immediate future that may be when the bulk of our business is, since that's what our customers are presently accustomed to."

Erica: "I really appreciate that, Jane. Is this a permanent assignment?"

Jane: "Not really, since right now it's impossible to anticipate our needs on the various shifts. My gut feeling is that we will only need minimum coverage on the early shift, with most people working the 9-5 and 11-7 shifts, but we'll have to wait and see. In any event, don't you worry about it. I'll do everything I can to accommodate your needs."

Jane then holds another group meeting, tells everyone that the assignment they now have will be their basic assignment, but that some adjustment may be required down the road if circumstances so warrant. She also states that if anyone wants to swap shifts on a temporary basis, it's fine with her as long as she receives prior notice.

Comments

There are several valuable pointers in this example as to how best to handle new procedures. First of all, notice how Jane involved her employees in deciding how the schedules would be handled. The employees decided, of course, to work the same hours all the time rather than alternating shifts. They also participated in deciding seniority was the fair way to allow a choice of shifts.

Unfortunately, there was no prior involvement of either Jane or her group in any discussions with upper management before the new working procedure was implemented. This wasn't the best way for top management to handle this. Giving people more than two weeks notice before the new schedule went into effect might also have been better. Nevertheless, despite top management's failings, Jane refrained from criticizing the top brass in front of her department. She also took a positive tack and got her people involved in working out the scheduling.

Something else to remember is that Jane didn't tell anyone to see her if there were problems until after she had given out the assignments. Certain management actions that impact employees are guaranteed to upset some, if not all, employees. In these instances, although you want to be as accommodating as possible, you don't want to be bogged down by a lot of bickering. For this reason, if it's feasible, implement the decisions and then give people the opportunity to complain.

There's a very practical reason for doing this, which is that people are far less likely to protest a done deal. Most people see it as impossible to make changes in anything that's already been done, whereas they will argue forever about something beforehand. This isn't to say that employees shouldn't be involved in discussing how the work should be done. But at some point after that is accomplished, decisions have to be made and implemented. You can't discuss things forever, and in some situations that would be precisely what would happen.

Another point to keep in mind is not to make gratuitous offers before you have to. For example, Jane waited until she had only Erica to contend with. If at the initial meeting Jane had offered everyone an opportunity to work the shift they wanted, she would still be trying to work out a schedule. It's one thing for a supervisor to accommodate real problems, such as Erica had with her children, but it is impossible to satisfy the personal wishes of every employee in the unit. You have to be flexible, but you also have to know when to help out and when to hold the line.

Last of all, notice how Jane offered employees the opportunity to swap shifts from time to time with prior approval. Giving employees this sort of flexibility is an approach that works well in selling new policies and procedures. Whenever you hold out the promise of some benefit to the employee, no matter how remote it may be, there's a lot better chance of employee acceptance.

PRUDENT WAYS TO SEEK SUPPORT FOR UNPOPULAR POLICIES

As discussed earlier, selling new policies and procedures to employees is never an easy job. It's especially troublesome when a given policy is unpopular with employees. Sometimes, of course, as was demonstrated, you can overcome initial employee reluctance by pointing out the advantages of a new policy. In some cases, however, its benefits may inure completely to the company and in reality be a distinct disadvantage to workers. These types of policies and procedures arouse opposition that goes beyond the natural resistance to anything new. Here the emphasis is on what to do when workers have an out-and-out distaste for a policy which they find is detrimental.

You, of course, would like to muster support for the policy. Otherwise you could be facing morale and productivity problems within your unit. Here, though, you have to be practical and not try to oversell something you don't believe in yourself. Look for prudent ways to rally support to your side from your employees. Although in any specific situation you may be able to come up with a key selling point, here are some more generic ways to seek support.

The Old College Try

When you face a lot of frustration over an unpopular policy change, sometimes the best way to deal with it is some variation of "Let's give it a try." Many times you can rightly argue that until the policy has been in force for a period of time there's no real way to assess its impact. As a matter of fact, employees often take exception to a new policy even though it won't have any negative impact on them.

For instance, Joe B., a ten-year employee, starts ranting and raving about a new policy that will prohibit carrying vacation time over from one year to the next. Ironically, a check of the records shows that in ten years Joe B. has never carried as much as a day of vacation from one year to the next. You could argue that he is planning otherwise for the future, but the more likely answer is that Joe B. just likes to gripe. Every group has a griper or two and the introduction of a new policy or procedure is just the thing to get them going. Given the likelihood that no new policy will be anywhere near as disastrous as employees perceive, counseling patience will let the anger fade away with time.

Let's Not Worry Since the Policy Is Sure to Change

One approach to take with an unpopular policy is to convince your people that it is quite likely to be modified once the problems involved in implementing it are realized. Sometimes a new policy may come down from above that you know is doomed to fail from the start. In such a situation the best approach is often to sit tight until it is revised.

The alternative, of course, is to do battle to get the policy changed. This isn't always the wisest course of action for a couple of reasons. First of all, the policy was conceived somewhere in higher management so there are very real career risks involved in sticking your neck out. If a policy is really a bad one, it will become evident, so why burn up your good will in fighting a battle you don't have to fight? From another angle, if you get all fired up about the policy, this will inspire your subordinates to follow your lead. This doesn't make you look good as a manager, and it probably won't do much for the productivity of your group.

Divide and Conquer

Opposition to unpopular policies is usually most vehement among one or two people within a group. Most workers tend to accept changes from on high with varying degrees of reluctance, perhaps accompanied by a little profanity and a few choice words about the intelligence levels of those running the company. In all, the people you have to convert are relatively few.

One good way to get these people on your side is to convert them to your cause one by one. Once you can convince a ring leader to see things your way, then everyone else will quickly swing into line. To accomplish this goal, solicit the input of the individual you're trying to win over. The policy may have already come down, but that doesn't mean it won't eventually be modified.

Ask for the dissenter's ideas as to what could be done to make the policy a better one. Give assurance that you will consider the suggestions when you forward your own ideas on changing the policy. Of course, you may not be preparing any position on the policy, but the dissenter will never know that anyway. In fact, not forwarding nonsensical suggestions from a worker may help keep the individual employed. As you know, some comments employees make about top management aren't of the type that contribute to job security!

Soften the Blow of the Policy

No matter how burdensome a new policy or procedure may be, there are always ways to soften the blow. Most policies are written loosely enough so you can find all sorts of loopholes to justify whatever it is you want to do. If a provision isn't specific, interpret it the way you see fit rather than asking for an interpretation. Once you've been doing something in a certain fashion it's less likely you'll be challenged. Even if you are, you can point to the fact that you made a reasonable interpretation of what you thought the policy to be.

Policies are also usually broad enough so that you can adjust them to make them more palatable to your employees. What about all of the detailed procedures somebody might dream up to provide guidance on how to implement a policy? You have probably seen enough of those to know that the more detailed the procedure, the harder it is to understand. If that is the case, it is easier to make your own interpretation.

The bottom line when it comes to winning support for unpopular policies is to do the best you can. It's neither an easy nor pleasant chore when you have to try and defend something with which you don't agree yourself. So do the best you can, but keep in mind that you can't win them all. Whatever you do, don't take it personally when your subordinates react unfavorably to a particular policy change. Remember, their anger is directed toward the policy—not you.

10
Reaping the Benefits of the New Workplace

Although the continually evolving workplace presents many challenges, its potential gains are many both in terms of efficiency and employee involvement. One of your supervisory tasks is to provide the leadership that yields the maximum benefits from the new technology and changes in management practices. To do this successfully it's important to look for ways to continually improve day-to-day operating practices.

Many ways to improve operations on a daily basis are discussed in this chapter. These include changing routines and encouraging small ideas rather than looking for the "big fix." Of course, implementing ideas—large or small—requires a selling job. You, as a supervisor, need to have a two-pronged approach: on the one hand, you have to learn how to sell the benefits of the new workplace to those you supervise, while on the other hand you must convince upper management of the wisdom of implementing new ideas. Plenty of tips for doing both are given in the pages that follow.

STRATEGIES FOR CONTINUOUS IMPROVEMENT IN DAILY OPERATIONS

All too often, top management adopts the latest in trendy quick fixes which will supposedly cure everything from poor quality to low levels of employee morale. As a supervisor, you have probably had more than your fair share of these buzzword strategies foisted upon you. What usually happens is that there's much initial fanfare and top management enthusiasm when these new techniques are introduced. Then, top management transfers its interest to other matters, and the allegedly sure-fire solutions fade away after proving they didn't do much of anything except fatten some consultant's bank balance.

Despite all of the hoopla surrounding these canned cures for what ails a company, it's the gradual day-by-day implementation of minor changes that over the long haul improve the productivity and efficiency of any organization. These sorts of improvements in operations are made at the working level, by the people who actually perform the work. Therefore, ignore the ballyhoo from above; improvements in the operation of your own department will for the most part be those that you and your employees implement.

Make Improvements Part of the Regular Work Routine

Rather than rely on a haphazard method of making minor improvements in how the work is done, it's far better for you to devise a strategy for doing this on a continuing basis. However, it doesn't have to be founded upon any particular program started by upper management. You can establish your own procedures for working with your employees in solving workplace problems and looking for ways to do things better. In fact, the very informality associated with how you do this will encourage a greater level of participation. In effect, you will have a team effort within your group aimed at identifying areas where improvements can be made.

It isn't difficult to get such an informal practice started once you have established credibility with the people who work for you. In terms of procedures, hold short informal gatherings where you kick around possibilities for changing how certain aspects of the work are performed. Once these gatherings become routine, individual employees will make suggestions for changes. Until that time, or at meetings when ideas aren't flowing too well, ask for workers' thoughts on ideas that you may have dreamed up yourself. Just make sure that you don't dominate discussions so that workers feel they are only there to agree with you and not to be equal participants in coming up with ideas.

If there are specific areas where you would like to see improvements, bring the topic up at the close of a meeting and ask if people will think about possibilities for making improvements in that particular area to discuss at the next meeting. Incidentally, looking for improvements should be an on-going exercise, and not limited to meetings held once a week or at some other interval. The purpose of the regular meetings is to provide continuity to the approach lest it get lost in the shuffle of a busy workplace.

Take the Time to Listen to All Suggestions

There is one key principle for encouraging employees to participate in recommending workplace improvements: do not give short shrift to their ideas. Often there will be suggestions made that obviously aren't workable. However, rather than arbitrarily dismissing the idea, take the time to hear the person out. In fact, if another employee cuts the person short, interject and say something such as, "Wait a minute, Jack. Let's hear what Buzz has to say. This is an area of operations we certainly need to make improvements in."

Ordinarily you will only need to do this a few times and employees will quickly learn that the practice is to let everyone have their say. Furthermore, when it becomes necessary to turn an idea down, take the time to explain why this is so. That way, you will sustain the person's confidence so that the particular individual will continue to contribute recommendations in the future. Surprisingly, even a consistent originator of totally unworkable suggestions will ultimately come up with a good idea or two.

Use Rewards to Encourage Worker Participation

One of the toughest hurdles to overcome in encouraging workers to make recommendations for improvements relates to "what's in it for me?" After all, why should an employee make suggestions on something such as speeding up the work, if the worker receives no benefit from it? The biggest negative of improving operations from a worker standpoint is that it may contribute to putting the employee out of work in the future. After all, the more productive the company becomes the fewer workers are needed to produce any given output.

Of course, if your company has a formal program that rewards employees for suggestions, then this isn't so much of a problem. Naturally, though, such a program must offer rewards of sufficient size to encourage participation. Furthermore, the program has to be structured so there isn't a lot of time between when an employee's idea is adopted and when the formal recognition is given. Another past impediment to many of these programs has been the extensive paperwork and involved administrative procedures which tended to frustrate both workers and supervisors.

One good way to work around this angle is to concentrate on areas which make the employee's job easier to do. For example, changing the way a task is performed so the employee has to exert less effort is something any worker will relate to. You can also implement your own reward system, such as giving workers longer breaks because they came up with an idea that saved significant amounts of time. With a little thought you can come up with simple rewards of one form or another.

Beyond anything else, showing respect for the employee's knowledge of his or her job will contribute the most in making them active participants in the innovative process of how the work is performed. The more involved employees are in the operations of your unit, the more interested they will be in how efficient it becomes. When workers feel they are respected as genuine contributors in making decisions, they will think of themselves as managers of a small segment of the business. And since they will perceive the department as "their department," there will be a concerted effort to make it superior to other units within the company.

HOW TO ENCOURAGE SMALL IDEAS THAT CAN REAP BIG BENEFITS

Beyond encouraging employees to participate in making suggestions for continuous improvements of departmental operation, the big payoff comes from those simple ideas that cut costs substantially either directly or indirectly. Frequently, these are changes that have utility beyond the boundaries of your department. For example, perhaps a change recommended by one of your workers in how her job is performed can be used throughout the company and, on a cumulative basis, can result in some serious money being saved. A program that encourages workers to continuously look for improvements can be beneficial far beyond the scope of any one individual's job.

Avoid Emphasizing Major Recommendations

Despite the potential benefits, it's important not to place too much emphasis on coming up with the big idea that yields important cost savings. Why not? In the first place, changes that yield substantial benefits in one fell swoop are few and far between. After all, it should be relatively rare that work processes, or other operations, are so poorly organized that a change of any great magnitude is called for. That's not to say it doesn't happen, but the chances of workers making these discoveries are rare. Once workers see how difficult it is to recommend changes that yield substantial benefits, they will get discouraged and will not even bother to come up with any suggestions.

From another perspective, placing emphasis on looking for changes that yield high-value cost savings will have employees focusing just on this area. They will stop concentrating on the day-to-day minor changes that are the bread and butter of any program for continuous improvement. Yet it's the cumulative impact of these many small changes that is most beneficial in the long run. So it's far better to emphasize looking for little ways to change how the work is done. It also keeps employees more interested in making recommendations. It may occasionally yield the big idea that can be implemented beyond one job or department, but even if it doesn't, the many minor changes will be invaluable in and of themselves.

Techniques to Encourage Workplace Improvements

What are the appropriate methods to use in encouraging employees to come up with ideas for improvements in the workplace? Specific tactics used can vary, but there are some common measures that apply across the board. First, it's important to have a strong sense of teamwork within the group you supervise. This allows for cross-fertilization of ideas among workers. If teamwork isn't a strong trait within the unit, then workers are much less likely to accept suggestions from their peers. And it's often someone who works next to you who may have a good idea on how to make your job easier to do. So teamwork is fundamental for the necessary discussions to take place that are likely to yield ways to improve the way jobs are done.

Beyond teamwork, good communication between you and the members of your department is essential to accomplish several things. For one, solid one-on-one interchanges guarantee for employees that they are able to be straightforward in discussions they have with you. Getting to know you this way also assures them that you won't be critical of suggestions they make. This is important since all people are self-conscious about appearing to look foolish, some much more than others. The fact that you are also the boss—with power over pay raise and promotion decisions—adds to this factor in a boss/subordinate relationship. After all, saying something stupid in front of the boss doesn't earn someone too many points as one of the best and brightest workers in the department. This barrier can be overcome where a boss has good rapport with employees.

Where such communication exists between a supervisor and his or her direct reports, a familiarity develops that encourages workers to view you as someone who has their best interests at heart. This means a lot when it comes to encouraging workers to recommend ways to do their jobs differently. A supervisor who communicates well with employees will be viewed as a manager who is on the employee's side, while a boss who remains aloof may be viewed as a member of management who is only interested in squeezing more work out of employees.

This brings us to a sensitive issue which can't be ignored. If surveyed, most people might not admit that many of their actions are focused on advancing their own self-interest. Yet in reality the recommendations workers make are often viewed from a personal benefit angle. Therefore, the discussion on self-interest in the preceding section applies equally here. As pointed out, however, the more workers see themselves as contributors in managing the unit, the more likely they are to subvert self-interest to department-wide improvements.

Incidentally, one of the best ways to pick up small ideas that can improve your department is to look at the way other departments handle their day-to-day operational details. Such seemingly insignificant matters as where a machine is located can impact efficiency. The processing of routine paperwork is another example. A good approach to take in this area is that there is no idea too small to be of value. Along the same line, never be too proud to adopt another department's ideas. Who cares where the idea came from as long as it makes your job a little bit easier.

JUSTIFYING THE BENEFITS OF NEW IDEAS TO SENIOR MANAGEMENT

It requires considerable effort on the part of a supervisor to establish a system where workers routinely recommend changes that will possibly improve some aspect of department operations. This can turn out to be a frustrating exercise if you succeed in establishing a climate where suggestions thrive, only to encounter bottlenecks in selling the changes to upper management. Remember, of course, that many ideas such as a change in how a worker performs certain duties can be implemented without higher level approval.

On occasion, however, because of budgetary or other considerations, higher level management will have to approve any new idea. Frequently, this is the case when funding approval is needed for new equipment, even though the expenditure will quickly be recouped by greater efficiencies. Whatever the purpose, whenever you need higher level approval, you have to be prepared to justify your request.

The degree of difficulty in obtaining approval will vary from company to company. Layers of bureaucracy, resistance to change, and a general attitude that "if a change wasn't originated by top management then it can't be of value" will all work toward making it difficult to secure approval. On the other hand, a company which encourages change and has both flexible policies and forward looking management will make it much easier to gain acceptance for new ideas. However, even where new ways of doing things are encouraged, it will still be necessary to document any request for a significant change.

Tailor Your Presentation to Your Audience

Naturally, gaining approval for any new idea will be based upon the benefits to be gained by making the change. What you can't neglect when you're selling the idea for doing something differently to senior management is that you have to make your pitch based upon their perspective. This can differ with the level of management required for approval.

For example, a division manager is looking at things from the division perspective, whereas a senior vice-president will consider the recommendation from a company-wide angle. This isn't insignificant because, while you may have assessed the idea for the benefits to your department, senior managers will be considering the big picture. Of course, you believe that a change improving your department's operations will generally benefit the company as a whole, but that's not necessarily true. Even when it is, if funding is required—such as for a new piece of equipment—your idea is in competition for limited resources with those from other departments. As a result, those presentations with the best justification will be the ones that are approved.

All of which leads to the question, What is the best form of justification to use? This will depend to some extent on the position of the person whose approval you are seeking. For example, the technology chief of a division may love the idea for new machinery which speeds up the production process, while the division financial officer may be more interested in its cost. Conceivably, both can be convinced of the merits of the idea, but from different angles. With the technology chief the emphasis will be on technical improvements, while the best justification with the financial manager will be how money can be saved by this purchase. In brief, the trick is to tailor your arguments toward the perspective of the person you have to convince.

Proposal Guidelines

The extent of your presentation and the detail required will vary with the scope of the new idea being proposed. If significant sums of money are involved and/or substantive changes in some aspect of company operations, then a great deal of time and effort is needed to adequately prepare your case. On the other hand, most ideas for changes won't be that significant and won't require an extensive level of preparation. Here are a few guidelines for preparing requests for approval to senior management that can serve you well:

- Focus on what the benefits of the change will be in terms most desirable from the perspective of the person whose approval you're seeking.

- If there are potential difficulties involved in implementing a new idea, point them out and identify how they will be overcome. Don't ignore them since that indicates you either didn't recognize the problems or are trying to be deceptive. Neither angle will get your idea approved.

- Whenever possible quantify benefits in specific terms, for example, cost savings, revenue increases, and so forth. Be as specific as you can be since this may be the most convincing argument of all. Pie-in-the-sky estimates are worse than nothing since they will just make people skeptical, and skeptics don't approve requests. Incidentally, don't neglect to include any implementation costs, since a failure to do so may be construed as a deliberate attempt to overstate the benefits and minimize any liabilities.

- If whatever is being proposed will have benefits beyond your immediate department, then try to enlist the beneficiaries in your cause. For example, a change which will benefit three departments besides your own will be an easier sell if you have the wholehearted support of the three department heads.

- If you know there is potential opposition to what you want to do, try to eliminate it before you formally start through the approval cycle. Talk informally with those who object and see if you can win them over. Even if you're not entirely successful in overcoming skeptics, if you have consulted with them beforehand, you may minimize their opposition. The very fact that you made the effort to consult with them may lead them to go along with your proposal, albeit reluctantly.

One of the things that can't be overlooked in pitching new ideas to management is the timing. If you're looking for money to install expensive new technology, the best time is when business is good, not just after a round of layoffs. On a smaller scale, don't try pitching ideas to people at times when you know they aren't in the best frame of mind. You can't be expected to be able to predict all of these things, but if there are obvious reasons to postpone a presentation, by all means do so if it's at all feasible. It's a lot easier than a rejection and only a faint hope of trying again some time in the future. When you're looking for approvals from on high, use every advantage you can think of and avoid every potential pothole that comes to mind. That, at least, will give you a fair shot of getting what you're looking for.

HOW TO AVOID TURNING BAD IDEAS INTO BAD PRACTICES

On occasion, changes made in the workplace with good intentions can have bad results. Something may not have been completely thought out before being implemented. As a result, unforeseen difficulties either require extensive effort to cure what went wrong, or the change has to be completely abandoned. On other occasions, a change is made even though the potential problems were pointed out beforehand. This can happen in circumstances where something new is introduced based upon upper management direction, even though lower level managers counseled against making the change. A senior manager with a pet idea is often the initiator of this sort of failed scheme.

Another all too common cause of workplace changes that result in chaos is when new technology is introduced without full knowledge of its capabilities and suitability for the job at hand. Sometimes a salesperson's product pitch is seductive enough to overcome practicality. So new equipment is purchased without determining whether or not it will perform as promised by the vendor. A failure to discuss requirements with those workers who will be using the equipment and know the details of the tasks that must be performed is a frequent cause of such disasters.

Voice Your Objections

As a supervisor, you want to avoid the problems that can result from making changes that don't work out. There are a number of things you can do to minimize the chances of bad ideas being put into practice within your department. Above all, don't be afraid to make your objections known when something new is suggested. This isn't always done, because of a fear of being characterized as someone who opposes progress.

Indeed, it's not always easy to object to something, especially if it has the support of top management. Nevertheless, you have to put your apprehension aside and make yourself heard if you don't want to be saddled with equipment that doesn't do the job, or if a new operating procedure causes more headaches than it cures. You can make your thoughts known beforehand without career damage if you take the right approach.

One of the first things to do whenever you hear of something new being suggested for your department is to determine who initiated the idea. One or two people are generally the catalyst behind any new equipment purchase. So whenever you get wind of new equipment being planned for your department, find out who the sponsor is. This gives you an immediate indication of how outspoken you can be in opposing the purchase.

Obviously you have to be more subtle if the idea originates with a senior manager or someone else who wields a great deal of power within the company. However, more often than not, the originator of the idea may be a peer in another department who has gone through the ropes of the approval process. It might also be a staff member who for one reason or another finds it advantageous to have the new equipment purchased. The proponent, however, probably didn't bother to consider its potential problems. In fact, many times there may not even be a discussion with those who will use the equipment.

Despite these failings, quite often a good proposal pitch will generate enthusiasm within top management. Then it's easy to assume the purchase is the idea of someone in top management, when in fact the potential problems have never been brought to the attention of senior managers. This is why, at the first inkling that new equipment is being planned for your department, you should find out where the idea originated. If it didn't really come from the top, then the political angle of making your objections known isn't as much of a problem.

Whatever you do, when you object to new technology or equipment, be explicit as to why something won't work. Senior managers tend to get caught up in the new technology trap and accept without question the wisdom of jumping on the bandwagon for the latest update. To overcome this bias you need to be able to show why the equipment won't work as expected.

Incidentally, always make your objections known as early as possible. Once a new idea gathers momentum it can acquire enough supporters to take it on a path of its own which defies any criticism. This is particularly true if one or two top managers are convinced of the potential of what is being proposed. When that happens, your immediate boss and others—even though they may agree with your reasoning—might think, "I'm not going to buck top management on this issue."

Look for Alternatives to Avoid Getting Stuck with Something

Sometimes you may not want to out-and-out recommend that new technology not be bought. But you can still minimize its negative impact on your own department. For example, you might want to point out your objections, and suggest that new equipment be bought on a trial basis. This is a good angle to use, especially if the equipment is expensive. Furthermore, you might suggest that the equipment be tested in someone else's department, preferably one of your peers who is a vocal supporter of the idea. That way, when the problems start, they will be happening to someone else.

Another alternative might be to recommend the approach that is the stalwart of politicians who don't want to make decisions on politically sensitive subjects: conduct a study of the pros and cons of the new idea before implementing it. This suggestion can have appeal. After all, it will not only be an opportunity to prevent expensive mistakes, but it has another advantage from the viewpoint of proponents. It gives them cover if the study recommends going ahead and, at a later date, the idea turns out to be a bad one. For this reason, some supporters of new technology may not object too strenuously to this suggestion. One good offshoot of this approach is that you may be selected to participate in the study, or in some fashion provide your input. This gives you a golden opportunity to make your objections known. Of course, recommending further study is only practical where the expenditures involved are substantial or the overall impact on operations is severe.

Despite the difficulties involved in being a dissenter to the purchase of new technology or the implementation of new working procedures, it's worthwhile to have your say. Otherwise you may be saddled with equipment or practices that aren't so easy to get rid of. Once they are in, there's a great deal of reluctance to scuttle any equipment and/or policy even after it's obvious they won't do the job. Those who sponsored the purchase won't want to admit a mistake and will go with the notion that a little tweaking here and there will make everything run smoothly. You might well have an extended period of frustration in trying to work with equipment that won't do the job. A similar problem exists when new policies and procedures don't work. Once they are introduced, if problems develop, they are attributed to everything but the new policy.

THE NEGLECTED PAYOFF IN CHANGING ROUTINE WAYS OF DOING THINGS

New and grand ideas are consistently touted as the means to improve different aspects of the workplace. What's not always recognized is that some of the greatest productivity benefits won't come from new technology or some grand reorganization scheme. Instead, they will result from incremental benefits achieved by changing some of the routine ways that the work is done. It's always assumed, of course, that things are being done in the most efficient manner possible with the available resources.

The common view is that the only way to make improvements in productivity is by expenditures for new machinery and equipment, employee training, and the like. Yet some of the easiest ways to reap benefits in the modern workplace are to eliminate some ingrained habits that are of little or no value to the productive process.

It's easy to assume your group doesn't have work methods or procedures that are outdated or wasteful. This thinking isn't so much a matter of not wanting to admit such conditions may exist, but rather the fact that many ingrained work practices are accepted as proper when, in fact, they are outdated and may have outlived their usefulness completely. Broad examples would include periodic reports and work procedures that were initially instituted for a specific purpose. That purpose may no longer be valid, but the report is prepared, or the work practice is continued, because its current usefulness has never been challenged.

One common failing is to neglect to review existing practices when new technology is introduced. Such a review, however, can eliminate obsolete practices and avoid unnecessary duplication of effort. This was widely ignored when computers first became a mainstay of business, and there was a widespread practice of having duplicate paper copies of computer files. While less prevalent now, however, it still exists to some extent. Other inefficient practices also occur, such as sending e-mail messages to a string of recipients who have little or no use for the information. The list of sins could go on and on, but the point is that it makes no sense to add expensive technology in the workplace if the basics of doing the work aren't up to date.

Recognizing the Hidden Benefits of Revising Workplace Procedures

Whenever workplace procedures are changed, it's usually for a very specific reason such as improving workflow, eliminating unnecessary steps in the work process, or some other commendable purpose. What's often missed are some of the hidden benefits of this revision. Being able to identify some of these potential benefits can help to convince employees of the wisdom of changing the procedures.

For example, eliminating a couple of steps in the work process of an employee may decrease the amount of time necessary to perform certain tasks. Workers may well view this as one more attempt to get more work out of them for the same amount of pay. In fact, in a union environment, changes such as this are sometimes the grounds for grievances. Yet there may be benefits to workers which are ignored because they are a secondary result of the intended purpose which was to speed up the work. For example, eliminating steps in a process may also improve safety if they were conducive to accidents.

Another benefit of periodically reviewing routine practices is the opportunity it provides to eliminate bad habits. Over a period of time, workers can adopt techniques which aren't necessarily the most efficient way of doing things. As time goes by, these practices are passed on to new employees who continue them. No one ever stops to think about whether or not there may be an easier way.

Work routine is a habit that isn't always easy to break, particularly with long-time employees. You probably know from experience that it's not always easy to suggest to a veteran employee that perhaps there's a better way to perform one of his or her tasks. Nevertheless, with the new workplace emphasis on teamwork, cooperation, and worker involvement, this is still easier to do than in the past.

HOW TO SELL THE BENEFITS OF THE NEW WORKPLACE TO EMPLOYEES

The new workplace with its heavy use of technology, changing employment practices, and a more flexible work force will continue to evolve as companies constantly search for an edge in the worldwide competition for customers. About the only constant you can depend upon is that changes will continue to take place. Many will be beneficial to employees, even though they may not always see them as such. After all, anyone who has experienced a reorganization or layoff isn't easily convinced that things are going in the right direction.

Change, even for the better, always brings a certain amount of upheaval and confusion which can reinforce a worker's perceptions that all of the benefits of workplace change accrue to the company— not to the worker. Yet many aspects of change in the new workplace directly or indirectly benefit employees. Even severe actions taken to remain competitive, which may result in job losses, are beneficial to the survivors if the company manages to turn things around.

Technological changes also offer benefits to workers. Much of the drudgery of many jobs has been alleviated by computerization and other aspects of high technology. The increased skill levels required for many new jobs offer workers the chance to learn and to enhance their career opportunities. Naturally, there are and will continue to be pitfalls along the way as the business world continues its transition to meet the needs of the future. But on balance, the new workplace offers substantive benefits to workers, and the burden of convincing them of that rests largely with their immediate supervisors. This may not be a task you particularly relish, but it's essential to maintain the morale and loyalty of your workers.

In terms of specifics, selling the benefits of the new workplace to employees is a one-on-one exercise. You will have to focus on any particular changes taking place within your company that affect your working group. For example, one of the main concerns for some supervisors may be trying to justify the virtues of a layoff to the survivors, while supervisors at other companies where layoffs aren't a problem may have other issues to deal with. Introduction of new technology always presents a set of problems concerning employee acceptance of the equipment and training in its use. Whatever the issues may be, supervisors must be able to point out the benefits of these changes. Otherwise hostility, resistance, low morale, and poor productivity will result.

Of course, before you can convince an employee of the benefits of some aspects of the new workplace, you have to have a handle on what they are from the worker's perspective. Sometimes this will be easy to do; other times it may require some thought. In all cases, it will require patience and understanding on your part if employees don't immediately see things your way.

HOW TO HANDLE THE CAREER ASPECTS OF THE NEW WORKPLACE SUPERVISOR

The new workplace with its slimmed down management structure, high technology utilization, fierce external competition, and overall flexibility presents many career challenges for anyone in a supervisory position. First and foremost, it requires you to consistently stay on top of potential changes that may impact your job. It also means you have to spend more time planning your future career, no matter how secure your future may appear at the moment. It takes only one merger to result in plants, divisions, and subsidiaries to be closed or combined, with a resultant loss of jobs.

For this reason alone, it pays to be prepared for that day in the future when you may hear at an all-hands meeting that the XYZ Company has bought your employer. At this meeting you will doubtless also hear comforting statements about how great this will be for everyone's future. Take this with a grain of salt, especially if the guy making the pronouncement just made a bundle by exercising a golden parachute with megabuck benefits that came into play upon the company being sold. It's easy to be positive when your future is a beach chair in the Bahamas with no financial worries. For you, and countless other employees, jobs may be at stake. This alone is reason enough to be prepared to seek employment on very short notice.

What to Do if Your Department Is Downsized

With reorganizations in one form or another a constant part of the modern business scene, you may one day find out that your department is being downsized. This could take a couple of forms. One could be a complete elimination of your department as it currently exists, with employees—and yourself—either reassigned to other groups or terminated from employment with the company. The other, less painful possibility is that your department could lose a number of slots, but would continue to function as before.

As you may recall, strategies to protect your job in a reorganization were discussed in Chapter Nine, so let's look here at the worst case scenario when your department is abolished. There are two prime considerations when this happens. The first is whether or not you are being retained in another position, and the second, what is going to happen to the employees you supervise. Of course, the specifics of how you handle the latter situation will vary, but do whatever you can to help your employees obtain reassignments or employment elsewhere.

It's logical to assume that you will know beforehand about the abolition of your department as well as your job. Perhaps you will also know of your reassignment, which may even be to a bigger and better position. However, as you may have experienced in the past, the way things should be done and the way they are actually done aren't necessarily the same. So it could well be that you are unceremoniously informed without notice that your job and department are no more. That, of course, probably won't happen. Nevertheless, it pays to be prepared, which is simple enough to do. The following steps are basics for successful career survival:

- No matter how secure your job may seem, always have an up-to-date resume ready to go.
- Always keep in touch with your contacts throughout the industry you work in.
- Keep your skills up-to-date.

- Decide if and whether you would relocate if you lost your job.

- Try to give yourself some financial security which will give you greater flexibility if you should suddenly lose your job.

- Don't burn any bridges if you lose a job. You never know when paths will cross again.

Career Adjustments for the New Workplace

Aside from the career planning aspects, which the relative job instability of the new workplace seem to dictate, there are a number of on-the-job adjustments you have to concentrate on to succeed in the new work environment. These include expanding the range and scope of your skills so you can easily shift jobs from one area to another, and working at improving all aspects of your people skills. Let's explore each of these areas separately.

As technology expands, it's essential for your skills to keep pace. Work continually to upgrade your technical skills, not only specific ones for your present job, but also general skills which are transferable to other employers. One hallmark of the new workplace is that the more you know, the greater your job security. Incidentally, if you are a veteran supervisor, be as active in improving your skills as less experienced counterparts. With the exception of those who are financially independent, you never know how long you will want to—or have to—work.

As you are aware, the new workplace emphasis on teamwork, cooperation, and employee empowerment requires supervisors to sharpen their people skills as well as their technical skills. You have to be better prepared to see other viewpoints, and encourage two-way communication with everyone you deal with. Persuasion is replacing the threat of discipline, and coaching is displacing caustic criticism. You may have to do a little bit of self-analysis to decide if your people skills need to be sharpened. If so, avail yourself of any training you think you need. For the most part, an awareness of the need to adjust attitudes may be all that is required.

The new workplace presents a wide variety of challenges for you as a supervisor. You will frequently have to do more work with fewer people than in the past. Your range of duties and scope of responsibilities may continue to increase as slowly but certainly as more management tasks are pushed down to the operating level. More often than not, when a middle management or staff position is abolished, the work doesn't cease. It just gets reassigned, which means first level supervisors can expect their duties to continue to mount. You will also have to be flexible in dealing with a diverse workforce along with savvy suppliers and demanding customers. It has never been easy to be a supervisor, and it may get worse before it gets better.

On the other hand, the new workplace gives you greater freedom to influence your own job as well as the operations that you supervise. It also provides the opportunity for greater cooperation with your workers. This should go far toward eliminating the hostility that sometimes existed in the past when supervisors and their subordinates operated in an "us versus them" environment. The tension and stress this brought about was never pleasant for any supervisor. There should be far less of that sort of pressure in today's workplace.

Index